The European Community in the 1990s

The transformation of the European Community into a single market in 1992/3, together with the changes in Central and Eastern Europe, have given new life to Jean Monnet's grand ambitions for European integration. The essays in this volume examine some of the key issues facing the EC in the 1990s, focusing on three important areas: the politics of integration, economics, education and science, and foreign policy and defense.

Brian Nelson is Professor of French and Director of the Centre for European Studies, **David Roberts** is a Professor of German Studies, and **Walter Veit** is an Associate Professor of German Studies, all at Monash University, Melbourne.

International Issues / Collection Questions Internationales

Presses de la Fondation Nationale des Sciences Politiques
and Berg Publishers

Françoise de La Serre, Jacques Leruez, Helen Wallace (dir.), *The Foreign Policies of France and Great Britain since 1945. The inevitable adjustment* (Les politiques étrangères de la France et de la Grande-Bretagne depuis 1945. L'impossible ajustement).

In Preparation

Zaki Laïdi (dir.), *Power and Purpose after the Cold War* (L'ordre mondial relâché. Sens et puissance après la guerre froide).

Jean-François Bayart (dir.), *Trajectories of Politics in Africa and Asia* (Les trajectoires du politique en Afrique et en Asie).

Jean-François Guilhaudis, *The Diplomacy of Disarmament* (La diplomatie du désarmement).

Pierre de Senarclens, *From Yalta to the Iron Curtain. 1945–1948* (De Yalta au rideau de fer. 1945–1948).

Sami Naïr, *The Mediterranean World in Conflict* (La Méditerranée en conflits).

Wrench, Solomos, eds., *Migration and Racism in Europe* (Racisme et migrations en Europe).

The European Community in the 1990s

Economics, Politics, Defense

Edited by
Brian Nelson, David Roberts, and Walter Veit

BERG

New York / Oxford

Distributed exclusively in the U.S. and Canada by
St. Martin's Press, New York

Published in 1992 by
Berg Publishers, Inc.
Editorial offices:
165 Taber Avenue, Providence, RI 02906, U.S.A.
150 Cowley Road, Oxford OX4 1JJ, UK

British Library Cataloguing in Publication Data
The European Community in the 1990s: Economics,
politics, defense.
I. Nelson, Brian II. Roberts, David
III. Veit, Walter
320.9172
ISBN 0–85496–758–3

Library of Congress Cataloging-in-Publication Data

The European community in the 1990s: economics, politics, defense /
edited by Brian Nelson, David Roberts, and Walter Veit.
p. cm.
Includes bibliographical references and index.
ISBN 0-85496-758-3
1. European Economic Community. 2. Europe 1992. I. Nelson, Brian, 1946- . II. Roberts, David, 1937- . III. Veit, Walter.
HC241.2.E83423 1992
341.24'22--dc20 91-33213
CIP

Printed in Great Britain by
Billing & Sons Ltd, Worcester

Contents

Preface

The present collection of essays is based on an international conference ("Europe Today") organized by the Centre for European Studies at Monash University, Melbourne, in July 1989. The essays included in this volume represent a selection of the papers presented at the conference. They have all been thoroughly revised, and as much account as possible has been taken of recent changes in Europe.

A major international conference would not be possible without the cooperation of numerous bodies. We would like to express our warm appreciation of the generous support given to us by the following persons and institutions: the German Research Association, the German Academic Exchange Service, the French and Italian Governments, the Government of Victoria, Austrade, and the Vice-Chancellor of Monash University, Professor Mal Logan.

Preparation of the volume was greatly aided by the work of Jill Anderson and Jan Lapinskus.

This volume is one of a pair. Its twin is *The Idea of Europe* (Berg, 1992). Each volume is complete in itself but reinforces the other.

EDITORS

Introduction

BRIAN NELSON AND DAVID ROBERTS

The European Community (EC) is a direct heir to the Europe of nation states. It cannot be forgotten that the nation state, which was enshrined in the nineteenth-century European system of states, the concert of Europe, exhausted itself at great cost in two major conflagrations of our own century, in strife that started as European civil wars and soon engulfed the world. The new Europe rising from the ruins of 1945 deliberately sought to transcend the previous excesses (territorial, ideological, economic) of a nation state system that had reached its historical apogee. Though the nation state in Europe remains generally intact, it is also a fact that the present twelve member states of the EC have opted, freely and democratically, for membership of a community in which sovereignty is partially transferred, especially (but not exclusively) in the economic sphere, to common institutions established in Brussels, Strasbourg, and Luxembourg for the benefit of all. The present European system may be described as a pre-federal one. It is this voluntary transfer of autonomy, and therefore of powers, to common institutions that distinguishes the EC from all previous attempts to unify the old continent, whether we speak of a classical Rome, of the Carolingian Empire, of the imperial Europe of Napoleon, or of the totalitarian hegemonies that arose in the Europe of the 1930s. The vision of Robert Schuman, Jean Monnet, Alcide de Gasperi, Konrad Adenauer, and Paul-Henri Spaak – the founding fathers of the European Community – was one of gradual union by popular consent; a far cry from previous European empires and also generically different from the organic union resulting from the settlement and expansion of "neo-European," federally organized pluralist entities like the United States, Canada, and Australia. The EC is a unique, and a uniquely successful, experiment in collaboration and common decision making between independent democratic countries.

It is not our intention to describe the history of the European integration process or the institutions that enable the EC to function: the aim of the present volume is to explore some of the key issues facing the Community in the 1990s. A crucial point of reference is, of course, the Single European Act, which ended fifteen years of stagnation caused by the petty intra-European protectionism of the 1970s and early 1980s. A legal instrument for the strengthening and acceleration of the integration process, the Single European Act, which became law on 1 July 1987, reflects the member states' resolve to advance the progress of the Community through: improving its decision-making procedures, chiefly by providing that many more decisions could be taken by majority decision rather than requiring unanimity; increasing cooperation in monetary matters, and in research, technology, and the environment; formalizing European political cooperation (i.e., the coordination of decision making in foreign policy); enhancing the role of the European Parliament in the legislative process; and, not least, creating an internal market without frontiers (the Single Market) by the end of 1992, when the physical and fiscal barriers to mobility between the twelve are due to disappear forever.

The most far-reaching of the Act's provisions will be the realization of the Single Market, which will literally change the face of Europe. By the end of 1992, the EC will be transformed into a unified market of 320 million consumers in which the following elements will be prominent: the elimination of customs posts and checks on goods; the harmonization of technical standards; the mutual recognition of university diplomas and apprenticeship courses; a common market in services, including a single broadcasting area; and the approximation of national value added tax and excise tax systems. It is projected that the completion of the internal market will increase the overall wealth of the European economy by 4.2 percent to 6.5 percent of its gross national product. In some important sectors, like energy, transport, banking, and insurance, appreciable cost and price reductions may be achieved. As for employment, about 5 million new jobs could be created. All of this would be in addition to normal economic growth. Competition among enterprises in a larger, unified market will give them a better chance to survive and expand than in a narrow national market. Moreover, the Single Market will benefit not only Europeans but foreign firms as well. Exporters to the EC will find themselves selling into a huge single market with a uniform set of norms, standards, and procedures. They will no longer have to face twelve different sets of requirements or border controls between one of the Community's member states and another. Foreign firms, like Community operators, will enjoy economies of scale and greater marketing flexibility.

The EC was thus relaunched under the catchword "1992," and the momentum created by the 1992 project has been remarkable: the plan for full economic and monetary union within the EC is being pursued with vigor; other countries have turned toward Brussels to seek new or improved trading relationships with the Community, or even to join it; and new life has been breathed into the old idea that the member countries of the Community should transform themselves from a group of sovereign nations into a European political union.

The timing of this Western European relaunch was extremely fortunate, for it was soon followed by the dramatic events in Eastern Europe, which have led to the dismantling of Stalinism and the ending of the postwar anomaly whereby the COMECON countries turned a blind eye to the unification of Western Europe. We cannot pretend that the Community's Single Market plan was the spark of democracy in Eastern Europe and the Soviet Union; the credit for that must go to Poland's Solidarity movement and, above all, to Mikhail Gorbachev. But even though 1992 had no hand in destabilizing a sick Communist order, it can now help to stabilize the countries of Eastern Europe with offers of aid and trade into a vast market. It can also offer these countries a context in which they can plan their futures, beginning with associate membership of the EC and leading later, perhaps, to membership. The EC has become the center of a new European order.

Germany, the Community's biggest and richest member, occupies a pivotal position in the new Europe. German reunification, laden with historical significance and political and economic consequences, may be seen as a culmination to the relaunch of Europe. It entails, of course, formidable problems. The economic cost of the absorption of the GDR is massive, and the political and social implications of the economic cost are no less great. Timothy Garton Ash has written:

> With the combination of political liberalism and economic disintegration in the former Eastern Europe, and the Soviet Disunion, the press of would-be immigrants or *Gastarbeiter* ('guest workers') will increase,

> adding to the existing pressure from across the Mediterranean. A new specter is haunting Western Europe: the specter of a postcommunist *Völkerwanderung*. This is a formidable challenge for the whole European Community, but for Germany above all.[1]

There are fears, on the other hand, of German domination of the Community. There are strong grounds, however, for thinking that Germany unification will enhance the EC's standing, strengthen its institutions, and stimulate greater integration among EC member-states. This is not, of course, simply because of the good intentions of German political leaders, or the concern of Germany's partners that the greater Germany be locked inside the EC, but because of the increasing autonomy and robustness of the EC institutions themselves – a development created by the Single European Act, which has transformed the Community's political system. Once the principle of majority voting was accepted in certain key areas of Community business, the practice spilled over into others. National interests are still fiercely defended, but, with the virtual abandonment of the national veto, there has been a marked tendency to temper unilateral ambitions and initiatives to the prevailing wind. It is difficult to see how a united Germany can modify this trend.

The essays in this volume examine some of the key issues facing the EC in the 1990s. Those in Part I explore the question of political union and the special role of Germany. Jacqueline Dutheil examines, in a historical perspective, the EC's progress toward realizing the federalist ambitions of Jean Monnet and speculates on the future of European federalism in light of the 1992 phenomenon and the new climate in Central and Eastern Europe. Philomena Murray shows how the Single European Act has enhanced the decision-making processes of the EC, but stresses that the concept of sovereignty remains a major stumbling block on the road to political union. Similarly, Werner Weidenfeld contrasts the grand vision of the founding fathers of European integration with the special interests and national selfishness that beset the integration process, and suggests ways of overcoming these difficulties, stressing that the unification of Europe needs a cultural bond as well as practical policy. Wolfgang Gruner and Christian Hacke analyse the "German Question," and the conditions of its solution, against the background of German and European history. Gruner, adopting a

1. Timothy Garton Ash, "Germany Unbound," *New York Review of Books* (22 Nov. 1990), 11–15, 13.

broad historical view, shows how the political and social system of the German nation has always been a European issue, and affirms the determination of the new Germany to become an "ensemble player" and seize the opportunity to draw a line under history by linking its own unification to the furtherance of European political union. Hacke examines the "tyranny of choice" that marked German politics after 1945, i.e., the dilemma between its pursuit of a pro-Western integration policy and its desire for national reunification. He discusses Germany's central position in postcommunist Europe and its special historical, political, and economic responsibility for future developments, in particular the enhancement of democratic civilization for the whole of Europe.

Economic, educational, and scientific issues are addressed in Part II. Stuart Rosewarne argues that the economic integration of Europe, together with the increased authority of the European Commission as a regulator of this process, will facilitate the Europeanization of business enterprise, creating the basis for a new regime of capital accumulation. Daniel Van Den Bulcke examines EC policy toward multinational companies and shows how the multinationals will be among the main beneficiaries of the Single Market, given the growth of cross-border mergers and collaborative projects. The common EC budget, from which Community policies are financed, is perhaps the single most important practical indicator of the movement toward economic and political integration in Western Europe. Heather Field, focusing on the vexed question of the Common Agricultural Policy, hitherto the major recipient of Community expenditure and the focus of Community activity, examines the nature of the EC budget and the consequences of changes to the system of budgetary funding made as part of the 1988 attempt to stabilize agricultural production. Corrado Paracone argues that the challenge of economic and technological change must be met by more, and more flexible, technical and managerial training, while Martin Mruck underlines the need for European cooperation in basic research.

Some of the international implications of European integration are explored in Part III: the developing international role of the EC in world affairs and its future priorities (Wolfgang Wessels); the impetus toward greater European defense integration and the obstacles that stand in its way (Joanne Wright); and the impact on European security and NATO of recent changes in the world order (Magnus Clarke and Joseph Camilleri).

The essays in this volume all point, from different perspectives, to the challenges and opportunities of change in Europe. The momentum of the organized change within the EC must be maintained; moreover, the new, dynamic role of the EC in what Gorbachev called the "common European home" makes further development of the Community more necessary than ever. The EC offers a center of gravity and political stability in Europe. It has become a natural political and economic focus for the emerging democracies in Central and Eastern Europe and provides a mechanism for immediate common action to help the processes of political reform and economic reconstruction in these countries. The enhanced status of the EC, and the changes taking place in Central and Eastern Europe, offer the Community unprecedented opportunities for the development of a common foreign and security policy and the further development of central democratic institutions.

The need here is above all what Werner Weidenfeld calls the step from negative to positive integration, from the progressive removal of barriers and obstacles to integration, to the creation of new supranational decision-making structures. Here one notes the absence of a security forum that could become the political voice of Western European security policies. Equally, the lack of linkage between the Council of Ministers and the European Parliament diminishes the scope for a common foreign policy. The EC has not as yet developed the consensus necessary for it to play an international role fully commensurate with its economic importance. Moreover, as the General Agreement on Tariffs and Trade negotiations show, the tendency toward protectionism, toward a "fortress Europe" mentality, has not yet been overcome. And yet the need for the Community to remain open to the world has never been greater. The most pressing challenge is of course that of Eastern Europe. It is crucial that the old cold war divisions are not replaced by a new economic divide, which would inevitably reinforce the danger of political instability. If the EC is to be the heart of Europe, the path to federation in the West must be matched by the prospect of a European confederation embracing East and West. The collapse of the Soviet satellite empire in Eastern Europe has opened up such a wider vision while at the same time posing, with renewed force, the question of a European defense policy. European defense policy can only be credible and viable if it offers a compelling vision of the future, a vision of the new Europe, based on human rights, self-determination, and economic and political democracy. This is the true European horizon of the European Community in the 1990s.

Part I

The Politics of Integration

–1–

Toward a Federal Europe

JACQUELINE DUTHEIL de la ROCHÈRE

The adoption of the Single European Act on 17 and 28 February 1986 appears to have given a fresh impetus, not only to the establishment of an internal market in 1992, but also to the political construction of Europe as envisaged by Jean Monnet and Robert Schuman at the time of the elaboration of the treaty that created the European Coal and Steel Community (Treaty of Paris 1951). The effects, however, of the media-promoted "1992" phenomenon, engendered by the adoption of the Single European Act, had not yet been fully absorbed by the twelve member states of the European Economic Community (Treaty of Rome 1957) when, at the end of 1989, crucially important events overturned the established order in Eastern Europe. The Communist regimes in Poland, the German Democratic Republic, Czechoslovakia, Romania, and Bulgaria, in existence since 1948, collapsed in less than three months, without any bloodshed (with the exception of Romania), and have chosen parliamentary democracy. East Germany has been reunited with West Germany and absorbed into the European Economic Community (EEC). Consequently, the assumptions that hitherto have been used as a basis for analysis have now lost their value.

Does the European Community, originally envisaged as a framework for the reconciliation of France and Germany, and as bulwark against the threat believed to have come from the East still have a reason to exist now that the Berlin Wall has collapsed and Czechoslovakian soldiers have dismantled the Iron Curtain? If the Europe of "the twelve" is to continue, having given an appropriate place to a united Germany, will it follow its original path confirmed in the Single European Act, toward greater political unity and toward federalism? Beyond the hard core of twelve, what perspective could be opened to new parliamentary democracies anxious to join the European structure?

In his speech on 31 December 1989, President Mitterrand launched the idea of a confederation of all European states, with the exclusion of the Soviet Union, which is itself in the throes of transformation, in addition to the federation of the European Community. This means that, even in this new period, the federal idea remains the central issue for discussion.

The term "federalism" carries with it a certain number of myths; in particular, the image of a peaceful unification process that preserves the right to be different. The federal state system is not a miraculous formula: compared with the exceptional successes experienced in the United States or Switzerland, the experience of federalism in countries like India, Brazil, and the Soviet Union has been much less convincing. This, however, is the formula most frequently advanced to describe the construction of Europe. In order to avoid, as far as possible, subjective assessments of the greater or lesser federalist nature of the European framework, a definition of federalism must be adopted – such as, for example, that retained in classical constitutional law, according to which a federal state implies:

1. The existence of common institutional mechanisms in which the member states participate, the decisions of which are made by majority vote rather than unanimity, which could have the effect of transforming the federation into a confederation.
2. The transfer of a certain number of internal powers to the federal government, member states preserving the right to exercise non-transferred powers.
3. The exercise of the external powers of the federal state by one federal government only.

Does the European Community at present come within such a framework? It should be remembered that the European Community is not a state. Its existence is not based, in the words of the French writer Maurice Barrès, on "an expressed desire on the part of the European people to live together." On the contrary, various national components of Europe have fought each other relentlessly over the centuries. One cannot discover at the heart of the European Community a "social contract" as the expression is used by John Locke or Jean-Jacques Rousseau to describe the foundation of the democratic state or parliamentary government. At the very most, what one can find in the founding treaties of the Community, the Treaties of Paris and Rome, is a contract between governments, or a pact between executive powers, which has received the approval of the respective national parliaments.

As it has become customary to conceive federalism as a form of state organization, it is somewhat difficult to consider the European Community outside the concept of the state. This, however, is what must be done in order to imagine, on the basis of a past and a present that are well known, what the European Community will represent at the end of the century in the new climate developing in Central and Eastern Europe.

The European Community Was Conceived as a Prefederal System

The authors of the Treaties did not make any definitive choice between cooperation and integration, leaving things to be decided by events. In certain circumstances, however, despite the fact that the governments had been unable or had not wanted to decide, the European judges have used the rule of law as a means of advancing in the federalist direction. This represents one of the most distinctive characteristics of the Community framework.

The Authors of the Treaties Did Not Make a Definite Choice in Favor of Federalism

As early as 1951, some federalist elements were apparent in the system instituted by the Treaty of Paris for the European Coal and Steel Community (ECSC). Important powers were transferred to the High Authority, an independent executive body. Certain decisions were to be taken with the approval of the Council voting by a mere qualified majority and not unanimously. Such decisions could have a direct effect on firms in member states. A Court of Justice was established as a permanent judge with the mission of ensuring the proper application of the Treaty. It could be referred to by the Community institutions, member states, and companies. However, some of the features of an international organization based on pure cooperation remained. The Council, which in reality was nothing more than a kind of diplomatic conference bringing together all the member states, played a decisive role in the decision-making process. The Assembly, elected by indirect suffrage, was confined to a purely consultative role.

A few years later (Conference of Messina, 1956), the authors of the Treaties of Rome (EEC and European Atomic Energy Commission (Euratom)) did not proceed any further along the path of supranationality. The European Community of Defence (ECD) plans, proposed less than ten years after the end of World War II in order to revive the German army under a supranational European command, had recently failed (1954), opposed by an anti-federalist French Parliament.

The six founding member states of the ECSC decided to proceed demonstratively with the construction of Europe by degrees, as advocated by the Schuman Declaration of 9 March 1950. The first and most important proposal in the Schuman Declaration, which was in fact drafted by Jean Monnet, was to assist the reconciliation between France and Germany by progressively binding these two states in a network of obligations, which were to become increasingly onerous and restrictive, the other European states acting as guarantors of the strength and durability of the agreement. Thus, the initial treaty, limited to coal and steel (1952), was followed by an agreement on nuclear energy and subsequently by the Common Market Treaty (1958).

In the longer term, the ambition of the Schuman Plan is a political one and involves a federalist approach. In order to eliminate any risk of war between the European states, these states must develop similar attitudes in all their foreign policies and perhaps even a common defense system in or parallel to NATO. A feeling of solidarity between the peoples of such states would also be needed, the ultimate objective being the creation of a "European citizen." This in turn would engender the creation of a European nation.

This federalist ambition, expressed for the first time at the Congress of The Hague in 1948, has never been completely lost from sight by a number of politicians who, for three decades, have been the defenders of the construction of Europe. The more recent conversion to Europe of other politicians may have had at its roots different aims, namely electoral on the national level (e.g., the French Socialist Party). This could, in the end, help to achieve the same federalist objective.

Community Practice Has Hesitated between Simple Cooperation and Greater Integration

For many years various political and economic factors have reduced the prefederalist nature of the Treaties in the operation of the Common Market. Although the removal of customs barriers was achieved in 1970, well in advance of the dates set by the EEC Treaty, the creation of a Common Market has raised considerable problems: the necessary legislation for the implementation of the free movement of persons and the free supply of services was not adopted before the end of the transitional period (1970). The common policies set out in the Treaty, which were to make the European Community more than a simple customs union, met with insuperable hurdles and difficulties in their adoption and implementation. Not only did the cost of the common agricultural policy weigh tragically heavily on the Community's finances, but also economic and monetary policies, as well as industrial and transport policies, proved impossible to formulate.

In order to attempt to analyse the causes of the difficulties encountered by the European Community on the path toward greater integration, three points should be emphasized:

1. The role of General de Gaulle from 1958 to 1969.

   It is well known that the former President of the French Republic vetoed several times the United Kingdom's application for membership. Suspicious of any form of integration, General de Gaulle advocated a "Europe of nations." This is a favorite formula of Mikhail Gorbachev when he invokes the common European forum "from the Atlantic to the Urals." In the 1960s however, the French President's desire to limit the European framework to a "Europe of nations" had some very definite consequences, causing what has been called "the crisis of Luxemburg" (1966). Faced with an important problem concerning the common agricultural policy, the French government refused to allow the qualified majority voting rules contained in the Treaty to apply, demanding a unanimous vote whenever their national interest was at stake. France's partners had to accept this huge backward step, contrary to the prefederalism of the Treaty, in order to avoid the breakdown of the Community.

   From 1966 onward, all the important decisions of the European Community were taken unanimously, just as in any other international organization of mutual cooperation. In France, both business circles, which were ill-disposed to accept competition from companies in other member states on their own territory, and intellectual and political circles more or less welcomed the government's anti-federal attitude. As for France's partners, their criticism of the principle behind the decision that had been made did not prevent them in turn from claiming at appropriate moments the right to benefit from the "Luxemburg compromise" and from using their veto to prevent the adoption of measures considered contrary to "a crucial national interest."

2. The accession of new member states.

Outside the Community institutions, the heads of state (in the case of France) and governments (in the case of the other five member states) formed the habit of meeting regularly to discuss common problems. This type of meeting, originally called a "summit" and then the "European Council," was by its very nature a challenge to the prefederal institutions created by the Treaties: the supranational Commission and the Council of Ministers, where votes should usually have been taken by a qualified majority.

At the Hague Summit in December 1969, the first summit at which France was not represented by General de Gaulle but by President Pompidou, three key words were adopted for the Community's future: achievement, reinforcement, enlargement. As a result, in 1972 the United Kingdom, Denmark, and Ireland signed their entry into the Community with effect from 1975, and in 1981 Greece joined the Community, followed by Spain and Portugal in 1985. Each new member was granted an adaptation period of two to five years before having to fully submit to Community legislation.

While strengthening the potential force of the great European market – 325 million consumers, whose average standard of living is among the highest in the world – such expansion created new problems, which were not solely of an economic nature. The unanimity necessary when a member state invoked a crucial national interest proved to be more difficult to obtain with twelve members than with six. New rifts appeared between Northern and Southern Europe, between the more liberal and the more protectionist countries, between the partisans and adversaries of political and monetary union. The United Kingdom continually refused to join the European Monetary System and to bring the pound sterling into the ECU. Major disputes arose over the vote to approve the budget, the Common Agricultural Policy (CAP). The United Kingdom was highly critical, not without reason, of the CAP and took over the position of eternal objector previously occupied by France. Prime Minister of England Mrs. Thatcher, refusing the principle of solidarity between Community member states, insisted that her country obtain from the Community a financial benefit in direct proportion to the sacrifices made (e.g., abandoning traditional sources of supplies from the Commonwealth): this is not permitted, however, by the system of common resources established in the Community since 1975.

The vote on the budget has become more difficult each year. It has become necessary to resort to a fourth source of revenue of a much less Community nature, calculated on the basis of the Gross National Product of each member state. This represented a further step backward in relation to the objective of integration, which, in contrast, would have resulted in the acceptance by member states of a certain degree of solidarity and cost sharing.

3. The Economic Crisis of 1978 to 1984.

The poor economic situation, accompanied by an ever-rising unemployment rate, did not help to develop feelings of solidarity between the European states or the acceptance of common legislation. Member states that had implemented the removal of the customs barriers in the 1960s surreptitiously reestablished their protectionist policies. Impeded by the multiplication of quality standard regulations and measures having equivalent effect to quantitative restrictions, goods circulated less freely. No notable progress was achieved in the field of free movement of persons, capital, transport policy, etc.

Faith in the concept of Europe began to falter, even in the most ardent federalist sectors. Was the Monnet method of the "construction of Europe by degrees" to lose its merits? Was the European Economic Community going to be reduced simply to a free trade area? In the pervasive pessimism of the 1980s, while Japan and the United States increased their market shares in international trade, the European Community hesitated as to the response to adopt. It must be emphasized, however, that even during this difficult period, the development of Community law continued to serve European cohesion.

The Role of Community Law

While at the beginning of the 1980s, in political circles, the federalists were themselves close to having doubts as to the Community's future, the lawyers never ceased to play, discreetly, an extremely constructive role.

1. The development of subsidiary Community Law.

   In a task such as the construction of the Community, which has not matured through a natural process of evolution but derives from deliberate action taken by governments involved, the law can play a decisive role. The law is the instrument whereby new institutions and regulations are created; the law enables potential abuses to be controlled and limited. Even though the European Community is not a state, it is a "state of law."

   The Council and the Commission, working together, have developed an impressive apparatus of regulations and directives with which to harmonize the member states' legislations, to ensure the existence of free competition within the EEC (by means of Community anti-competition law, which is highly sophisticated) and to prevent any discrimination on the grounds of nationality. Week after week, the Official Journal of the European Community spreads this new flow of regulations throughout the Community, translated into the nine official languages of the EEC.

2. The constructive attitude of the European Court of Justice.

   In any federal system in which the question of the division of power between the federal government and the member states frequently causes problems, the federal judge has to intervene as arbiter. The Court of Justice in Luxemburg, created as the permanent judicial organ of the European Community, has not hesitated, whenever the opportunity arose, to fully exercise its role as interpreter of the common law of the Community, in particular by means of referrals for preliminary rulings from judges of the national courts.

From the ambiguities contained in the text of the Treaties, the Court, in an empirical but perfectly coherent manner, has established the main principles of a prefederal Community law. It has laid down, for the benefit of nationals of the member states, the principle of direct applicability of Treaty provisions, which are sufficiently clear and precise to be capable of creating rights [case 26/62 van Gend en Loos, 5 February 1963]. The Court confirmed the supremacy of Community law over the national laws of member states regardless of any provisions of any national constitution [case 6/62 Costa v. Enel, 18 July 1964; case 106/77 Simmenthal, 9 March 1978].

The Luxemburg Court was criticized at the time for acting like the Supreme Court of the United States, as a type of government of judges. In reality, however, apart from a few token protests, the member states accepted that the Court of Justice should take on the task of completing the legal construction of the Community, which they themselves had not yet achieved due to being unable to vote either by qualified majority or by unanimity.

The Court of Justice, faced with the task of having to interpret texts that were susceptible of several meanings, has regularly chosen interpretations that are the most apt to guarantee the unification and cohesion of the supranational legal system and to conserve a Common Market. The absence of any formal objection on the part of member states can be seen today as amounting to acceptance. Accordingly, behind the European political scene, which consists of clashes between states, tension and dead-ends, Community law has prospered and allowed the creation of a new area for the expansion of business. At the end of the 1980s, while the European Community was uncertain of its future, the rest of the world recognized its existence in a positive way and saw its power of attraction as important.

It is against this complex background that the Single European Act was adopted in 1986, followed by the enormous upheaval in Eastern Europe in 1989. These two events have led to a general questioning of the future of European federalism.

What is the Future of European Federalism?

More than the Single European Act, which has proved to be essentially a media-based operation, it is the changes in Central

Europe, and in particular, the arrival of a reunited Germany, which should create a new challenge for the European Community.

The Single European Act: An Essentially Media-based Operation

The new European Parliament, elected in 1979 for the first time by direct universal suffrage, and anxious to fully exercise its role as a representative assembly of the people, relaunched the idea of a political union. In order to be true to its original vocation, the European Community should not be satisfied to be simply a common economic organization.

At the initiative of one of its members, Mr. Spinelli, Parliament prepared and then adopted in 1984 a plan for a Treaty of European Union, in which a Community with increased powers in the field of security and human rights would assume the functions of a proper federal government. This proposal for a Treaty, inspired by pure federalism, had little real chance of being ratified by the member states. Parliament's initiative did, however, lead the states to undertake a minimal revision of the Treaties in order to reactivate the Community spirit and to achieve in 1993 what, according to the terms of the original Treaties, should have been achieved long ago in the area of free movement of goods, services, and capital. As a result of noteworthy cooperation between the Commission and the Council, a heterogeneous text was prepared, the Single European Act, which was adopted at the beginning of 1986 and came into force on 1 July 1987.

Progress toward federalism has not been enormous, but the "Monnet method" for the construction of Europe by degrees had once more shown itself to be workable and this is what has most struck the experts.

1. The provisions of the Single European Act.

New institutions and new procedural measures were introduced, inspired by a common desire for greater integration. A new court of first instance should serve to lighten the daily caseload of the Court of Justice without damaging its role as supreme court of the Community. The Council of Ministers has been given the right to decide more often by a qualified majority rather than unanimously. The powers of Parliament have been increased. In collaboration with the Commission it can block a decision of the Council, except if the Council has acted unanimously. The granting of Parliament's basic request to participate actively in the exercise of the regulatory power has not, however, reawakened the interest of the European electorate, which abstained in alarming proportions (40 percent abstentions) in the June 1989 elections.

Under the Single European Act, new powers in the field of environmental policy, research, and technology, and economic and social cohesion, have been transferred by the member states to the Community. Nevertheless, however extensive the transfer of powers may be, in the crucial fields of education and culture, power remains within the exclusive competence of the member states. Finally, a completely new chapter has been introduced in relation to political cooperation. This is perhaps the most clearly federal aspect of the Single European Act. The member states have decided to formalize a practice that they have exercised since 1974. The regular meetings of the heads of state and governments should permit the member states to consult each other regarding foreign policy matters.

2. The psychological impact of the Single European Act.

It is the media's representation of the Single European Act, more than its contents, which are, after all, quite modest, that has enabled 1993 to become a "new frontier."

It was formally agreed by all the parties that the internal market, which would already have existed since the end of the transitional period if the decision-making process had worked properly, would definitely be achieved by 31 December 1992. The message was relayed by every modern means of communication, which transmitted it as an event and thus, created the event.

Consequently, the French Government, after years of hesitation, decided to progressively liberalize its national system of telecommunications and to adjust taxation on savings in line with the system that exists in other member states, in order to make the freedom of movement of capital workable. Suddenly, the conservation of Europe, undertaken thirty years ago by governments, was considered by everyone to be a necessity.

The operation is quite remarkable but does not owe a great

deal to the law. It must be emphasized that, after having adopted the Single European Act, the heads of government signed a joint declaration in which they stated that the date set of 31 December 1992 was devoid of any legal effect. This prevented the European Court of Justice from declaring, as it has not hesitated to do in the past, that certain provisions concerning the establishment of a single market are directly applicable for the benefit of nationals of the member states.

In this way, in a context of increasing prosperity, the Europe of the twelve was slowly proceeding toward its goal of 1993. At the beginning of 1989, President Jacques Delors had launched a plan for economic and monetary union, which was to be achieved in three successive stages, leading to the creation of a single issuing bank. This would be an essential preliminary achievement, in the minds of its supporters, of a new movement toward federalist reform.

The advisability of launching a new revision of the Treaties while the effect of the Single European Act remains unknown, was being questioned when Central and Eastern Europe were plunged into an era of turbulence that is likely to confuse the layout of Europe for a long time.

The Future of European Federalism in the New Climate Emerging in Central and Eastern Europe

In recent years there has been a great tendency to link Europe solely with economies, with the single market, forgetting at times that the primary aim of the European edifice was political: to ensure peace in a continent where, in this century alone, two world wars have arisen; to restore European influence over the rest of the world; and to concentrate on a world order no longer dominated by recourse to arms. Current changes in Europe require a return to these original aims. How should the Community react to these prodigious transformations, which are progressively liberating the eastern half of the continent of Europe? Should a slowing down of the Community process, which had just been reactivated by the Single European Act, be expected?

Some people, viewing what they see as uncertainty as to the future of Germany, predict a return to the diplomacy that consisted of a balance of power and backdoor alliances. Others are of the opinion that, due to the fact that Eastern Europe has been liberated, a new concept of a "grand Europe" should replace the Community concept, which is considered already to be out of date. In light of these new events, the idea of a great European Confederation proposed by President Mitterrand has the advantage of offering a new perspective and a new framework to the Eastern countries currently in the process of becoming democracies.

At the same time, the idea reopens the debate on a political Europe. Would the path toward a confederation lead to the abandonment of any prospect of the economic and political reinforcement of the Community of the twelve? Jacques Delors does not envisage this to be the case. On the contrary, he sees a Federation between Western European countries as a means of accompanying the reunification of Germany and an essential preliminary requirement for the launching of the great Confederation.

It is certainly too soon to outline the possible structure of plans that have been launched in an exceptionally unsettled European context. In conclusion, however, one can make three observations:

1. The reunification of Germany will depend on the freely expressed wishes of the German people within the exercise of their right to self-determination. A reunified Germany may easily take part in the European Community, which has for a long time already included East Germany within its free trade area. The EEC Treaty regards any German person as a national of a member state; however, the expansion of the Community's territory to the eastern part of Germany may appear to be incompatible with the maintenance of this eastern part in the Warsaw Pact. In view of this, the question of security and defense in Central Europe is bound to be raised.
2. The process of transformation commenced in the Soviet Union seems to be a long-term one. As long as a risk of instability remains in the Soviet Union, the preservation of links of solidarity with the Atlantic and an efficient defense system will continue to be necessary in Western Europe. Furthermore, it seems that the time has not yet come for the transfer of power, in the area of defense, from member states to the Community. If the plan for a Federation of Twelve, extended to East Germany, were to be implemented in the next few years, NATO would very likely continue to exist in parallel.
3. Freedom in Eastern Europe is accompanied by risks of instability and struggles caused by low economic standards and the

resurgence of nationalist feelings that have been held in check for a long time. The development of these countries and their peaceful evolution toward democracy require extensive outside help. Community aid would be even more effective if it led to the signing of association agreements without excluding the prospect of future membership. For the majority of Eastern countries, however, such a prospect can only remain distant. A suitable means of preparation could be membership of the Council of Europe during the period of democratic apprenticeship, as Community discipline may only be borne by countries with more or less comparable economies and standards of living.

–2–

Who Legislates? Institutional Developments in the European Community and the Single European Act

PHILOMENA MURRAY

The European Community (EC) is a new form of political community that does not conform to existing definitions either of an international organization or of a federation of states, while it displays features of both.[1] The Community is a political organization of twelve democratic states, which are to some extent interdependent and hence have surrendered a measure of national sovereignty in order to cooperate on specific policy areas. EC laws are binding on the member states, with direct effect in the states. This interdependence of national and EC laws is the crux of the interrelationship and the mosaic of complex relations in the EC. It is the only international organization that involves a consistent transfer of power and functions of state administration to new European institutions, and these for economic and social objectives. These EC institutions form a system of checks and balances in an institutional structure that possesses no government or opposition, no media or distinctly European citizens.

The EC is based on the policies intrinsic to the four freedoms of movement of goods, persons, capital, and services and the growing realization that certain problems could not be solved by national means exclusively. The EC's main legal base, the Treaty of Rome,

1. The EC or European Community refers to the European Coal and Steel Community, the European Economic Community, and the European Atomic Energy Community.

sets out the aim of free trade and free and fair competition, with a single internal market for the four freedoms. The Single European Act (SEA) prepares the Community for the practical implementation of these four freedoms throughout the twelve member states.[2] The SEA provides the legal framework for improved decision making in order to complete by 1992 the Internal Market, an area without internal frontiers in which the four freedoms are ensured.

Background to the SEA Initiative

Over the last decade, it has been persuasively argued that the member states had reached a stage of interdependence where they needed a common economic policy, to maintain equilibrium between the imbalance of their economies, provide a framework for their economic development, safeguard their interests in and contribute to the management of the wider international economy.[3] It has been commonly held that, despite the fact that the EC is a major trading power, "far too little" had been done in order to build up an internal market, with common policies and a transfer of powers to the Community. Interdependence, critics argued, merits further integration with a further transfer of sovereignty to the Community. The SEA of 1986 established the institutional and decisional structures for a single internal market, with the target date of 31 December 1992. This involves both negative integration (the abolition of national barriers in order to set up the Internal Market) and positive integration in the form of implementation and coordination of common policy by the EC.

The original conception of the EC was of a community of economic or functional integration by sectors, beginning with the areas of coal and steel production, which would then lead to a political community in a federalist United States of Europe. Over three decades later, the internal market proposed by some early federalists is now approaching realization.

2. The SEA was approved at the Luxembourg European Council in December 1985.

3. See for example J. Pinder, "Economic and Social Powers of the European Union and the Member States: subordinate or coordinate relationship" in *An Even Closer Union: A Critical Analysis of the Draft Treaty Establishing the European Union*, ed. R. Bieber, J. Jacque, J. Weiler (Luxembourg, 1985), 123.

While there is no central executive or European party system, there are four main EC institutions, provided for in the founding Treaties and the 1965 Merger Treaty. These are the Council, the Commission, the Parliament, and the Court of Justice, and there are some auxiliary institutions and "complementary entities" that have legal status.[4] The EC possesses a body of law, upon which it is based, and although it has been called an "incomplete legal framework," nevertheless, the Community's legitimacy is largely based on its legal system.

The Intergovernmental Conference and the SEA

The 1985 IGC, the Intergovernmental Conference of EC member states, which resulted in the Single European Act, further reinforces the Treaty-based nature of the EC, including the decisions to incorporate European Political Cooperation (EPC) and the European Monetary System as they operate at present in the EC, despite the evolving nature and previous extra-Treaty status of these means of cooperation. The fact that the EC is not simply a legal entity, but now affects the lives of the citizens of Community member states, is recognized in the incorporation into the SEA of such policy areas as a People's Europe, the environment, monetary policies, and economic and social cohesion.

The IGC amendments to the Treaties have illustrated that the EC is still largely intergovernmental in structure and decision making. It is the member states that possess the power and authority, as a body in Conference, to amend or increase the competences accorded to the institutions.[5] The involvement of the EC institutions in the IGC was minimal.

The politicization of the EC in the 1970s and 1980s had seen a substantial increase in the exercise of non-Treaty-based functions and powers in the Community in the areas of EPC and monetary cooperation, for example. The SEA accords Treaty status and recognition to such cooperation, although in effect it describes the situation as it existed and so served to "freeze" in a legal framework those cooperation processes that were still in a state of evolution.

4. R. Bieber, "The Institutions and decision-making procedure in the Draft Treaty establishing the European Union" in Bieber, et al., *An Even Closer Union*.

5. This is provided for in Articles 235 and 336 of the EEC Treaty, by means of an Intergovernmental Conference.

The April 1989 Delors initiative on Economic and Monetary Union (EMU) goes beyond the provisions of the SEA, for example.[6]

The EC's Institutional and Decision-making Crisis

The Community has been challenged by the enlargement of the scope of its activities with the politicization of its role. It has also been challenged by the successive enlargements, which resulted in the doubling of its member states. This has inevitably placed severe strains on institutions created in the 1950s for a six-member Community with defined short-term aims of economic integration and long term objectives of political integration. The Community had been further rendered less effective in decision making by the emphasis on the primacy of national interests in the light of the Luxembourg Compromise in 1966, which rejected majority voting on issues of "vital national interest." No criteria were ever actually established by the EC as to what vital national interest actually means.

Institutional reform of the decision-making processes of the EC was therefore proposed as a cure to the malaise of institutional inertia. The malaise was always the same *lourdeur*, democratic deficit, and irrelevance.[7] The proposed cures are always the same: improved decision making, more powers to the European Parliament, and an increase of the competence of the Community.[8] The political will, it was constantly stated, was lacking, while the *lourdeur* of the Community's institutional procedures reinforced the Community's negative image, some national governments' disillusionment with the Community, and the weakening of European cooperation in general.

The Three Wise Men's report in 1979 validly pointed out that institutional reforms alone were unlikely to improve the "climate," particularly in the absence of the priorities of the Community itself. Rather, many observers placed the responsibility for Community

6. See Committee for the Study of Economic and Monetary Union, *Report on Economic and Monetary Union in the European Community* (Brussels, 1989).

7. J. Weiler, "Supranationalism Revisited – A Retrospective – The European Communities after 30 years" in *Noi Si Mura* (Selected Working Papers of the European University Institute, Florence, 1986).

8. See, for example, the Vedel Report, the Tindemans Report, the Report of the Three Wise Men.

inertia on the national governments. The issue of institutional reform was reopened in 1985 by the IGC in the wake of attempts by the European Council to improve the institutions and to make the Community more relevant.[9] The European Parliament's (EP) Draft Treaty on European Union also challenged the political actors to envisage an EC government directly elected by the people, with federal power centralized in the EC institutions. This initiative was not adopted by the member states but it served as a useful and thought-provoking catalyst for institutional reform and the adaptation to the challenges facing the EC, especially at the Milan European Council.

The SEA is significant as a political compromise between those participants at the Milan European Council who favored major institutional reform, and those adamantly opposed to it and who favored the retention of the veto. The SEA links institutional changes to efficiency in decision making by greater use of majority voting in specific areas – such as the internal market, harmonization, freedom of establishment, mutual recognition of qualifications, and the Regional Fund – although it has not abolished the veto.[10]

The SEA: An Improvement of EC Decision Making

The Single Act (Article 10), while conferring on the Commission powers to implement EC rules laid down by the Council, also allows the Council to reserve the right to exercise powers of implementation itself, in an amendment of Article 145. This illustrates that while the Commission has more latitude in its role, the Council reserves the right of a final say. It is the Commission that monitors the implementation into national law of EC directives, regulations, and decisions, takes infringement proceedings against member states and manages the Community funds.

Under the SEA, the Council of Ministers continues to make the final decision on what becomes EC law. There are legitimate concerns about preserving democratic accountability in the Community, as the Council is not directly accountable to either the

9. The Dooge Report; The Adonnino People's Europe Report.

10. J. Fitzmaurice, "An Analysis of the European Community's Co-operation Procedure," *Journal of Common Market Studies*, 26, 4 (June 1988).

European Parliament or even national parliaments.

The European Council, the Conference of Heads of State, and Government, which was outside the Treaties and institutional structure, now, under the SEA, meets at least twice a year in order to iron out major problems of coordination of EC policy in a top-level intergovernmental structure.

Within the EC, legislative and executive functions are divided between the Council and the Commission. The Parliament fulfills co-decision and control functions and judicial control is exercised by the Court of Justice. The Council, however, remains the closest to an executive decision maker within the institutional structure, while the Commission has management competences and proposes legislation. The Parliament's co-decision powers had been limited to the conciliation procedure on the Budget until the Single Act expanded this procedure somewhat, while not going as far as the Italian proposal on co-decision put forward during the IGC.

The Commission is endeavoring to improve the balance of powers in the institutional triangle and to reduce conflicts between the institutions through interinstitutional dialogue, which has been intensified since the SEA, particularly with regard to the cooperation procedure. The Commission-Council link is the strongest side of the institutional triangle, followed by Commission-Parliament linkage; the weakest side is that of relations between the Parliament and the Council. The Commission therefore plays an important role in cooperation procedure, in acting as mediator in Council-Parliament conflicts as well as in informal negotiations or inter-institutional dialogue under the 1988 agreement and encouraged by Delors.

The European Parliament is still far from becoming a legislative body but alterations of its role are apparent. With the exception of the cooperation procedure on the Budget, the EP had minimal influence over the Council and limited power over the Commission until 1986. The SEA altered the balance of power of the EC institutions with regard to the cooperation and assent procedures, as here the EP's active legislative involvement is now essential. In addition, the Council is now obliged to adopt a common position on draft EC laws, a position that it must now justify to the EP, and decision making has now been speeded up as there is a strict time scale for the adoption of common positions.

The EP is now becoming adept at flexing its muscles and at attempting to exercise its budgetary and control powers, and its new powers under the assent and cooperation procedures, particularly since the implementation of the SEA. It is particularly in the assent procedure in external relations, that the EP's role has been enhanced under the SEA.[11] Now the EP's assent is required for all such agreements as well as for the renewal of agreements and their related financial protocols.

The SEA's "cooperation" procedure applies to very specific cases between the Council and the Parliament. These cases include legislation on the elimination of discrimination under Article 7 of the Treaty on the freedom of movement of workers, the right of establishment (Articles 49 and 54) and on the establishment of the free movement of services (Article 57) and finally harmonization directives under the new Article 100a on the functioning of the Common Market. This latter provision excludes tax harmonization, major aspects of freedom of movement, and provisions relating to the rights and interests of workers, thereby limiting the scope of the EP's involvement.

The Parliament has pointed out difficulties with the cooperation procedure.[12] Despite the political will expressed, when the SEA was finalized by the Council, for more involvement of the EP in the EC legislative process, in the first twelve months after the entry into force of the SEA fewer than half of the amendments that the EP had adopted at first reading and less than 25 percent of those adopted at second reading had been incorporated into legislation that the Council adopted. The Parliament has also criticized what it regards as the Council's failure to participate adequately in the planning of legislation introduced by the EP and the Commission and the fact that there is no requirement on the part of the Council to complete its first reading "within a reasonable time limit." The EP has also taken the Commission to task for not always publishing its modified proposals following the EP's first reading and for abandoning positions of the EP that it had previously accepted. The EP is seeking to make maximum use of this cooperation procedure in order to combat its perceived marginalization in EC decision making.

The Parliament's dissatisfaction with the SEA in general with regard to its limited scope, and the fact that it falls short of the EP's

11. Under Article 8 of the SEA, applied to Article 237 (accession agreements) and Article 238 (cooperation agreements) of the EEC Treaty.

12. European Parliament: Resolution on the Results obtained from the SEA's implementation, 27 October 1988. Doc. A2–176/88.

own project for European Union, has prompted the Parliament to consider drawing up a new draft proposal for European Union "before the 1992 deadline and it will be for the Parliament elected in 1989 to accomplish this task."[13] It should be pointed out that the position adopted by the Parliament on the SEA in October 1988 was a majority, not a united position, as there are distinct differences of opinion within the Assembly on the SEA and the Parliament's role under the new procedure. In addition, the EP decided to reap the benefits of the SEA by amending its working methods in order to exploit its participation in the legislative process, to comply with the strict deadline during the second reading in accordance with the SEA, and to ensure a political link between the first and second readings as well as the achievement of an absolute majority of the EP as a whole. The 1990 EP Martin Report envisages a more active role for the EP in the Intergovernmental Conference of late 1990, with co-decision powers with the Council.

The literature on the EC's institutional reform suggests that by giving the EP co-decisional power, the democratic deficit will be reduced and the SEA goes some way in that direction. Fears that reform would "render a decisional process which is already heavy almost unbearably so"[14] have not been borne out. Institutional reform by its very nature involves extensive review of the present system, streamlining of the decision-making process, as in the case of the 1985 IGC on the SEA, and hence a less cumbersome decision-making machinery.

The allocation of co-decisional powers to the EP, for example, (already initiated in the SEA) merits the risk of complicating the decisional process if it serves in some way to legitimize the EP's role and involve it in the legislative process in a more active manner than hitherto. The July 1990 session of the EP adopted the Martin proposed Treaty Reforms on co-decision with Council and on increased use of majority voting in Council on social and environmental legislation.

The provisions of Article 149 on the Internal Market have been substantially amended in the SEA in favor of speedier and more efficient decision making by the Council and fuller consultation of the Parliament. For example, the Council and Commission should now inform the EP of the reason for the Council's common

13. European Parliament: Resolution Doc. A2–176/88, point 23.
14. J. Weiler, "Supranationalism Revisited," 13.

position, and also of the Commission's position on draft legislation (new Article 149, 2a and 2b). Hence, answerability is strengthened in the EP's favor. Parliament is to approve the common position of the Council, or to take a decision on it, within three months, thereby reducing some delays in the process of making EC law. Specific time stipulations for the reexamination of the EP's position by the Commission are also laid down in the Single Act.[15] The assent of the Parliament, by absolute majority of its members, is also required, under the new Article 237, paragraph 1, with regard to applications for EC membership and regarding agreements concluded by the Council under Article 238. This process has worked smoothly in the first year of implementation.

The SEA has challenged the EP to become aware of new procedural demands, as it realizes that it needs to fully utilize its role under the SEA in order to attain political leverage with the other institutions. The provisions of the SEA offer the party groups of the EP a new objective rationale to strengthen group cohesion and leadership control of those groups. The SEA has also given rise to new procedures in the EP and its decision-making circuits as well as a widespread desire for increased legislative decision making. Under the SEA, the EP is now obliged to come to a decision on its strategy by the second reading, particularly on the EC Budget, in order to form a coherent long-term strategy. For this it is obliged to trust the group whips and expert MEPs to attempt to reach consensus. In order to achieve consensus, therefore, the coalition-building process must be handed over to the political groups, and this constitutes a new political configuration in the EC with repeated scenarios of control by the two major groups, the Socialists and the European People's Party in the 1984–1989 EP and the present Parliament.

Conclusions

The EP, like the Commission and some member states, is of the opinion that much remains to be achieved in the quest for European Union. The EP has in the past denounced the democratic deficit in EC decision making, which alienates them from the representation of the voters in decision making and from control and scrutiny over the other EC institutions. The majority of the MEPs consider that

15. New article 149, 2(c) to (g) inclusive.

the SEA has led to some progress and believe that due to improved decision-making procedures the EP is more closely associated with the legislative tasks of the Community. "Association" does not, however, denote "powers," and the EP itself has pointed out that decision making still lacks "democracy," as the Council can adopt a text rejected by the Parliament.

The SEA has altered the institutions of the EC by adding new chapters that deal with previously understated or ignored policy areas, such as economic and social cohesion, the environment, monetary affairs, research, and the social sector; second, by formalizing the process of foreign policy coordination known as European Political Cooperation; and third, by setting the year 1992 as the deadline for the completion of the Internal Market. The allocation of adequate financial resources to the Community in order to ensure the success of the SEA has been welcomed by the institutions. The SEA has sought to enhance the effectiveness of the EC in decision making. In this area, the number of Council decisions taken by majority vote, rather than unanimity, has increased. Nevertheless, with regard to the EP's role, the Parliament is aware that the genuine power of co-decision of the EP and the Council is at present very limited, and the EP's current majority position is for co-decision making on EC legislation in a shared desire for political union.

The EP has criticized the Council and Commission on several counts. It believes that the fact that the Council can adopt legislative texts that it has rejected is anti-democratic. The EP has called on the Commission to provide an undertaking that it will withdraw proposals rejected by the Parliament "in order to ensure that Community legislation is acceptable to the elected representatives chosen by the electorate specifically to ensure democratic control at this level."[16] In this way, the EP is emphasizing its representative role as a watchdog of Community legislation. It further wishes to extend its exercise of this watchdog function, and its information function, by recommending that it be informed of the Council's position, under the cooperation procedure, and of the position adopted on each amendment and vote of each member state. The EP also sees a role for active involvement in European Political Cooperation, including security questions, under the Martin Report, where its role could be "extended," where it could "exercise political con-

16. E.P. Doc. A2–176/88.

trol," and in the appointment of the Commission, which under the Treaty is limited.[17]

Under the SEA, the EP needs to decide on strategy early in the legislative cycle and evolve a coherent long-term strategy on the Budget in particular. Consensus can best be achieved by handing over coalition-building to the political groups. The committees would thus be allocated the very substantive technical details of the political agreements, once they have been elaborated by the groups.

It is incumbent on the Council and the European Council to express the political will to comply with deadlines for the legislative proposals on implementation of the Internal Market, some 300 of which were contained in the Commission white paper and over half of which had been implemented by mid-1989. This is not simply an institutional matter, but rather a political matter at the highest level. It is encouraging that decision making has already improved under the SEA and that the President of the Commission has attributed this improvement to the SEA; the 1990 IGC on political union should promote a quasi-federal institutional system of decision making.

The removal of fiscal barriers remains a matter of reservation for some member states. In addition, the effectiveness of the Delors EMU package will depend on decision making at the European Council, that is, intergovernmental level. Such decision making is not regulated by the other institutions. The concept of sovereignty still remains a major stumbling block and this is reinforced by the predominantly intergovernmental, rather than federal, nature of the 1985 Conference on the SEA. The Community is only as strong as its least enthusiastic member when it is a matter of surrender of sovereignty. The protection of vital national interests is still the top priority on the EC agenda for many member states, whether made explicit or not. The centralized decision making with more majority voting, which is so necessary in order to achieve the Internal Market in the SEA, will be undermined by national interests or derogations for some time to come, although the 1990 IGC should challenge member states to take another step in the direction of a federal-style political union.

Finally, it is important to place the SEA in the context of the institutional and political developments of the EC as a *sui generis* political community. The SEA is less innovative than the EP Spinelli

17. E.P. Doc. A2–201/88, point C of Resolution on the SEA.

Draft Treaty, it is true. Yet, the SEA contains commitments that amount to the handing over of decision-making sovereignty by member states to supranational EC institutions on specific aspects of the Internal Market. The success of the SEA will depend on the political will of the member states and on whether they adhere to the spirit of European Union, which prevailed at some of the 1985 IGC meetings. The efficient operation of the SEA also depends on interinstitutional cooperation, particularly on the will of the Council of member states to adhere to deadlines and to its commitments to European Union in the 1990 IGC. The very fact that political union, although not clearly defined, is the focus of the 1990 IGC is a step forward from intergovernmentalism to tentative federalism, and it remains to be seen if this will be followed by other steps along the long road to European federalism.

–3–

Basic Questions of European Integration

WERNER WEIDENFELD

Careful observers of the process of European integration over the last few years will have gained very mixed impressions: the undeniable achievements of integration constantly contrast with new tasks and difficulties; alongside progress there have always been signs of crisis and stagnation.

Thus, the European Community presents a very varied and not entirely clear picture in which light and shade are closely interwoven. The consensus of the early days has disappeared. Controversy concerns no longer only individual positions in European policy but the fundamental question as to whether there is any point to further integration at all. The visions of the founding fathers of European Integration have been replaced by the cool calculation of statistics and net payments.

What is the reason for all this? What are the root causes of the basic trends of recent years? And what can be done to overcome the fundamental difficulties?

I should like to respond to these questions with answers in the form of theses, five theses that illustrate the difficulties and then four theses suggesting reforms.

First Thesis

The original reasons for European integration have lost their urgency. Thus, the question arises as to the current justification for European unification.

There were five reasons for the path taken in European policy during the 1950s:

- desire for a new identity: Europe became the alternative for the discarded national identities, an alternative to all those perversions of political thinking that had led to world war;
- the wish for security: Europe was to provide a bulwark in the emerging East–West conflict against Communist expansion;
- the desire for freedom and mobility: Europe was to help overcome the restrictions on freedom of movement for people, goods, and capital, which the war had imposed;
- the hopes of economic prosperity: the large common market was to allow economic recovery;
- the expectation of a new shared power: it was hoped that by forming a political alliance the member states could gain much of the power that they had lost individually.

Although these great historical motives have not entirely lost their political importance, they certainly no longer provide the psychological impetus they once did. The pictures of enthusiastic Western Europeans joyfully tearing down border posts is today nothing more than a faded recollection. The question therefore arises of how the historical justification can continue in a valid form. What real reason is there nowadays to favor the unification of Europe?

Reference should here be made to three reasons related to structural aspects of international policy, which are likely to become more important as time goes by:

- European integration is an attempt to reconcile the structure of problems with the decision-making structure; this means that in the Western European countries we can see that the problems are becoming international. For a long time they have transcended national borders with respect to energy supplies, environmental protection, and economic groupings, but the decision-making structures for dealing with these international problems are antiquated because they have remained largely geared to the nation state. As problems have become more international, politicians have lost more and more of their scope for maneuver. European integration is therefore at least an attempt to modernize the political system.

- European integration is a prerequisite if the Western European states are to act effectively at the international level. The countries of Western Europe are faced with enormous international power groupings. No single Western European state is likely to be taken seriously as a credible partner if it acts in an isolated way. Together, however, the countries of Western Europe represent an important power factor in the world.
- European integration offers an opportunity to exert political influence on social development, which means democratic control as well. At the social level, internationalism has made great progress. Economic entities, banks, companies, associations, even tourism have led to greater involvement between societies. The question is whether or not we wish to exert political influence on these developments in Western Europe, and thus democratic control.

These are three essential, forward-looking reasons for European integration, which are derived from vital international issues of the day and provide a realistic assessment of the need for, and limits of, integration.

Second Thesis

In the European Community at the present time there is a discrepancy between the expectations placed on the Community and the Community's scope for action.

The view of history taken in discussions of European policy that there was simply one successful founding generation followed by nothing but stagnation and disappointment is clearly wrong. It ignores the failures of the 1950s (European Defense Community, European Political Community) and the latest successes in the 1970s and 1980s. For example:

- Community financing from its own resources;
- direct election and expansion of powers of the European Parliament;
- creation of European Political Cooperation and inclusion of security policy in such cooperation;
- creation of the European Monetary System;
- conclusion of the Lomé Convention for development policy; and
- creation and reform of the regional fund and social fund.

Throughout this period, however, European integration has been seen as being in crisis. This could be summarized as follows:

Europe suffers not only from its failures but also from its successes, because these successes are "consumed" politically, (i.e., they are taken for granted without any explicit connection being made to the process of integration). If we look more closely, we find that the social-psychological problem in European integration has been that by more or less working it has itself removed the grounds for enthusiasm among the people. The grand notion of "Europe" has become everyday reality, with all the everyday conflicts, compromises, and cumbersome procedures this implies. Any political system, any state, any local authority is subject to this wear and tear, and we regard it as normal; in fact, as democrats in a positive light. But, strangely, we seem to combine with the idea of Europe a particularly marked sense of harmony and regard any controversy and conflict as disruptive. The gap between the hopes and expectations on the one hand and the concrete political potential of the Community on the other, has become a supremely important problem in European policy. We need, therefore, to acquire a realistic view of the possibilities and difficulties, the achievements and shortcomings of the European Community.

Third Thesis

The European Community has not yet succeeded in moving on to its second stage (i.e., from "negative" to "positive" integration).

European unification has entered a new phase: originally it was a question of eliminating obstacles; the frontiers were to lose their divisive effect. In political science this is often defined as "negative integration." Consequently, the Treaty of Rome concentrated on the question of the freedom of movement, the Common Market, customs union, the agricultural market, and common external trade. This "negative integration" has long since reached its limits. The market requires a general political system, competition and concentration require the appropriate intervention measures. Freedom of movement requires supplementary social and economic safeguards. The Common Market calls for uniform representation in international politics.

This means that negative integration now requires additional features of a different kind, "positive integration," requires giving political substance to the social area that has already been created. It means the positive formulation of a common policy, in which matters of substance come to the fore. Political programs need to be formulated and discussed with more attention focused on the structures of society. But this qualitative leap – from the observation and follow-up of quasi-diplomatic procedures in the past, to active use of traditional instruments of domestic policy – has not been achieved.

The unfavorable effects of this transition have already become very apparent. The practical constraints on internal policy are determining the European landscape to greater extent; internal policy considerations and difficulties are increasingly restricting the European Community's room to maneuver.

Fourth Thesis

The heterogeneity of the European Community is proving a major obstacle.

The Community includes large and small states with different positions on security policy, with very different economic structures, and very different national traditions and temperament. It includes members who take a very different view of Europe: Europe as a political union, Europe as a free trade area, Europe as a loose confederation of states. When political and economic conflicts intensify, these differences are of course felt more strongly than in periods when it is simply a question of distributing high growth rates.

These difficulties can be illustrated in a particular context: the economic disparities within the European Community. The differences in economic development in Western Europe are proving to be an obstacle to integration.

The scope for the European Community to react effectively to basic economic challenges has remained severely limited until now. A glance at the budget of the European Community is sufficient to dampen any expectations that might exist, that the Community has an efficient range of financing instruments.

Fifth Thesis

There is a lack of transparency and efficiency in the political decision-making structure.

One thing is clear: the institutional structure of the European Community in no way satisfies the great demand for initiative and leadership on the one hand and coordination on the other. First, it lacks an executive body endowed with all the necessary political powers; and second, there is no clear procedure to give due weight to the various political forces. This overall impression is revealed in a large number of current institutional difficulties:

- The Council of Ministers remains the dominant decision-making body, and because of the present practice of unanimity with its tedious consensus procedures, it has become the sticking point for all proposals. It is very strange to see that the advocates of decentralized power, the representatives of the national governments, have become, as it were, the guardians of the centralized power in Europe.
- The European Council has in no way eased the burden on the Council of Ministers with regard to the backlog of matters requiring decisions. It has not lived up to expectations. Indeed the European Council tends to refer difficult cases back to the Council of Ministers, thus making the whole process longer.
- The Commission has lost a great deal of its political influence. Since the Council of Ministers operates according to the principle of unanimity, the Commission's right of initiative has largely lost any political relevance. The Treaty of Rome set up the Commission as a source of initiative and guardian of Community interest. Its monopoly as regards initiative in the legislative procedure was given particular weight in that the Council of Ministers could only deviate from a proposal unanimously. But if unanimity is the rule, then the Commission has largely been removed from political responsibility in the legislative process.
- The directly elected European Parliament has so far not succeeded in becoming the focal institution representing the citizens of Europe in their eyes.

In general it may be said that the founding fathers of the European Community saw the institutional framework as a dynamic area designed for further development. They formulated concrete proposals on further development, which so far have scarcely been realized. This area of activity is bound to lose its dynamism, and thus its appeal, because the process of institutional development is stagnating.

So much for the problems of European policy, the scenarios of European difficulties, and European crises. What can be done? How can the problems be solved?

First Thesis

European policy is not short of ideas, but short of implementation; thus, the question of strategy becomes the main concern.

The rapid increase in the reports on the reform of European policy indicates a growing loss of confidence. The history of these reform reports, such as the Vedell Report (1972), the Tindemans Report, and the Genscher/Colombo initiative is largely a history of "lost opportunities."

The question of strategy in this concentrated form is one of the aspects of European policy that has been wickedly neglected. Which agency of European policy should take which step, how, and with what effects? Or to be more specific, who can provide an impetus for fresh progress toward integration: governmental conferences or popular movements; European elites – parliamentarians, intellectuals, journalists, academics; a jointly developed leadership of France and West Germany, pulling the other along in its wake as envisaged by Adenauer and de Gaulle when they concluded their treaty of friendship?

Who then is to bring Europe together? I should like to examine this question:

- The integrating element can only be found in those states in which the political and economic power is sufficient to supply the necessary leadership. Calculations in European policy must take account of the real power potential. Illusions quickly fade in the harsh reality of power politics. And it is perhaps one of the stranger illusions of European integration that the draft plans for reform are often left to the smaller states, which means that they then at best find employment as the plaything of seminar organizers and visionaries of various kinds.
- The integration element can only be found in states that believe

the unification of Europe means more than pragmatic economic cooperation. The writing was already on the wall for the political union of Europe when the European Community allowed the accession of states that were only interested in the Community because of its economic success. Today that means we must note carefully which members of the European Community are generally satisfied with the status quo that has been achieved and which states wish to go further toward political union. The solution is then quite simple: those who want a politically united Europe should build it, even if at first there are only two, three, or six of them; those who are only interested in the status quo of European policy should continue to focus their attention on crisis management as in the past.

Second Thesis

The European Parliament could provide an important impetus if it were to strengthen its political position.

If the European Parliament wishes to strengthen its influence in the framework of the decision-making centers (national governments, national bureaucracies, Council of Ministers, Commission), then I believe that the key issue for central changes is for the Members of Parliament to increase their influence on internal, national policy. Those taking decisions on European policy at the national level must not simply be exposed to the pressure of national power centers. The development of the European party system is also essential if the power of the European Parliament is to grow. Generally it is important to have a well-developed political infrastructure (parties, pressure groups, mass media; i.e., all the relevant bodies). Complicated industrial states cannot simply be ruled by decisions taken by statesmen sitting around the fireside.

But it is also important to extend the power of the European Parliament, which means especially:

- effective participation in the legislative process;
- greater budgetary powers;
- greater influence of the European Parliament on appointments in the other bodies.

Third Thesis

European policy must once again take up the successful strategy of the founding fathers: it must conclude European deals.

What does this mean? At the founding stage, one particular technique was always employed in negotiations: different items on the agenda, interests and conflicts were not allowed to stand in isolation but were closely linked. For example, the European Coal and Steel Community was only achieved because at the same time the discriminatory practices toward the German steel industry on the basis of occupation laws were abolished. In return, the German steel market was integrated into the newly created European steel market. The European Atomic Community only came about because the Common Market was achieved at the same time. The military reservations on the part of the French against extending the Atomic Community were only accepted because the appropriate European economic community was set up. In the course of these deals even conflicting interests were used to benefit European policy. Single endeavors, which taken singly appeared hopeless, were brought to a stage where compromise was possible as part of an overall formula, and this is a recipe for success that need not be confined to the founding years.

Fourth Thesis

The unification of Europe must be seen as the long-term task of political life.

The limited attention paid to the subject of Europe is due no doubt to a number of reasons. One of these is that it is not a subject of interest to intellectuals who could in turn transmit it further. We must go beyond the details of everyday policy and consider the cultural aspects of Europe. A healthy portion of intellectual confrontation would be of great benefit to the idea of Europe.

The relatively arid intellectual discussion on Europe nowadays confirms only too well the old argument of the German philosopher Karl Jaspers that the only role left to Europe is "care of the holy places" of world civilization, i.e., that Europe only has a function as a museum. I would like Europe to come more to the fore as the long-term aim of political life. The task of uniting Europe, which is so beset by special interests and national selfishness, needs a cultural bond as a part of the European identity.

–4–

European Integration and the German Question: Drawing a Line Under History

WOLF D. GRUNER

Preliminary Considerations

By 1 January 1993 the Single European Market will be established. Will 1992, the "annus mirabilis of the European Community," as a commentator aptly put it recently, be Europe's last chance to stay in business politically and economically? What will be the impact of the peaceful revolutions in Eastern and Central Europe on the process of integration in the EC? Will the unification of the Federal Republic of Germany and of the German Democratic Republic mean a "complete German takeover of all Europe" and a subjugation to "Deutschmark"-imperialism?[1] Why is 1992 important for world trade, for the whole of Europe and not just for Western Europe? Why are 1992 and its implications important for Germany as a whole?

Let me briefly provide some basic facts:[2]

1. "Speaking for England: Saying the Unsayable about the Germans. Dominic Lawson meets Nicholas Ridley" in *The Spectator*, 14 July 1990, 8–10.

2. Paolo Cecchini, *The European Challenge 1992* (Aldershot, 1988). Victoria Curzon Price, *1992: Europe's Last Chance? From Common Market to Single Market* (London, 1988). John Fells and Michael Newman, *The European Community and the Superpowers* (London, 1989). Ernest Wistrich, *After 1992: The United State of Europe* (London, 1989). Ralph Dahrendorf, et al., *Whose Europe? Competing Visions for 1992* (London, 1989). John Palmer, *1992 and Beyond* (Luxembourg, 1989). Werner Weidenfeld, et al., *Binnenmarkt '92: Perspektiven aus deutscher Sicht* (Gütersloh, 1988).

1. On 1 January 1993 the mass of (West) European legislation, which has to be passed on an EC-level and on a national level for the completion of the Common Single Market, will come into force.
2. Economically and politically speaking, 1992 means some 300 regulations and directives have to be enacted. This project is so far the "most sustained attempt towards the further economic integration" (Arthur Hanhardt) of Western Europe.
3. It is also the intention of the Internal European Market to reap the benefits of scale afforded by a market of 320 million people. This vast market – the biggest single market in the world – will provide the framework for Western Europe to become a giant, single industrial world power, setting standards on a global level.
4. The Single European Market will inevitably further the political, monetary, fiscal, and social integration of the West European democracies and will at some point definitely bring about a European Political Union, thus fulfilling the dream of generations since the fifteenth century.

I shall not be able to deal with all these aspects. Thus, I would like to concentrate on the "problem of Germany," Europe and the Single European Market 1992. What are the implications of the process of European integration for Germany as a whole? They are manifold. I believe that we can understand the impact of West European integration and the process toward further integration only if we analyse the historical role and function of Germany in Europe. This includes the motives for European integration in the early 1950s and today as a means of containing the German nation-state. Much will depend, of course, on the developing framework for a future European Union or, perhaps, a United States of Europe. Will a United Europe be based on states, on nations, on regions, or on traditional nation-states? How will a united and democratic Germany fit into a European constitutional federal system? Will such a solution settle the German problem as a historical, political, and psychological issue once and for all?

Despite the fact that the democratic Germany of 1990 is totally different from Imperial or Nazi Germany, fear still prevails among Germany's neighbors that Germany might once again aim at European hegemony. Take Nicholas Ridley's "verbal Gatling gun assault" on European Union and Germany: "It is all a German racket, designed to take over the whole of Europe. It has to be thwarted. This rushed takeover by the Germans, on the worst possible basis, with the French behaving like poodles, is absolutely intolerable."[3] Whenever the role of a new and united Germany in a new Europe is discussed, the historical dimension of the German problem, especially the negative image of the Germans still prevailing among parts of the ruling elites, comes to the surface. Thus, it will be appropriate first to discuss the historical dimensions of the German question, as the Germans call it, or of the German problem as it is termed by their neighbors.

The German question cannot be regarded as a phenomenon that in 1946 was suddenly brought on the stage of international politics. It was not just the result of National Socialist policy since 1933 nor an immediate consequence of the "policy of Yalta." The German question implies more than the division of Germany after the war. The German question, past and present, and its solution cannot be understood unless we consider its historical and European dimensions. This perspective will provide insights into German historical traditions and types of statehood in Central Europe.

In discussing the historical dimension of the German question and its impact today, I would like to emphasize four aspects that I believe are essential for understanding the problem of Germany:

1. What do we understand by "German question" or "German problem" from a political perspective? What does it mean historically?
2. Was the foundation of the *kleindeutsch* German Empire in 1870 to 1891 the only and inevitable solution of the German national question in the nineteenth century?
3. What were the aims and ideas of the National Socialists concerning the German question and the unification of Europe under German rule? How did the Allies react and what were their plans for Germany and the reconstruction of Europe after the War? Did they expect to solve the German problem once and for all?
4. What was the impact of the German problem on the process of European integration since the 1950s, and what would have happened to the GDR if the "silent revolution" of November 1989 had not occurred?

3. "Saying the Unsayable," *The Spectator*, 8.

My concluding remarks will deal with the more recent debate on the German question and the conditions of its solution against the background of German and European history and the necessary conditions for establishing a European Germany in a United Europe.

The Political and Historical Meaning of the German Question

Does the term "German question" necessarily imply that it was a German question? Most citizens of the new Germany ("We are *one* Volk") certainly believe that this was the case. They associate the "German question" with the problem of overcoming the division of their country, which took place after the war without their consent. Thus, the German question has become a political term in the history of postwar Germany. Reunification of Germany became a political goal in both Germanies. The Federal Republic of Germany and the German Democratic Republic, established in 1948 to 1949, both claimed to be the legitimate agent for the whole German people. Whereas the Federal Republic aimed at German reunification in peace and freedom on the basis of a democratic and federated political system, the GDR of 1948 to 1949 considered a socialist system based on democratic centralism as the best means for the whole of Germany and its people. The political dimension of the German question, however, covers only one aspect of a rather complex problem. We cannot understand the genesis and the reality of two states in Germany without keeping in mind their historical quality and setting. As a political concept, the German question brings together all problems concerning Germany since 1945. Notwithstanding existing interdependencies, we have to make a distinction between the national, German level and the international, European level.[4] From a German perspective, between 1946 and 1948 to 1949 it meant the maintenance of the political, legal, territorial, and economic unity of Germany. After the foundation of two states in Germany in 1949 it implied the problem of overcoming the division of Germany by reunification or by a new union of the German people. The Federal Republic of Germany constantly stressed that the continued division of Germany must be regarded

4. Wolf D. Gruner, *Die deutsche Frage. Ein Problem der europäischen Geschichte seit 1800* (Munich, 1985), 15ff.

as a threat to European peace in the long run. Thus, the German question, with all its security implications, was and still is, as the "Four-Plus-Two" Talks and the calling of a special meeting of the CSCE in November 1990 show, an important element of international politics.

From the perspective of international politics, the German question means the problems and questions the victors had to face after the unconditional surrender of Germany on 8 May 1945. As such up to the present they have not been settled. To give some examples: the reintegration of Germany into the European and global system after the war; Germany/the Germanies and European security interests; Europe's reconstruction and the role of Germany; the decision on the political, social, and economic order of Germany after the war; a peace treaty with Germany determining the future international boundaries of an all-German state or the successor states of the German Reich; German-German relations; the geopolitical and geostrategic position of Germany in Central Europe; and the political, military, and economic integration of both Germanies into the Eastern and Western alliance systems.

From a historical perspective, the German question means a lot more than the division of Germany after World War II and the right of self-determination for the German people. The impact of World War II and its results gave a new quality to the "historical German problem." This is true whether we approach the problem from a national perspective or from a European-international viewpoint. Alfred Grosser has rightly reminded us that "a purely contemporaneous approach gives a misleading, two-dimensional impression."[5] On the other hand, there are dangers if we overemphasize historical continuities and historical traditions to throw light on the present, or if the historical approach is used as a vehicle to support political and/or ideological objectives.

The German question became a major issue of the European states system and the European Peace Order long before World War II. It has been a European and international problem at least since the turn of the eighteenth century, when the idea of the nation, as a result of the French Revolution of 1789, obtained a political dimension initiating the epoch of the nation-state. From the viewpoint of the national state, the German question became a primary

5. Alfred Grosser, *Germany in our Time. A Political History of the Post War Years* (New York, 1973), 1.

problem of the European states system. The entry of the U.S. into World War I in 1917, and its impact on the peace negotiations of 1919, showed that the German question had become a global issue. The Germans and other nations should remember that the German question is not just a German issue. A historical approach provides the insight that the political and social system of the German nation today, and in the past, has always been a European-international issue. We have to consider the following interrelated facts as being essential:

1. *The image of Germany*, i.e., the problem of how Germans see themselves and how their neighbors perceive them: As a result of German self-assessment, the German image abroad gradually turned negative from the mid-1850s onward. After the miscarried revolutions of 1848, many pamphlets and books on the German heritage and the need for a national state were published. Over and over again, irrespective of a *kleindeutsch* or *großdeutsch* viewpoint, one finds phrases like: the Germans "are the most civilized race on earth"; "the Germans are the leading nation"; "the nature of the state is power, power, and power again."[6] The generally positive view of Germany disappeared and the ambivalent image of Prussia, its militarism and efficiency developed since the late eighteenth century, became a substitute for "German" after the foundation of the Prussian-German Empire. "Prussian militarism" and its synonym "Nazism" played a major role in Allied considerations on Germany in World War II.
2. *The geography of Germany*: In contrast to Italy or Britain, there are no natural boundaries in Central Europe. There are lowlands extending from northern France to western Russia. Being the heartland of Europe means that major lines of European communication necessarily pass through Germany. Thus, from a geopolitical and geostrategical viewpoint, "Mitteleuropa (Central Europe) occupies a key position in any European order."[7]

6. Heinrich von Treitschke, "Bundesstaat und Einheitsstaat," *Historische und Politische Aufsätze*, vol. 2 (Leipzig, 1886), 71–214 (p. 152).

7. As in the case of "Germany," there is no agreed political and geographic definition of *Mitteleuropa* (Central Europe). See Henry Cord Meyer, *Mitteleuropa in German Thought and Action 1815–1945* (The Hague, 1955), 1ff., K. Sinnhuber, *Transactions of the Institute of British Geographers*, 20 (1956), 19, Fig. 2; the area indicated in the *Journal of Central European Affairs* (1941 ff.), and the articles

This may be one of the reasons why the German fear of encirclement, (*Einkreisungssyndrom*), can be found in Germany's geographical position ever since the end of the eighteenth century, leading to attempts to provide secure boundaries for Germany through territorial expansion.

3. *The nature of German statehood*: The conceptions of German statehood oscillate between centralized unity and union in diversity, between fragmentation and cohesion, between central and federal forms of government. The constitutional order of Germany, however, is of major importance for the functioning of the European state system. Thus, the neighbors of the Germans have a vital interest: that any constitutional bond for the German nation will not destabilize the European system. From this perception, the process of German unification will be watched carefully by the states bordering Germany. The "Four-Plus-Two" Talks also serve to find a solution acceptable to the Germans and their neighbors in Europe.

After World War II the French poet Paul Claudel focused the problem when he wrote: "Germany does not exist to divide nations, but to gather them around herself. Her role is to create agreement, to make the different nations surrounding her feel that they cannot live without one another."[8] A centralized German nation-state most probably would aim at European hegemony, whereas a solution along federal lines would show a stronger tendency for European cooperation. The political system of the new Germany will be democratic and federal, forming an integral part of a European architecture. The majority of the Germans are not aiming at a German-dominated Europe; their preference would be a European Germany as part of a united Europe.

---

printed; on the recent revival of the *Mitteleuropa*-idea see Timothy Garton Ash, "Does Central Europe exist?," *The New York Review of Books*, 33, 15 (9 October 1986), 45–52. Garton Ash was one of the experts invited by Mrs. Thatcher to the Chequers Meeting of 25 March 1990 (the published memo in the *Sunday Independent* of 15 July 1990); Renata Fritsch-Bournazel, "The Permanent Quest for Security," *AEI Foreign Policy and Defense Review*, 4, 3–4; Joyce Lasky Shub, ed., *Germany: Keystone to European Security. A Symposium* (Washington/London, 1983), 35–39.

8. Quoted from Richard von Weizsäcker, "The Germans and their Identity," speech at the 21st Convention of the Evangelical Church in Germany, Düsseldorf, 8 June 1985 (excerpt), *Statements & Speeches, Federal Republic of Germany*, 7, 20 (25 June 1985). I am grateful to the German Information Center in New York for providing the English version of the text.

4. *The demographic factor (population potential)*: According to population figures, Germany is the dominant nation in the heartland of Europe. It has borders with almost every European nation. Germany's neighbors feel uneasy about its demographic potential. This feeling does not emerge from security considerations alone.
5. *The economic potential*: Germany, possessing insignificant natural resources, is dependent on international trade and the state of the world economy. It has to sell its goods on the world market, competing with other industrial nations. The raw materials have to be purchased at international prices. Germany's position within the international economy and world trade implies both strength and weakness. The ambivalent economic situation of Germany has repeatedly furthered efforts toward German self-sufficiency.

From the historian's point of view, these five determinants, indissolubly interrelated, have to be regarded as decisive components of the German question.

The German Problem, the Impact of National Socialism and Allied Responses

With the coming of Hitler and the National Socialists, the German question achieved new domestic and international dimensions. National Socialism combined both traditional and revolutionary elements in its ideology, which had a decisive impact on its domestic and foreign policy. When the National Socialists talked about Germany's just demands for great power status as well as political and military equality, they appeared concerned for the interests of the German nation. To all appearances they were pursuing traditional German foreign policy goals. Open support for these traditional/revisionist aims had a twofold function, for the Nazis realized that:

1. these aims were popular with the German nation and could rally the Germans behind the Führer, who seemed capable of bringing Bismarck's policy to fruition; and
2. the state of rearmament, during the early stages after the National Socialist seizure of power, demanded a policy that

was seemingly headed for a peaceful revision of the Treaty of Versailles.

The racist-ideological goals of National Socialism could be realized only if the "Government of national revolution" (as the Nazis liked to call themselves) succeeded in activating the material and human resources of Germany. Its "biological nationalism" (Thomas Nipperdey) and its policy of race and *Lebensraum* necessarily pointed to a policy of expansion and aggression. The results of this policy provided the political framework for postwar developments.

In analyzing the foreign policy of Nazi Germany and comparing it with traditional German foreign policy (which was, until Munich, represented to some extent by the bureaucratic elite of the *Auswärtiges Amt* or Foreign Office), we find a qualitative difference in approach to both the theory and practice of foreign affairs. Despite the fact that economic and also, in the beginning, military and security determinants influenced the foreign policy of Hitler's Germany, there are good reasons to believe that Hitler, the "unprincipled, opportunistic Machiavellian," had to some extent a programmatic conception of National Socialist policy. Indeed, the global aims of the National Socialists, with their strong interdependency of domestic, ideological, and foreign policy factors, could only be attained through military force. While publicly maintaining a revisionist and even peaceful stance, the National Socialists in reality were aiming at an expansionist and aggressive realization of their schemes.

When, in the pressing circumstances of summer 1939, the British government elected to achieve military security, even at the cost of economic security, it was convinced that the only way to safeguard the continued existence of the British empire and to shore up Britain's dwindling status as a great power was through declaring war on Hitler's Germany. This did not preclude, however, the danger of being downgraded to the status of a second-rate power in a qualitatively different postwar system. The political elite was convinced, however, that the British nation would close its ranks again and win "a victory for right." Defeating Hitlerism had thus become the only remaining hope for establishing a new European order on British terms. At first, Britain's struggle for a military victory against Hitler held few prospects for a quick and successful termination of the war. After the crushing defeats of its continental allies, Britain had to bear the brunt of the war alone, especially throughout 1940 and early 1941. The military and material situation was improved, however, when the United States "expressed open support of the cause of democracy against aggressive dictatorship," passing the laws necessary for supporting Britain financially and materially in her struggle against Nazism.

German-American relations had deteriorated dramatically since mid-1940. Hitler accused Roosevelt and the Americans of "moral aggression." On Navy Day 1941, President Roosevelt "gave even more severe expression" to the already forthright tone that he had used in his message to the annual Forum of the American Foreign Policy Association.[9] In his speech Roosevelt also referred to detailed plans for German world domination, which the government had "in its possession." In his outspoken address, delivered six weeks before the Japanese attack on Pearl Harbor, the President made it clear that the United States had long since abandoned the role of a disinterested power. Within a few months after the entry of the United States into the war, the anti-Hitler alliance had been forged. The mutual aim of the "unholy alliance" was the complete defeat of Nazi Germany and the overthrow of Hitler. Both camps waged a grim and total war that increasingly took on ideological overtones.

Within the political and bureaucratic elites of the United States and Britain, different solutions to the German problem were under discussion. These discussions, however, concerned not only the destruction of German militarism and Nazism, but also the reconstruction of postwar Europe. Moreover, the lessons from the Treaty of Versailles as well as perceptions of the German character and of German history also acquired major importance in these discussions. To avoid a new "stab in the back" legend being created in postwar Germany, the Allies agreed to terminate hostilities only after the unconditional surrender and the complete occupation of Germany.[10] In addition, planning staffs considered military,

9. Samuel I. Rosenman, comp., *The Public Papers and Addresses of Franklin D. Roosevelt* (New York, 1950), v. 10, 438–45. On the early Germany policy of the United States see Marie Louise Goldbach, comp., "Amerikanische Deutschlandpolitik," *Dokumente zur Deutschlandpolitik*, 1, 2 (11 August 1941 to 31 December 1942) (Frankfurt a.M., 1986).

10. Inter alia see Lothar Kettenacker, ed., *Das 'Andere Deutschland' im Zweiten Weltkrieg. Emigration und Widerstand in internationaler Perspektive* (Stuttgart, 1977); Lothar Kettenacker, *Krieg zur Friedenssicherung* (Göttingen, 1989); John H. Backer, *The Decision to Divide Germany* (Durham, 1978); Detlef Junker, ed., *Deutschland und die USA 1890–1985* (Heidelberg American Studies Background Papers No. 2, 1985).

economic, and political solutions to prevent future German aggression. While the general public discussed various options as to the treatment of postwar Germany and the prerequisites for a lasting peace, most often within a Carthaginian framework (see for example the partition plans of Henry Morganthau, Jr. and Summer Welles), various committees of experts in Washington and London discussed the pros and cons of German partition or unity.[11] In general, these committees approached their task soberly and thoughtfully, and therefore less vindictively than the extremists.[12] The arguments put forward for or against the "desirability of a partition of Germany" ordinarily focused on economic and security questions. Whereas Robert Vansittart, the political advisor of the British government, was strongly in favor of a partition of Germany for economic reasons in order to avoid a sixth German war against Europe, John Maynard Keynes, as early as 1940, warned against partition.[13] Keynes stressed the necessity of "creating and preserving economic health" in every European country after the war. The "same principle must apply to the German people themselves." He was convinced that "Germany under new auspices will be allowed to resume that measure of economic leadership in Central Europe which flows naturally from her qualifications and geographical position. I cannot see how the rest of Europe can expect effective economic reconstruction if Germany is excluded from it and remains a festering mass in their midst."[14]

All memoranda discussing the future of Germany and her role in postwar Europe make it quite clear, however, that there would have to be certain international controls over Germany. Whether divided

11. Henry Morgenthau, Jr., *Germany is our Problem* (New York, 1945); Summer Welles, *The Time for Decision* (New York, 1944).

12. For sober and thoughtful approaches see Edward Halled Carr, *Conditions of Peace* (London, 1941); James Kerr Pollock, *What shall be done with Germany?* (Carlton College, Northfield, Minnesota, 1944); Kurt R. Grossmann and Hans Jacob, "The German Exiles and the 'German Problem'," *Journal of Central European Affairs* 4 (1944–1945), 165–85 (181ff.): "It is essential for the economic future of Europe and the world that Germany's productive power be conserved. If it were destroyed, the economic conditions would become hopelessly depressed in all countries of Europe . . .Germany's productive strength should be integrated in an international system of production and consumption . . ."

13. PRO F.O. 371/22986 "The Origins of Germany's Fifth War" (Memo by Lord Vansittart, 28 November 1939); PRO F.O. 408/70 No. 84 "The Nature of the Beast" (Vansittart's Memo of 14 March 1940).

14. PRO F.O. 371/28899 "Statement to counter the German 'New Order'" (Keynes, 1 December 1940), most passages printed in Blasius, "Britische Deutschlandpolitik" I: 248–46.

or preserved as a body politic, it was the intention of the planning staffs that Germany should contribute to the economic recovery of Europe without threatening its security. One argument against the partition of Germany that appears repeatedly in the files is that a division of Germany would make no contribution to security; on the contrary, it would constitute a permanent danger to future world order. British and American experts, in their considerations on solutions to the German problem, therefore repeatedly expressed the view that it would be more appropriate to further the political and economic decentralization of Germany that "might arise from the living tradition of federalism in Germany and from a reaction to Nazi centralization."[15] Consequently, to overcome the dilemma of "partition or unity," the British Foreign Office in the autumn of 1944 proposed the dismemberment of Prussia instead of Germany.[16] This would further European interests and at the same time provide the best means for a positive development of postwar Germany. Prussia, not Germany, it was argued, constituted a grave security risk for Europe and for the world. A dismemberment of Prussia would be beneficial because it would provide a better territorial balance among the German states as well as an effective federal constitutional framework for Germany. The realization of these conditions would open up the best prospects for a stable and democratic system in Germany. Thus, conditions could be created "out of which a new Germany can arise and a new Europe be rebuilt."[17] The memorandum also stressed the psychological impact of the dismemberment of Prussia: "Prussia has undeniably been the focus of German militarism since the days of Frederick the Great. The elimination of Prussia would be a strong and symbolic action, clear to all; and the Nazis have shown that it is unwise to underestimate the power of symbolism, particularly in Germany."[18] Decentralizing Germany and eliminating Prussian militarism would be

15. Proposal of the Interdivisional Committee, 23 September 1943, U.S. Department of State, *Post-War Foreign Policy Preparation 1939–1945*, 558–60 (p. 560).

16. PRO F.O. 371/39080/C 16550 "Confederation, Federation and the Decentralization of the German State and the Dismemberment of Prussia," 27 November 1944. Lothar Kettenacker first drew attention to the "Prussian" factor in British policy during World War II: see Lothar Kettenacker, et al., "Großbritannien und Deutschland," 312–40; Lothar Kettenacker, "Die anglo-amerikanischen Planungen für die Kontrolle Deutschlands," in Joseph Foschepoth, ed., *Kalter Krieg und Deutsche Frage* (Göttingen/Zürich, 1985), 66–87, and in his habilitation thesis, Kettenacker, *Krieg zur Friedenssicherung*.

17. Pollock, *What shall be done with Germany?*, 6.

18. PRO F.O. 371/39080/C 16550 "Confederation."

tantamount to minimizing the historical "German peril."

As far as the future of Europe was concerned, the Western Allies, and Britain in particular, were primarily interested in bringing about economic recovery in Europe.[19] Britain especially was afraid of "economic turmoil" and "chaos," which would only further the communist cause throughout Europe. This becomes clear from a statement of Anthony Eden, who maintained that he was "personally inclined to think that out of chaos evil is more likely to emerge than good. It must not be forgotten that the great depression was one of the main factors in the growth of the Nazi party and we do not wish to destroy the Nazis only to put something equally evil in their place."[20] The fear that Germany or, even worse, all Europe, might become communist, was on the minds of politicians and officials.[21] In stressing the economic importance of Germany for European recovery (which would be undermined in the event of German partition), Keynes argued that German economic leadership would be inescapable "unless it is our intention to hand the job over to Russia."[22] Unlike the end of the Napoleonic wars or the First World War, there existed in 1945 no allied principles or agreements as to the future of Germany and Europe in the postwar world. The Allies had only reached agreement in 1944 concerning the zones/sectors of occupation and the control machinery for Germany.

At the Four-Power Conference of the Foreign Ministers in Moscow, the Allies (Great Britain, the United States, USSR, and China) also agreed on the restitution of Austria as a sovereign state.[23] Nevertheless, despite the existence in London of a European

19. See the files of the British War Cabinet (Cabinet Conclusions and annexes PRO CAB 65/61, 52), the documents for "Argonaut" (code name for the Yalta Conference) PRO F.O. 371/50838 and "Terminal" (code name for the Potsdam Conference) PRO F.O. 934/1 F.O. 2, F.O. 4; PRO F.O. 934/4(20) Economic Question Germany; PRO F.O. 934/6 and PRO F.O. 371/50864.

20. PRO CAB 87/67 (19 July 1944).

21. See the Memorandum "Will Germany go communist?" printed in Kettenacker, *Das 'Andere Deutschland'*, 212–17.

22. PRO F.O. 371/28899, Keynes, "Counter the 'New Order'," 1 December 1940.

23. See *Documents on American Foreign Relations*, 6 (1943–1944) (Boston, 1945), 228ff. It is quite interesting to see how the German Foreign office reacted to the Moscow Declaration: see PAAA Nachlaß v. Renthe-Fink vol. 11 note concerning considerations on how to counteract a "Propaganda Initiative" of the Moscow Conference on European questions (13 October 1943) and the reactions to the Moscow declaration. Note for the Foreign Secretary, 16 November 1943 and PAAA Nachlaß v. Renthe-Fink vol. 12, Memorandum by v. Tippelakirch concerning the

Advisory Commission (EAC), created in Teheran, the general lack of mutual agreement regarding the foundations of the postwar order was to prove fatal in the face of rapidly deteriorating relations among the wartime Allies. There were arguments about the British proposal for the zones of occupation. The Soviet handling of the Control Commission of the Balkans led to complaints and distrust. The documents dealing with the Conferences at Dumbarton Oaks (concerning the establishment of a World Organization) and Bretton Woods (International Monetary Fund), show a difference of opinion as to the questions of security, international cooperation, world economy, and the meaning of an international organization.[24] Additional problems were posed by the Soviet demand for reparations at the Conferences at Yalta and Potsdam.[25] A repeated disparity of views originated from different perspectives and approaches. Thus, Britain often totally disagreed with U.S. views. For example, the British Delegation at Potsdam suggested to the United States "the desirability of concluding early Treaties of Peace with the four satellites (i.e., Bulgaria, Finland, Hungary, Romania WDG.) as both desirable in itself and the only means of securing an early evacuation of their territory by the Soviet army."[26] Whereas Britain was interested in an early and stable settlement of the European question,

restitution of Austria in the Moscow Communique. Quite useful still is Heinrich Siegler, *Austria: Problems and Achievements since 1945*, Bonn/Vienna/Zürich, 1969.

24. Department of State, ed., Foreign Relations of the United States (hereafter FRUS), *Diplomatic Papers 1944*, vol. 1: General, Washington, 1967, 713ff. (Dumbarton Oaks Conversations), 614ff. (Organization for Peace and Security); FRUS, *Diplomatic Papers 1944*, vol. 2, General: Economic and Social Matters, Washington, 1967, 106–35 (Bretton Woods, International Monetary Fund); PRO CAB 65/50, 51; FRUS, *Diplomatic Papers 1945*, vol. 1, General: The United Nations, 108ff.

25. See PRO F.O. 934/1–6 (Potsdam); PRO CAB 65/51, 52; PRO F.O. 371/50838–39 (Yalta); PRO CAB 119/11 (Yalta); PRO F.O. 371/50863/50867 (Potsdam); some of the British material on Potsdam has now been published by Rohan Butler and M.E. Pelly, eds., *Documents on British Policy Overseas*, Series I vol. 1: "The Conference at Potsdam, July-August 1945," (London, 1984), including material on microfiche; still useful FRUS, *The Conference of Berlin* (The Potsdam Conference) *1945*, Washington, 1960, 2 vols.; FRUS, *Diplomatic Papers, The Conferences at Malta and Yalta 1945*, Washington, 1955; FRUS, *Europe* vols. 3–4, Washington, 1968ff; on the special issue of reparation see Otto Nuebel, *Die amerikanische Reparations-politik gegenüber Deutschland 1941–1945* (Frankfurt a.M., 1980); Josef Foschepoth, "Britische Deutschlandpolitik zwischen Jalta and Potsdam," *Vierteljahrshefte für Zeitgeschichte*, 30 (1982), 675–714. *Alliierte Deutschland- und Reparationspolitik und die Anfänge der westdeutschen Außenwirtschaft* (Düsseldorf, 1978).

26. PRO F.O. 934/6 Note by the Foreign Office "Considerations affecting procedure for reaching a 'peace settlement'."

acting as "representative of European culture" at Potsdam, the United States was mainly concerned about an early entry of the U.S.S.R. into the Pacific War. Regarding the procedures for reaching a peace settlement for Germany, the Foreign Office took up an idea that had been much discussed by the British government and postwar planning committees, e.g., the Armistice and Post War Committee (AWP). Should there be a German Central Government or should Germany – in the "absence of potential democratic leaders after ten years of Nazi repression"[27] – be governed like a protectorate?[28] As a result of the signing of the terms of unconditional surrender by the German High Command and the assumption of the administration of Germany by the four Commanders-in-Chief governing the four Allied zones, there was "no German Government" and the central German Government had disappeared. Since it would be "impossible to put through a treaty of the Versailles type in any foreseeable future, even if this were desirable," the Foreign Office proposed to use the supreme authority over Germany, conferred to the Allies by the Declaration of 5 June 1945, to "impose the Allied peace terms upon Germany by Allied 'Declaration'."[29] This procedure would be preferable, because the Allies would not have to wait for an indefinite period until there was a suitable government in Germany that could sign a "formal treaty for peace." The Foreign Office officials gave good reasons for adopting the course of peacemaking by declaration.

In face of the growing friction among the Allies, the decision to divide Germany into four Zones of Occupation and the postponement of settlement of the "most pressing" issues turned out to be fatal. It took the Council of Ministers for Foreign Affairs almost two years to draw up treaties of peace for Italy, Bulgaria, Romania, Hungary, and Finland. The growing tensions between the Western Allies and the Soviet Union prevented a peace treaty for Germany and Austria.

The basic U.S. memorandum dealing with postwar policy toward

27. PRO F.O. 371/34460/C 11296. German translation of the Memorandum of 27 September 1943 dealing with the future of Germany printed in Jacobsen, *Weg zur Teilung der Welt*, 318–20. Quoted also by Lothar Kettenacker, "Großbritannien und die zukünftige Kontrolle Deutschlands," Foschepoth and Steininger, *Britische Deutschland- und Besatzungspolitik 1945–1949* (Paderborn, 1985), 39.

28. PRO F.O. 371/39116/C 9330 (Note of the F.O. 15 July 1944) printed in: Kettenacker, *Das andere Deutschland*, 203–10. See also Kettenacker, *Krieg zur Friedenssicherung*.

29. PRO F.O. 934/6 "Peace Settlement."

Germany, as agreed in July 1944, strongly opposed the creation of Zones of Occupation, which would amount to a de facto division of Germany. The State Department Officials predicted that these zones would fall under the control of the three great powers, which would "find themselves bidding for German support by promising to work for the reunification of Germany."[30] Thus, Secretary of State Cordell Hull suggested to the President in September 1944 that "no decision should be taken on the possible partition of Germany until we see what the internal situation is and what is the attitude of our principal Allies on this question."[31] The deteriorating relations between the United States, Britain, and France on one hand, and the USSR on the other, together with tensions and disagreement among the Western allies, precipitated a chain of measures and countermeasures based on misunderstanding, fears, and suspicions on both sides regarding the division of Germany and Europe. The partition of Germany along a military frontier was unnatural and moreover unhistoric.[32]

Germany and European Integration: Fears Despite Containment

The foundation of the Federal Republic of Germany and the German Democratic Republic in 1948 to 1949 must be considered as the result of, not the motive for, the development of a bipolar international system dominated by the two superpowers that emerged from the war. The two states in Germany were integrated into the camp of their protecting power (i.e., the political, economic, and military integration of the Federal Republic of Germany into the Western alliance) just as the German Democratic Republic became an integral part of the Eastern bloc.[33]

30. Cit. in Backer, *Decision to divide Germany*, 26.

31. Cordell Hull, *The Memoirs of Cordell Hull* (New York, 1945), 1622.

32. An interesting view is taken by Frank Ashton-Gwatkin, an economic expert of the Foreign Office, on 14 February 1941: "(Amery) does not solve the essential problem of how Germany can be the centre of European economy without becoming politically paramount and therefore a danger to our own security. My own solution would be to divide Germany along the line of the Elbe and create a Western and Eastern European economic sphere; the one based on the coal and iron area of the Ruhr, Rhineland and Lorraine, and the other based on the coal and iron area of Silesia, South Poland and Czechoslovakia" (quoted from Blasius, *Bitische Deutschlandpolitik* I: 212 n. 8).

33. See for these aspects the more recent studies by Dennis L. Bark and David

As we have seen, the image of Germany was a major issue in wartime planning and all considerations concerning Germany and her future European role after World War II. It was an important aspect in all discussions of how to integrate West Germany into the community of West European democracies in the 1950s, and it still plays an important role in contemporary European politics, especially since November 1989 when the German question was put back on the political agenda of Europe, from which it had disappeared since the atomic stalemate of the mid-1950s.

Of course, the still negative overtones concerning the image of Germany or of the Germans are often used to divert attention from domestic problems and issues; nevertheless, they should not be underrated. We should keep in mind Germany's neighbors' historical experience since the late nineteenth century and during World War II, including German plans for a new European order and for a European Economic Community – and United States of Europe at a later stage – under German leadership. It has therefore been in the interest of the other European nations to agree on checks and balances in order to make Germany's quest for domination, or even leadership, divided or reunited, impossible. In this respect, integration becomes a key term. Integration could be approached as either a positive or a negative strategy for containing Germany in Europe. Both spring from the same root.

The problem of European security, as well as the image of the Germans, has been an essential determinant in all proposals and considerations on (West) Germany's European integration. Germany's European neighbors knew that a united Germany might come about at some stage of postwar developments, despite the fact that they would prefer two Germanies in postwar Europe. The public debates in neighboring countries, when the remilitarization

---

R. Gress, *A History of West Germany*, 2 vols. (Oxford, 1989), vol. 1: *From Shadow to Substance, 1945–1963*; vol. 2: *Democracy and its Discontents, 1963–1988*; Wolfram Hanrieder, *Germany, America, Europe. Forty Years of German Foreign Policy* (New Haven, 1989); Raymond Poidevin, ed., *Origins of European Integration* (Paris, 1986); Klaus Schwabe, ed., *The Beginnings of the Schuman-Plan* (Baden-Baden, 1988); Enrico Serra, ed., *The Relaunching of Europe and the Treaties of Rome* (Milan, 1990); Simon Bulmer and William Paterson, *The Federal Republic of Germany and the European Community* (London, 1987). For the GDR see David Childs, *The GDR: Moscow's German Ally* (London, 1983); idem, ed., *Honecker's Germany* (London, 1985); David Childs, et al., eds, *East Germany in Comparative Perspective* (London, 1989); quite useful J.K.A. Thomaneck and J. Mellis, eds., *Politics, Society and Government in the German Democratic Republic* (Oxford/New York/Munich, 1989).

of the two German states was being discussed, serve as a good example. Fear prevailed then, as it did to some extent in the early 1980s and does so now, that Germany might regain her military strength. The discussions heated up when after the beginning of the Korean War Winston Churchill proposed in 1950 a European Army and when the Western Allies favored a remilitarization of the Federal Republic of Germany. There were several proposals like the Pleven Plan and the plan to establish a European Defence Community (EDC). The treaty on the foundation of the EDC was signed in 1952, but the French National Assembly in 1954 refused to ratify it. The prospects and implications of the EDC were discussed at national party conventions. In November 1951 the congress of the Belgian Socialist Party (PSB) discussed the consequences of a West German military contribution to West European defense. In his speech to the party congress, the vice president of the Belgian socialists pointed out that a remilitarized Germany posed a threat to Europe as a whole. Referring to the Molotov-Ribbentrop pact of August 1939, the treaties of Rapallo (1922) and Tauroggen (1813), he concluded that the German military and German politicians had always been in favor of good relations with Russia. The experience of two German occupations in a lifetime and the fear that communism might take over in Europe, came together. Other contributors at the congress spoke up against any "precipitate organization of European unity." Paul-Henri Spaack was one of the few Belgian socialists at the convention who took a positive stand on the integration of the Federal Republic of Germany into the community of West European democracies. Because of the German problem, a European Federation was needed:

> Our policy towards Germany should be based on trust and confidence. We should not repeat the errors of the interwar period giving Hitler with an easy hand what we refused to concede to the friendly Weimar democracy. The only chance of solving the German problem will be to accept her as an equal partner within a European Federation.[34]

These positions, containment by negative integration versus positive integration, dominate to some extent the debate on Germany's present

34. See PAAA Abt. 2/245 Report of 19 November 1951. Wolf D. Gruner, "Deutscher Nationalstaat und Europäische Integration" in *Deutschland und Europa nach dem 2. Weltkrieg. Entwicklungen, Verflechtungen, Konflikte*, ed. Heiner Timmermann (Saarbrücken, 1990), 69–101.

position in Europe and her future role in a European architecture. The example of the Congress of the Belgian Socialist party seems to be symptomatic of the discussions on the problem of Germany from the early 1950s onward.[35] There still exists a strong belief, as a British memorandum in 1940 put it, that "Germany has shown that if she is sufficiently strong, no treaties or undertakings will deter her from taking by force anything she might happen to want. Therefore security in Europe is only possible if Germany is not strong enough to act in this way."[36]

When the Federal Republic negotiated in 1950 to 1951 the Treaty of the European Coal and Steel Community and the Treaties of Rome in 1956 to 1957, establishing the European Economic Community and the EURATOM, the government had to keep in mind the provisions of the Basic Constitutional Law concerning German unity and European integration. The Western Allies supported the FRG's legal point of view. Thus, in the negotiations leading to the Treaties of Rome, the demand of the Federal Republic that the "Soviet Zone of Occupation" not be considered as a foreign country was accepted.[37] A protocol to the Treaty of Rome stated that the trade between the Federal Republic of Germany and the "Soviet Zone of Occupation" (i.e., GDR) was considered as "internal German trade." Therefore, from 1958 onward, the GDR became an "invisible member state" of the EC. As long as the EC was not a Single Market, there were only minor problems arising from the special relationship between the FRG and the GDR. The approach of the planned establishment of the Internal European Market by 1992 would have put "inner-German" trade on a new basis, since there would no longer be any border controls for trade within the European Community. What to do with the GDR after 1992 is no longer an issue, given the reunification of Germany. Nevertheless, it will be interesting to see, when the respective archival material of the EC and member states is open for research, if there were communications, memoranda, and talks at the commission and intergovernmental level dealing with the future relationship of the GDR, the Federal Republic of Germany, and the European Single Market. Were there any blueprints for the final settlement of the problem of Germany?

35. See e.g. the debates in the Danish Folketing in 1951 or in the Dutch Chambers.

36. See PRO F.O. 371/24370/C 5155 "Post War Security," 12 March 1940.

37. Sekretariat of the Bundesrat, ed., *Bundesrat and Europäische Gemeinschaften. Dokumente* (Bonn, 1988), 29ff.; 105ff.

A European Germany as part of a United Federal Europe. The Solution to the German Question: A Perspective of Hope

Since the early 1980s, the problem of Germany has reappeared on the agenda of international politics, reviving all the fears, hopes, and prejudices that constitute the historical framework of the German question.

For most contemporaries the German question seemed to be settled. The topic was picked up dutifully only in speeches on special occasions. As the President of the Federal Republic of Germany, Richard von Weizsäcker, in an address delivered to the 1985 Convention of The Evangelical Church in Germany put it: "If we have a question to ask we want to be in a position to answer it and have done with it. And if it cannot be answered we would rather deny its existence. That is only human. But questions do not disappear simply because we cannot answer them. History has proved this time and again. While I was in Berlin someone put it very aptly: 'The German question will remain unanswered as long as the Brandenburg Gate remains closed.' "[38]

The debate on NATO's deployment of cruise missiles and Pershing Twos in West Germany resulted in a notable upswing of public interest in the German question in Germany, Europe, and overseas. The Germans on both sides of the line of demarcation feared that Germany would become the battleground of a nuclear conflict of the superpowers; this gave a new dimension to the German problem. Contrary to expectations, the German question was not a "dead issue" for Germany's "successor generation" in the East and in the West. The growing interest in the problem of Germany since the late 1970s, such as the demand of the new left and the new right, forming an "unholy alliance," for reunification through neutralization of Central Europe, the often irresponsible talk about "missed opportunities," the German peace movement, and the entry of the Green party into West German parliaments and the electoral successes of the Republicans in state elections, were closely watched abroad.[39] The media, public opinion, and to some

38. von Weizsäcker, *German Identity*, 4.

39. Wolfgang Venohr, *Die deutsche Einheit kommt bestimmt* (Bergisch-Gladbach, 1982); Herbert Ammon, "Plädoyer für deutsche Einheit durch Blockfreiheit," *Deutschland Archiv*, 8 (1983), 820–33; Ulrich Albrecht, "European Security and the German Question," *World Journal* (Spring 1984), 575–602; Herbert Ammon

extent the official attitudes in foreign countries reacted with "seismographic sensitivity" to any change in German politics.[40] There was and still is talk about a resurgent "German nationalism and even revanchism," the "German peril," the resurgence of a "Fourth Reich," the bad features of the German character, and the irrational search for "German identity." The reliability of the Federal Republic of Germany was often questioned; the same applies to a united Germany today.

In his last speech to the Bundestag, former Chancellor Helmut Schmidt reminded his fellow countrymen of some important aspects of the German problem: "As a consequence of the sufferings of partition there is a permanent danger that our existing propensity for emotional exuberance will break through dangerously. We Germans therefore are in urgent need of common sense, of political reasoning to provide the necessary compensating factor to balance our national abnormalities."[41] The changes in Eastern Europe and the unification of Germany after more than forty years of separation will certainly promote sensitivity and political reasoning. The developments since 9 November 1989 seem to prove this case. After some months, emotions were replaced by reasoning and communication with Germany's partners in West and East in order not to endanger the unification process.

During the 1980s, the only way out of the dilemma of neutralization and deployment of missiles seemed to be that both German states and their neighbors and Allies had to come to terms on a peaceful solution of the indissolubly interrelated European and German problems, allowing for a peaceful settlement of the German question. Certainly there are no "ideal" solutions for the "unfinished business of Germany." It cannot and should not be the task of the professional historian to present blueprints for this case. There are, however, some aspects, which I have dealt with, that could stimulate discussion on German statehood within the European framework. The German problem has always been a primary

---

and Theodor Schweisfurth, eds., *Friedensvertrag – Deutsche Konföderation – europäisches Sicherheitssystem* (Starnberg, 1985); from Steininger's more recent studies: Rolf Steininger, *Eine Chance zur Wiedervereinigung? Die Stalinnote vom 10. März 1952* (Bonn, 1985).

40. Dietrich Stobbe, "Germany – A Challenge to the Superpowers," West Germany, East Germany and the German Question. Five Lectures at the American Institute for Contemporary German Studies, *German Issues*, 1 (Washington, 1986), 13–22 (p. 13).

41. Printed in the *Süddeutsche Zeitung*, 208, (11 September 1986).

European issue since the days of Napoleon (i.e., German options for national statehood can only be realized in conformity with European and international interests and never against them). European interests demand a settlement that does not threaten the stability of the European regional system and at the same time provides a solid basis for overcoming the "historical German peril" forever. An associative solution will open channels for a necessary compromise between the Europeans' need for security and stability and the legitimate claim of the Germans to self-determination. These issues were discussed in the "Four-Plus-Two" talks, in particular the membership of a united Germany in NATO and the strength of a new German Army.[42] The decision of the two German governments that a united Germany should be a federal state like the Federal Republic of Germany, has to be considered as being the right option from a German and a European perspective. There are five *Länder* of the former GDR: Saxony, Brandenburg, Mecklenburg, Sachsen-Anhalt, and Thuringia.[43] They have adopted a political system similar to that of the Federal Republic. The first Landtag elections were held on 14 October 1990, putting the new states on a legitimate basis. The German question has seemingly been answered. Will the problem of Germany disappear from the political agenda forever? This will happen if the new Germany furthers the process of European political integration. President von Weizsäcker reminded us, in his speech commemorating the fortieth anniversary of the end of World War II, that Germany's aim is "to seize the opportunity to draw a line under a long period of European history in which to every country peace seemed conceivable and safe only as a result of its own supremacy, and in which peace meant a period

42. See the respective statements at the meetings of the Ministers of Foreign Affairs and of Defence since the Brussels meetings of 28–29 November 1989 (Nato Press Service, Press Communiqués); *Survey of Current Affairs*, 20, 4 (April 1990), 130ff.; "German Unification and East-West Relations"; Press and Information Office of the Federal Government, *Bulletin*, 74 (13 June 1990); "Meeting of Ministers of Nato at Turnberry," 645–49; *Bulletin*, 90 (10 July 1990); "London Declaration of the Nato Summit," 777ff.

43. For the debate on the restructuring of the *Länder* (states) of the FRG and the creation of three *Länder* instead of five on the former territory of the GDR, see Karlheinz Blaschke, "Alte Länder – Neue Länder. Zur territorialen Neugliederung der DDR," *Aus Politik und Zeitgeschichte*, 27, 90 (29 June 1990), 39–54, and the debate opened by the Hamburg senator for Federal Affairs Gobrecht, based on considerations and statements of the enquete commissions of the Bundestag, headed by Luther and Ernst since the early 1950s, e.g., "New Boundaries for the Länder," *Bayerisches Hauptstaatsarchiv München* (BHStAM), StK 110, 096ff.

of preparation for the next war."[44]

The democracies of Western Europe started in the 1950s on a process of economic and political integration. The EC is not a dream, it is real. Today the twelve states forming the EC are highly integrated economically, and the process of integration cannot be slowed down. The path to Europe is irreversible despite jealousies and tensions. The dynamics of German unification caught the EC by surprise; there was no agreed policy. The FRG's partners were hesitant for various reasons that have to do with the historical and European dimension of the German problem, which can be followed throughout the history of European integration. German-French relations deteriorated after Chancellor Kohl's unexpected proposal to the Bundestag on 28 November 1989 for German unification along confederate and federal lines.[45] There had been no communication about his intentions between Kohl and his colleagues in the EC, especially with his friend François Mitterand. Whereas President Bush at a very early stage favored German unification unconditionally, France and Britain were not very enthusiastic about the prospect of German unification with its impact on the European system and the balance of power in Western Europe. Mrs. Thatcher made this quite clear in public and private statements. To counterbalance the speeding up of the German unification process, President Mitterrand proposed the creation of a "European Confederation," *Confédération Européenne*.[46] In a letter in *Le Monde* on France and Germany, Michel Vauzelle warned his countrymen against an outdated nineteenth-century balance of powers policy to contain the new Germany. A policy of mistrust against Germany will not provide a solid basis for "a serious European policy." In the present period of rapid change it will be the wisest policy for France to cooperate with Germany.[47] In an interview for *Time*, Michel Rocard, the French Prime Minister, stated that German unification was not a threat. If "we get on quickly with building the European Community, the German

44. English text of the speech on 8 May 1985 commemorating the end of the war, provided by the Office of the Federal President.

45. Press and Information Office of the Federal Government, *Bulletin*, 134 (29 November 1989), 1141–48 and *Süddeutsche Zeitung*, 274 (29 November 1989), 3.

46. "Après les bouleversements à l'Est, quelle Europe? Quatre projets et des ombres. La 'Confédération européenne' après 'L'Europe de l'Atlantique à L'Oural'," *Le Figaro*, 18 January 1990.

47. Michel Vauzelle, "Paris, Berlin"; see also Jean François Deniau, "Mission Europe," *Le Monde*, 7 March 1990, 2.

problem will be diluted in a greater political entity."[48] This was in line with a proposal of the President of the Commission of the EC, Jacques Delors, who proposed a Federal European Union before the end of the century. It was also Delors who argued at an early stage that the GDR was a "special case" in Eastern Europe and would have a virtual right to membership in the EC.

In a television interview on 25 March 1990 President Mitterrand proposed the opening of talks on political union in the EC, which should be formed at the same time as the completion of the European Single Market.[49] The Kohl-Mitterand initiative for European Political Union at the Dublin summit of the EC Council pointed in the right direction.[50] There was no longer a question mark over the GDR's position toward the EC, for it would join the FRG and the new *Länder* of the former GDR would form part of the new Germany.

The new and democratic Germany will not pose a threat to Europe. It is different from the Wilhelminan Germany of the Kaiser or Hitler's Germany, which still dominate our neighbors' image of Germany. It wants to be European; if it is given a fair chance to work toward the European dream of unity, it will not drop out and lose interest. The question is, of course, how the new Germany will play her political and economic role in Europe. A leading American commentator posed the central question, asking "Will it act as Germania Rex, the haughty leading man who hogs the spotlight and steals the scenes? Or will it become more of an ensemble player, a willing partner of and respected spokesman for a more unified European Community?"[51] The Germans have learned their lessons from history. Their attempts at European hegemony by creating a German Europe have failed. They know of the fears still prevailing among their neighbors that they might attempt a German Europe once again, maybe this time by other means. Thus, they will do their best to become good and reliable European Germans, working for the European ensemble. Only then will the chapter on the German question, which has always been a European question, be closed for ever.

48. "A Vision of a New Europe," Michel Rocard interviewed by Henry Muller and Christopher Redman, *Time*, 2 April 1990, 24ff.

49. E.S. Browning and Mark M. Nelson, "Mitterrand calls for EC pact on Political Union by 1993," *The Wall Street Journal*, 26 March 1990.

50. Press and Information Office of the Federal Republic, "The European Council in Dublin," *Bulletin*, 84, 30 June 1990, 717ff.

51. Terence Roth and Mark M. Nelson, "Germany Prepares for a Leading Role," *The Wall Street Journal*, Europe, 9 July 1990.

–5–

Germany: Locomotive for European Integration or Pacemaker for Detente with Eastern Europe?

CHRISTIAN HACKE

The Division of Europe

At first sight German politics after 1945 faced a central political problem, which might be described as the tyranny of choice. This tyranny of choice offered in reality no options for German politics, only dilemmas: Germany was no longer a major continental imperial power looking for geopolitical space in the East of the continent. Germany's quest for global seapower in the tradition of Tirpitz was also over, and so was Germany's role as a balancer between Eastern and Western Europe, as an honest broker in the tradition of the foreign policy of Foreign Secretary Stresemann during the Weimar Republic.

After 1945 there emerged a completely new foreign policy environment and domestic setting for Germany:

1. The breakdown of the old balance of power in Europe: World War II reduced all European powers to the status of second or third rank countries, which had to lean for protection on one or the other superpower in the West or East. Furthermore, the European system of the balance of power had lost its classical function. It no longer preserved independence for each European power, but had led to extreme dependence and reliance on the Soviet Union or the United States.
2. The moral, political, economic, and military status of Germany

was at its lowest point in history.

3. The division of Germany, Berlin, and Europe reflected the division of the world into two camps.

This was the context for the tyranny of choice between 1945 and 1949; its central dilemma, caused by Hitler's Germany, forced the Germans after 1945 to opt either for integration with the West or Sovietization.

Adenauer opted for the West for two basic reasons: West Germany's Eastern frontier follows the line of military demarcation established between the Red Army and the Western armies at the end of World War II. The military governments established in the Western zones of occupation considered it their main purpose to preserve the status quo of that *de facto* partition. That purpose was powerfully and in all probability decisively supported by the refusal of the German people – freely and clearly in the West and mutedly in the East – to exchange the tyranny of the Nazis for that of communism.

Adenauer incorporated the national goal of reunification into the European idea and harmonized internal order and integration of West Germany with the West. This option prevented German isolation and also prevented the Western partners from simply ignoring the German question. It is doubtful whether the Federal Republic had a genuine alternative to Adenauer's policies of Western integration. His sense of priorities was shaped by choice as well as by necessity. In fact it would have been much more difficult to extract concessions from the Western powers with regard to the quest for sovereignty if the restored elements of sovereignty had not been subject to international surveillance. The creation of integrated West European and Atlantic structures had a decisive influence on the speedy political recovery of West Germany. They provided mechanisms for controlling Germany and they made the restoration of sovereignty less risky for the Western powers, especially for France. Adenauer's European and Atlantic oriented policy was an essential precondition for successful political and economic recovery, which were also complementary. A weak West German economy would have been a liability for the Western alliance, undermining political stability and opening up opportunities for Soviet policies.

The goal of unifying West and East Germany was of an entirely different order, because it could be achieved only with the consent of both Cold War camps. Stalin's reunification offer of 1952, which might have led to a neutral unified Germany, was an option that would have given Stalin more influence on Germany than otherwise: Stalin tried to prevent the integration of the bigger Western part of Germany into the American power structure. National unity might theoretically have been promoted, if Stalin's offer had been pursued, but it would have been a unity without democracy and human rights, without the freedom West Germany has enjoyed since 1949. All the Western powers, especially France and the United States, were against a reunited Germany without domestic freedom and without the freedom of choice in foreign policy that clearly would have resulted in Western integration for all of Germany. This option, however, was unacceptable for the Soviets.

As a consequence, the goal of unifying West and East Germany on the basis of democracy and freedom was an impossible task. Adenauer's long-range unification policy was thus based on the two central assumptions that with the passage of time the balance of power between the Cold War blocs would shift in favor of the West, allowing negotiations on the basis of strength, which would induce the Soviet Union to settle the German question on Western terms. But Western roll-back rhetoric and the so-called magnet theory failed under the dialectic of the nuclear age. The rhetoric of strength from Bonn and Washington sounded like the trumpets of Jericho, but the wall did not crumble, as the uprisings and revolutions in the GDR in 1953, in Poland and Hungary in 1956, and in Czechoslovakia in 1968 showed.

The Politics of European Integration or Germany as a Reluctant Locomotive

The basic attitude of the West Germans toward the postwar European border was shaped by very contradictory emotions: defeat, deliverance, and division. This triangle of cause and effect contained a moral logic, but also for the Germans a deeply ambivalent feeling about the new European political order. Basically, it confronted Germany with the tyranny of choice between pursuing an energetic, pro-Western integration policy and simultaneously trying to keep or gain German unity.

But for Adenauer, and then for a majority of the Germans, it became clear that under the dilemmas of East-West confrontation not territorial unity, but political equality, freedom, and democracy were of paramount importance. From the idea of a Western orientation to the reality of political integration in the West; that was the decisive step from the Weimar Republic, over the intervening episode of disaster, to the Federal Republic. Western integration in West German foreign policy represents the – in part involuntary – completion of what had already been formulated by outsiders in the years after 1919. The paradox here is that only in the frosty atmosphere of the Cold War did the pleasant warmth of democracy finally enter the homes of West Germans.

After 1949 it was possible to erect a canopy over the Western part of Germany and its immature democracy, which provided protection for its internal development. Western integration and European unification meant that freedom, democracy, prosperity, and security could be realized and secured. In the early years, the Federal Republic had a lowly international status. Konrad Adenauer managed, however, to turn the country into one of the co-founders of a West European democratic system of states. Another important factor – in contrast to the period after 1919 – was the development of material prosperity after 1949, which lent stability to democracy in the Western part of Germany. For Germans there was no alternative to democracy and Western integration. After all, the Federal Republic's foreign policy created a new dimension of possibilities within the framework of West European and Atlantic integration, not only economically but also in terms of security policy. This fundamental core of political détente, economic prosperity, and military security was lacking in the development of foreign policy in the Weimar Republic and was only able to evolve with Western orientation after 1949.

Furthermore, the policy of integration from the beginning combined two elements. First, the Atlantic security dimension, which stressed the role of the United States for German and West European security; nuclear guarantees and the strategy of extended deterrence must be seen in this context. The high point of this dimension of "Westpolitik" was from 1955 until 1960. It is interesting to note, however, that nearly all chancellors in the end developed, for different reasons, a critical attitude toward the United States. Adenauer in his final days became very suspicious of Kennedy's foreign policy; Chancellor Erhard felt left alone by President Johnson; Chancellor Kiesinger tried to keep a delicate balance between an American and French oriented outlook in German foreign policy;

and Chancellor Brandt felt very distant from President Nixon and realized from the beginning that his "Ostpolitik" would arouse deep suspicion on the American side. Of all European statesmen Chancellor Schmidt became the most intense critic of the foreign policy of President Carter. It is too early to say whether Chancellor Kohl developed, with regard to SDI and the American-Soviet double-zero-agreement of December 1987, a more critical outlook toward the Reagan Administration.

The relative decline of American power during the 1970s and 1980s marks the background of shifting priorities within the politics of Western integration: the second element, the continental West European dimension, became increasingly important.

At the beginning of the 1990s West Germany faces another tyranny of choice:

1. Although still dependent on America's nuclear guarantee, Germany's foreign policy concentrates now more on the West European continental perspective.
2. Germany, as well as the other Western European states, is confronted with the conflict between greater integration or enlargement of the community. The enlargement through the accession of Greece in 1981, and Spain and Portugal in 1986, complicated the coordination of economic and monetary policies and brought about a de facto dual membership. Many politicians now see the need for two types of membership of the EEC, which would allow members to proceed at different speeds and integrative intensity, leading to a Europe *à deux vitesses*. The doubling of its membership since the Treaty of Rome is a mixed blessing for the community. Enlargement has meant that the potential for integration has weakened and that quantity has increased at the expense of quality.

Aside from inherent economic and political difficulties, the coordination of economic policy and the harmonization of prices and taxes were complicated by the disparate foreign policies of the major members. Although the French and Germans remained conservative in the 1980s with respect to allowing drastic or rapid reforms of the Community's agricultural subsidy system, they are somewhat more venturesome on military issues, aiming for some degree of Franco-German collaboration and perhaps even a modification of NATO institutions. Britain, on the other hand, remained conservative with respect to NATO structures and their practical and symbolic value for continuing a special British-American relationship.

For reasons of domestic and foreign policy it remained highly questionable whether the community could coordinate its divergent economic policies and enable its institutions to foster imaginative and effective leadership. The failure of the Community to respond to the economic and political challenges of the 1980s was in essence a failure to come to terms with the contradictions of a modern system of states that was itself a mixture of the old and new. Again, coordination rather than integration appeared to be more acceptable. Western European integration remained incomplete even though intensified European integration might provide a more effective check on the political energies of the Federal Republic, which was a major reason why the community was launched in the first place.

The politics of the European Community has not led toward more integration and supranationality. It remains a halfway house between integration and disintegration. It is the prototypical phenomenon of a system of states in transition. The role of the Federal Republic as a locomotive in this process is a misconception since 11 members share the status of being locomotive and train at the same time. Furthermore, it is a long time since deeply convinced Europeanists such as Hallstein, Schuman, de Gasperi, and, last but not least, Adenauer were determined to strengthen the institutions and the process of Western European integration. In the 1950s there was a clear primacy of policy with an idealistic notion, which in the end fell short of its goals. Today the situation is the reverse: pragmatic politicians are led by the accelerated speed of economic and technological change, which forces them to find a common denominator for development under the primacy of economics, so that Western Europe does not fall behind the dynamics in the United States and Japan.

We may be watching the dwindling power of the nation-state, but the alternative is not necessarily political integration, as was hoped in Western Europe, but a corporation-dominated world. This possibility seems far more real as economies become increasingly linked through multinational companies and the sophisticated financial networks that service them. The reflex of these macroeconomic trends may be seen in the development of the Federal Republic: in a country torn between the aim of national unity on the one hand and economic and political integration with the West on the other hand, this conflict was transformed into an economically guided perspective.

The Role of the Federal Republic as Pacemaker for Détente

"Westpolitik" was never merely "Westpolitik," but from the beginning had an Eastern political function. In the 1950s, the hope was that by strength and military security Western Europe, and especially the Western European integration model, would serve as a magnet for Eastern Europe. Adenauer and Schumacher shared the idea of this magnet theory. Second, German Ostpolitik from the 1970s onward was anchored in West European consent, while the United States watched this development with tolerance but with mixed feelings. Consequently, two notions of détente developed in the 1970s: the American détente policy was from the beginning global and advanced under the aspect of indivisibility, while the West German and West European idea of détente was regional and under the aspect of divisibility.

Domestically the Social Democratic Party and the Free Democratic Party played a special role as trendsetters for détente. From Brandt to Schmidt to Kohl, West Germany has tried to reestablish Germany's role as honest broker between East and West, while standing firm within the Western alliance. Human rights and more freedom between East and West for people, information, and opinion, but also more human rights and more freedom within the Communist empire, were of paramount importance. The central German idea concerning détente can be put in a nutshell: the more the Soviets and the socialist regimes change the border between East and West in the direction of freedom, the more the West and especially Germany will be willing to recognize formally these borders and regimes. But the central problem soon became apparent: it is one thing to recognize a regime, a state, or a border, but quite another to adjust to greater freedom between East and West. The recognition of regimes and borders is a formal act, while opening borders includes, in a communist perspective, the freedom to close these borders or to counter Western détente with a policy of demarcation.

As a result, from the beginning of the 1970s until the threshold of the 1990s, only limited progress was achieved in changing the dynamic conditions of détente. The bi- and multilateral treaties did not solve the German and European security problems. The paradoxical result of German Ostpolitik was that the country had become politically more important and had gained more room for maneuver toward the West and within the Western alliance, while real progress with regard to freedom was limited.

The foreign policy of the Schmidt years, from 1974 until 1982, shows the transformation of West Germany from an economic power into a political power: as the importance of economic and monetary issues increased relative to military strategic matters. German political leverage also increased through Ostpolitik. Through Ostpolitik, Germany had become politically more important, had achieved greater independence, but still enjoyed no total freedom of action. But Bonn has always been highly effective in multilateral settings, and the Federal Republic has succeeded in turning international cooperation to national advantage, even if "Ostpolitik" did not produce transformation through rapprochement or reunification.

The Schmidt government took a much tougher stand than any previous German government on crucial issues. Although Schmidt was willing to be a good European and a good Atlanticist, he also demanded that fellow EEC members and the American government make reforms in return for Germany's heavy financial contributions to the common market and the Atlantic system. Schmidt also opposed Henry Kissinger's tough attitude on Eurocommunism, viewing it as nervous and shortsighted. During the Carter administration, the issues of human rights, export of nuclear technology by Germany, Washington's initial failure to support the dollar in international markets, Carter's anti-nuclear theology with regard to the neutron bomb, and his unclear view toward the Soviet Union aggravated the problems between Washington and Bonn. From Schmidt's point of view, the Germans were propping up the United States, as well as the European community, when they were asked to support the French farmers and the American dollar. Schmidt's foreign policy must be seen against the background of the obvious decline of American power and influence in the international environment. Within the alliance structure, the balance of power shifted toward Western Europe.

Thanks to Schmidt's leadership capability after this phase of severe economic crisis, the Federal Republic emerged at the beginning of the 1980s as one of the leading actors in the Western and world economic system. Under Chancellor Schmidt the Federal Republic of Germany reached not only an economic world power status, but for the first time fully realized and used the potential of its new leading position, which offered West Germany, under peaceful circumstances, many of the objectives of the old continental and worldwide options pursued by a united Germany before the Second and First World War. Especially in the context of East-West détente Schmidt played a predominant role, together with Giscard d'Estaing, as bridge-builder to the East. After détente broke down in the latter half of the 1970s, both Western European leaders tried to step into the power vacuum and to warm up the ice cold climate that Soviet intervention in Afghanistan had created also in the Atlantic and European system. Although many Americans felt that détente toward the Soviet Union had failed in essence because it was unable to induce the Soviet Union to exercise political restraint or military moderation, Helmut Schmidt and Giscard d'Estaing looked at détente more optimistically. In Chancellor Schmidt's terms the prerequisite for détente was equilibrium, a balance of power between East and West. It is thus not without tragedy to note that between 1974 and 1982 the Soviet Union shifted the military balance of power to its own advantage in Europe and worldwide by a massive military buildup on land, sea, and air, conventional and nuclear, which endangered Western Europe's security. The symbol of this became the new SS 20 rocket. The Schmidt/Genscher government accordingly pressed both superpowers to continue arms control policy. The *Ost- und Deutschlandpolitik* of the Kohl/Genscher government developed a dynamism in policy on Germany and central Europe that would have been dismissed as utopian just a few years earlier. It was able to achieve this by building dialogue and cooperation with the nations of central and Eastern Europe on the basis of a secure defense capability. The Kohl/Genscher government was able to prove that the change from a Social Democratic to a Christian Democratic administration would not lead to a deterioration in relations between the two Germanies; rather, a turn for the better was achieved through continuity and predictability.

The Kohl/Genscher government had urged the Reagan Administration since 1982 to reestablish close contacts with Soviet power. But Brezhnev, Andropov, and Tschernenko all died within 20 months. Diplomacy with the Soviet Union was reduced to funeral diplomacy until Mikhail Gorbachev came to power in 1985. In retrospect, his emergence to power marks the decisive watershed in the West-East relationship of the postwar world. Gorbachev's changes in foreign policy also had a distinct effect on Germany and Europe. The Soviet Union now reacted favorably to the proposals of the Western world to ease the East-West conflict and to give more room for human rights, freedom, and self-determination for nations and peoples in Europe. But between 1985 and 1989 Western reactions were mainly hesitant; it was still unclear where Gorbachev was heading. Nevertheless, Western governments were stunned, after forty years of Soviet false words and deeds, as they watched Gorbachev's breathtaking new initiatives. While most Western governments remained skeptical, it was the Federal Republic which again took the lead as at the beginning of the 1970s, in a new phase of détente policy. In July 1986 Foreign Minister Genscher picked up Gorbachev's formula of the European house, but demanded open doors outside and within. Genscher perceived the new foreign policy of the Soviet Union as a chance for the West: "A Soviet Union which bets on cooperation and openness is a better partner for the West than a Soviet Union which is dominated by the old thinking." Consequently Genscher favored new initiatives: "Let us not sit back and wait for what Gorbachev might bring! We must influence the developments ourselves."

When President von Weizsäcker visited the Soviet Union in July 1987 and Chancellor Kohl in 1988, the bilateral relationship reached a new intensity. In January 1989 Genscher reaffirmed his hopeful attitude toward Gorbachev's policies: "It is true that a Soviet Union, which is changing within, which is becoming more open both inwardly and outwardly, which participates pragmatically in coping with the world's great future tasks, is a gain for the international community."

American suspicion, always latent since the beginning of West Germany Ostpolitik in the 1970s, was stirred up again. "Genscherism" became the fashionable and often ill-chosen synonym to express not only a sell-out attitude and naive pro-Soviet perception, but also fear of German neutralism and anti-Americanism. In short, in the United States Genscher was suspected of selling out Western interests; in reality, American foreign policy had not adjusted to the new developments in Europe. As a consequence, U.S. and West German détente policy did not complement each other completely but became at times contradictory and fueled by suspicion.

The Gorbachev visit to West Germany in 1989 symbolized a new stage in the bilateral relationship. His enthusiastic welcome was not without paradox. On the one hand, he represented a superpower that is mainly to blame for the division of Germany and the suppression of 18 million fellow Germans and the nations of Eastern Europe. On the other hand, he personally represented rapid change and rising hopes for reform. His attitude toward West Germany was almost flattering when he described the relations as one of "two great powers, which are of central significance for the situation in Europe and for East-West ties in general." But Gorbachev's position on Germany remained orthodox. He described the wall as a guarantee of peace, the existence of the GDR and two German states as a guarantee for stability, and German reunification as dangerous. But in the joint declaration, Gorbachev acknowledged the decisive significance of the FRG. Now Bonn was finally raised to the status of partner in leadership by both Washington and Moscow.

Thus, before the outbreak of the great crisis in central and Eastern Europe in summer 1989, the FRG had established itself as a politically respected and economically powerful key state in European politics. West Germany, so it seemed, had overcome the old tyranny of choice between East and West. Without jeopardizing the close ties and multilateral integration framework of the Western European and Atlantic world, the FRG developed a rational bond of interests with sympathetic overtones toward the East. In pragmatic terms, *Deutschlandpolitik* had become an astonishing success during the Kohl/Genscher years. The bilateral relationship to Poland remained critical but was beginning to warm up slowly. The relations toward the Soviet Union reached a new peak. Together with the other European powers in the framework of the Commission on Security and Cooperation in Europe (CSCE) process, West Germany became one of the most important actors urging a new European order for peace and for self-determination and freedom. At no moment were Bonn's ties to NATO and the European Community the subject of discussion. The *raison d'état* of the Federal Republic was anchored politically in the mid-Atlantic, but the German question remained unsolved. When people in East Germany gathered in the streets, demanding freedom and democracy and shouting "We are the people," it became obvious that not only the dictatorship in the GDR was bound to fall.

Germany and Europe

The revolutionary changes in central and Eastern Europe since the summer of 1989 deeply affected West German *Ost- und Deutschlandpolitik*. It was not only the magnetic pull of Western civilization, but also technological revolution and economic integration, which have propelled the West, Japan, and the non-communist Asian countries into a new age of progress. The double success of Western détente policies and the technological revolution provided a depressing vision for Gorbachev: the rising gap between the bright future of capitalist democracies and the catastrophic outlook for the socialist camp. After only a few years of *glasnost* and *perestroika*, a second gap became obvious; Gorbachev's political intention to revive socialism and its real failure deepened the crisis of communism. In a political firestorm from summer to winter 1989, Communist regimes fell from power in Poland, Hungary, Czechoslovakia, Romania, Bulgaria, and the GDR. The developments in the GDR also reflected Gorbachev's impossible task in trying to confine reform problems strictly within the domestic context. They naturally spilled over into foreign policy and created a new complex of foreign and domestic reform patterns, sharpened in central and Eastern Europe by a rising anti-communist nationalism. The East German population started to oppose the Honecker regime in the name of *glasnost* and *perestroika* by welcoming Gorbachev personally on the occasion of the 40th anniversary of the GDR. The Stalinist phrase of the 1950s, "to learn from the Soviet Union means to learn how to win," was now paradoxically turned into a pro-Gorbachev reform slogan. Soviet encouragement became paramount for the revolutionary development in the GDR. The Hungarian contribution to the German upheaval in October/November 1989 was the decision to open its frontiers to Austria in August 1989. Some thirty thousand East Germans fled, others were looking for an exit via the West German embassies in Prague and Warsaw. Parallel to this rising exodus, the power of demonstrators and demonstrations in the GDR grew from a snowball to an avalanche. The spectacle of the 40th anniversary became a nightmare. On 18 October the Honecker regime fell. On 9 November the new Socialist Unity (Communist Party) (SED) government under Krenz was forced to open the wall in Berlin – a joyous and spontaneous reunification of Germans took place 28 years and 91 days after the building of the wall on 13 August 1961.

Most of the new opposition groups in the GDR opposed German reunification in the beginning. West Germans did not want to push their fellow Germans on this question. Within the West German parties the goal of reunification remained rather negative in the aftermath of 9 November. The Social Democratic Party (SPD) and Greens were against it. Willy Brandt's phrase, the "living lie of reunification" reflected the basic SPD attitude. The FDP and the vast majority of the Christian Democratic Union (CDU) had come to terms with the status quo of two states. Reunification was left to the extremes of the political left and very conservative intellectuals and politicians. In this period of extreme political turmoil, when neither East nor West Germans were sure about the political future, when neither the Western allies nor the Soviet Union were able to react to the revolutionary developments, Chancellor Kohl boldly took the political initiative. In his ten point plan of 29 November, Kohl outlined the essential cornerstones of the future *Ost- und Deutschlandpolitik* of his government:

1. immediate measures to provide aid;
2. cooperation with the GDR on the economic and cultural level;
3. fundamental political and economic change in the GDR;
4. a close-knit network of agreements;
5. confederative structures with the goal of forming a federation in Germany;
6. the future structure of Germany must fit into the future architecture of Europe as a whole;
7. the power of attraction of the European Community remains a constant feature;
8. the CSCE process remains a crucial part of the total European architecture, but new institutional forms for pan-European cooperation are required;
9. disarmament and arms control must keep step with political developments; and
10. freedom within Europe as the means whereby the German people can via self-determination restore their unity. Reunification, the attainment of German state unity by peaceful means, remains the political goal of the Federal Government.

Chancellor Kohl's ten steps toward reunification marked an astonishing reversal of attitudes. In the 1950s the Federal Republic rejected any confederation between the two Germanies while the

GDR toyed with it. In the three steps from confederation via federation, Kohl envisaged a transformation that might lead to reunification. Kohl moved forward obviously in Adenauer's tradition. He demanded a legitimate democratic government of the GDR as an essential prerequisite. Presenting himself as a true European, Kohl pointed out that the future development of inner-German relations must remain embedded in the pan-European process and in East-West relations. In stark contrast to the dangerous vision of a neutralized unified Germany, Kohl insisted that the center of political gravity, not only for the Federal Republic but also for the envisaged new German nation state, will and must remain within the Western European and Atlantic framework: "The powers of attraction and the aura of the European Community is and remains a constant feature in the pan-European development. We want to strengthen this further . . . we understand the process leading to the recovery of German unity to be one of European concern. . . . In keeping with this, the European Community must remain open to a democratic GDR and to other democratic countries from central and South Eastern Europe. The EC must not end on the Elbe, but must remain open to the East."

Kohl's ten point plan can be described as a high point of German *Ost- und Deutschlandpolitik*. Kohl avoided interfering with or making political demands on the GDR, but repeated instead his readiness to offer assistance. He made it clear to the three Western allies, as well as to the Soviet Union, that his perspective remains within the framework of existing agreements. He thus made it difficult for others to object. Kohl's remarks about structures of confederation could not be construed as demands, so the GDR leadership did not reject them. The GDR agreed, though grudgingly, to the immediate steps Kohl proposed. In his speech to the Bundestag Chancellor Kohl also revealed another diplomatic advantage: his proposals were set in motion by both German states without affecting the Four Power Status of Germany and Berlin. These ten points did not require the agreement of any third party. Membership of alliances is not an impediment to economic and political change. The significance to domestic politics of Helmut Kohl's initiative cannot be ignored, especially a year before a general election. With this plan Kohl seized the political initiative again.

Western reactions to Kohl's proposal were astonishingly mild given the fact that the West German Chancellor had proposed steps toward reunification, which essentially affected the rights of the four allied powers. The Paris summit of November 1989 showed that the twelve EC countries are basically in accordance with Kohl's ten points. In return, Kohl emphasized the FRG's commitment to the West and to European integration. Kohl's plan reflects the successful attempt to overcome that old tyranny of choice between integration in the West and the reunification of Germany. Adenauer had refused this simplified alternative between Western integration and national reunification; so does Chancellor Kohl. He and Foreign Minister Genscher stated that this plan for reunification did not alter West Germany's position within the alliance framework, but implied a Federal Republic and a Western Europe, which together would form the new framework for change in Europe in which the new integrative structures and democratic values would also make room for a reunified Germany.

The President of the EC, Jacques Delors, was among the first to welcome Kohl's initiative. For him, the idea of integrating the GDR into a West European framework had become central. If the GDR laid the groundwork for private investment and for a free market economy, economic links with the West would be strengthened. In January 1990 Delors approved the plans of the Kohl/Genscher government for the integration of the GDR. European-minded politicians like Delors realized that the Community could only help the reform-minded states in Eastern Europe if at the same time it gave a satisfactory answer to the German question. If the Germans decided for unity, the West European Community must be prepared for this. In a second step, therefore, Mitterrand proposed combining all these considerations in an all-European confederation. In the first stage, the European Community had to intensify its integration and solve the German problem, perhaps by incorporating the German problem within the European Union; in a second stage, pan-European cooperation should lead to a closer network. At its summit in Strasbourg in December 1989 the EC officially recognized for the first time the right of Germans "to unity through free self-determination" as already confirmed at the NATO summit in May 1989. German unity as a realistic option was now de facto accepted by the EC. The Community also outlined how Western Europe intends to help the process of reform through cooperation with Poland, Hungary, Czechoslovakia, and East Germany. One problem, however, is that Eastern European countries, as well as the GDR, belong to the Council for Mutual Economic Assistance (CMEA or COMECON).

The French reaction to Kohl's ten point plan was ambivalent: the Quai d'Orsay toyed with the idea of reviving neo-Gaullist thinking, that the two parts of Europe have moved out of the shadow of their superpowers, and, consequently, the French Foreign Ministry favors a united Europe as the third world power on the basis of two German states. French President Mitterrand seemed to fear that a too speedy reunification process would diminish France's political and economic role. Both Kohl and Mitterrand, however, agreed that the EC must grow as a cornerstone for a new European architecture and as the one pole of a future balance of power in Europe, while the FRG should remain firmly anchored in the EC and Atlantic Community. Prime Minister Thatcher showed the most reluctant attitude toward German reunification by pointing out that it could only be seen as the endpoint of a long pan-European process of integration. Nevertheless, the vast majority of public opinion in the Western world showed understanding and sympathy for the German wish for reunification. There was also great respect and admiration for the peaceful revolution in East Germany and for the national feeling that "what belongs together must grow together again," as it was put by Willy Brandt.

The European context is critical. Since the revolutionary events of autumn 1989 the disparity between Western and Eastern Europe has been growing. As Western Europe prospers, the former state economies in Central and Eastern Europe fall apart. As Western Europe integrates, the Eastern European economic block, COMECON, disintegrates. While West European reforms such as the Internal Market 1992 enhance economic progress, Eastern European economies will lead to further impoverishment before things improve, even where they decide for social market systems. Consequently, economic and social divisions between Western and Eastern Europe are increasing, as well as divisions within Eastern Europe. Another trend of conflict lies in the fact that while nations in Western Europe are integrating, nations in Eastern Europe, on the other hand, face new waves of nationalism. *Glasnost* and *perestroika* have strengthened the national consciousness of Balts, Latvians, Serbs, Ukrainians, Armenians, Slovaks, and Croatians. Some of these conflicts are fueled by religious conflicts, as the Armenian-Aserbaidjanian conflict shows. National and ethnic conflicts, cries for independence, and even civil war have become reality in Armenia and Aserbaidjan. Another element of future European conflicts lies in the shift from East-West conflict to new military confrontations within the new context of rising nationalistic movements. The distinct division between free and totalitarian societies, which marked the West-East conflict in Europe, is fading. But after the breakdown of Communist rule, democracy and freedom are not the automatic alternative. Some European countries have a distinct democratic tradition; others do not. Some are demonstrating, after the breakdown of Communist rule, a clear determination and ability to build new political structures and procedures for democracy; others are more reluctant. The wall between West and East has tumbled down, Cold War Europe is changing into post-Cold War Europe. This marks so far the happy aspect of the present moment, but further crisis lies ahead, new conflicts are being born. The momentum toward crisis is aggravated by the fact that forty years of Communist rule have deformed individual and societal life as well as political thinking. The West must first learn to understand this psychological situation in Central and Eastern Europe.

Many of these elements of crisis are reflected in the German problem. But, for better or worse, Germany carries a special historical, but even more a special political and economic responsibility for future developments. Every aspect of political, civil, economic, cultural, and private life is in one way or the other deeply affected by the ongoing process of unification on the federal or local level in Germany.

Twenty years of West German détente made the Federal Republic the foremost détente power in Europe. All German Chancellors from Konrad Adenauer to Helmut Kohl personify the spirit of a new postwar Germany that wants to live in peace and cooperation with its neighbors in East and West. It is this forty-year-old stock of credibility that gives historical weight to the Kohl/Genscher "Ostpolitik" and "Deutschlandpolitik" as outlined in the ten points. This genuine combination of two ideas is the essence of the ten point plan. Germany remains politically anchored in the mid-Atlantic, while the Western idea of magnetism after forty years of frustration is now beginning to shape reality all over Europe. The German reunification process is part of the Western idea of magnetism. This fact puts a heavy responsibility on the German government: to keep up the momentum of the process and to persuade friends and others alike that by reunification nobody will lose, but all will profit in East and West. There is good reason to have trust in Germany, described by Norman Stone, Professor at Oxford, in this way: "She is, easily, the outstanding European country. She fulfils the role that Britain used to fulfil of combining economic efficiency, educational excellence and all-round seriousness with political liberalism and respect for people's rights. She is now, in my opinion, the modern European country. A reunified Germany will not only remain a stabilizing force for democratic civilization but will enhance it."

The vision of the Kohl/Genscher government for Germany and Europe reflects a new kind of federalism on a continental level, which goes back historically to pre-Bismarck times, when Germany was decentralized and the individual states more powerful and the central government weaker than in any other Western state. The Kohl/Genscher government's vision of the postnation-state in a post-communist Europe builds mainly on the European Community. This vision is far from either the European superstate or the ambitious Europe most French have in mind. It is a vision in which Eastern Europe's nations can develop toward democracy and well-being without violent discontinuities. This vision is one of association and assimilation rather than of incorporation. It is open to links with the United States and Canada as friendly states with historical and strategic interests in the future of Europe. This model of a larger Europe may serve central Europe and Germany for a long time. It may overcome the European division and will finally give the Germans East of the Elbe the prospect of human rights, freedom, economic well-being, and stability in a mature new nation state. But the success of reunification will only be assured if the Kohl/Genscher government is not left alone or even isolated by its Western partners. The collapse of the GDR and the failure of communism also mark the end of the German problem. It is not a victory for Germany but a victory for freedom.

Part II

Economics, Education, Science

–6–

Toward a New European Regime of Capital Accumulation?

STUART ROSEWARNE

The formal integration of the European market in 1992 has been held out by some as a panacea for the economic woes of the 1970s and 1980s. The establishment of a single European market, it is argued, will generate new business opportunities, stimulate investment and employment, and generally promote economic growth. More skeptical observers have suggested that at best the claims that market integration will promote economic growth are exaggerated; or worse, that the integration movement is just one further step in a neo-liberal strategy to increase competition and deregulate capital and labor markets, which has proved decidedly unsuccessful to date.

The focus of much of the debate on the economic advantages of European integration has concentrated largely on the institutional transformations, and particularly with respect to state forms, and the way in which these have been necessary for securing the liberalization of the European economy generally. Essentially, proponents of integration have stressed the desirability of diminution in the power of nation-states across Europe at the same time as they have applauded the transformation of suprastate formations to oversee and manage economic integration. Critics have likewise focused their attention on the state, and particularly upon the inability of nation-states and the European Commission to lay the basis for sustained economic recovery. The focus is clearly quite limited, and in this essay I want to suggest that a better impression of the future shape of the European economy can be obtained by developing an appreciation of the changes in the broader political economy of Europe.

The formal economic integration of Europe in 1992 should be viewed as part of a longer term process of economic and political transformation. It is the contention of this paper that the formal integration of the European market has been partly engendered by the distinctive way in which private and state enterprises have restructured and rationalized their operations in response to the economic malaise overshadowing Europe. A key feature of this response has been the Europeanization of enterprise. Since the mid-1980s there has been a noticeable shift in corporate strategy, with industrial and financial concerns extending their reach by a range of means, such as entering new markets within Europe, setting up subsidiaries, merging with or taking over competitors, and generally adopting a more European profile. This restructuring of private and state enterprise has heralded a reorganization of production across Europe, promoting a more integrated economic region. Furthermore, the efforts of individual states and the European Commission to promote sustained economic development has tended to reinforce this Europeanization process. The market integration being promulgated in the institutional changes formalized in the Single European Act can be considered to be a corollary of the Europeanization of production and of the organization of enterprise.

From the Long Boom to the Economic Crisis and the Neo-liberal Agenda

The 1950s and 1960s was by and large a period of sustained economic growth or capital accumulation in Europe. The period was characterized by a transformation in the organization and location of production and substantial gains in worker productivity. This transformation was the basis for the extensive development in the mass production of commodities, and especially consumer goods. The economic growth generated employment opportunities and this corresponded with an expansion in the working populations' material needs. This, in turn, underwrote the dramatic growth in the European market. Rising profits fed into this by providing resources for investment and further stimulating productivity gains.

While growth, full employment, and increasing productivity were maintained, the competing interests of capital and labor could, for the most part, be accommodated. This made for a certain degree of social cohesion and, in most European countries, a substantially transformed state helped to reinforce this. States intervened more actively in economies, pursuing Keynesian-type stimulatory policies and developing state enterprises, particularly in infrastructure and basic industries. Social cohesion was further promoted by state provision of education, health, and welfare. This combination of factors underwrote the period of sustained capital accumulation and economic prosperity.

Some theorists have conceptualized this period as a regime of accumulation and, more particularly, the Fordist regime of accumulation.[1] What is regarded as significant about this period was the unique combination of forces that produced an order in which a generalized system of production relations formed alongside a distinctive pattern of consumption. It was the correspondence between these that sustained capital accumulation. But integral to this was the emergence of a range of institutional relations and sociopolitical norms, a mode of regulation, which operated to secure a degree of social and political order and, thereby, establish a system of reproduction. This is not to argue that there were no tensions or conflicts; on the contrary. But unions, capital, and the state, as well as the organization of production, the labor process and of consumption, operated in such a way, at least until the late 1960s, to contain these tensions and conflicts. In the process, the conditions for the reproduction of this system of relations were secured. The period of sustained capital accumulation, or regime of accumulation, is thus associated with the systematic regulation of conflict and tensions; the economic growth that arises out of this also secures the order.

The onset of economic crisis in Europe represented the collapse of the Fordist regime of accumulation. Regulationists explain this in terms of an increasing incongruity between production and consumption, borne of crises in the respective relations, and the dissolution of the prevailing modes of regulation.[2] It is argued that the success of the Fordist era of production was undermined by the failure of increased investment in capital equipment to generate productivity gains and enhance profitability. Profitability was also eroded by the ability of an increasingly segmented labor force to secure increases in real wages. In the face of falling profitability and excess productive capacity, corporate capital reacted in a number of

1. Michael Aglietta, *A Theory of Capitalist Regulation* (London, 1979). The analyses emerging out of Aglietta's research have been referred to as the *regulationists*.

2. For instance, see Alain Lipietz, *Mirages and Miracles: The Crisis of Global Fordism* (London, 1987).

ways that tended to exaggerate the emerging imbalances. For example, production was decentralized and more "flexible" modes of production substituted for mass production; these sorts of changes dismantled the previous articulation of systems of production generally, as well as the links with markets. Rising levels of structural unemployment, alongside the increasing segmentation of the labor market, reinforced the lack of correspondence between production and consumption.

Changes in the role of nation-states tended to exacerbate this situation. The pursuit of monetarist policies was one dimension of the ascendancy of a more liberalist outlook on the part of states right across Europe. Privatization of certain state activities and the deregulation of various sectors of the economy, occurred alongside policies that reduced redistributive taxation and cut back on the provision of health, education, and social services generally, and brought an end to the explicit pursuit of Keynesian-type expansionary policies. On the other hand, the adoption of neo-mercantalist policies to protect markets and local industries, when generalized across much of Europe and the globe for that matter, had a contractionary effect.

The ascendancy of the neo-liberalist state also transfigured a breakdown in the ensemble of institutional relations and socio-political norms, which had helped to secure the order of the postwar period as well as underwrite the economic prosperity. The accord between capital and labor, which had been possible because of the increasing productivity and the resultant economic prosperity, was torn asunder by labor's ability to organize successfully while full employment prevailed. Capital could not meet labor's demands in the face of falling profitability, and the tenuous nature of the postwar social contract was revealed as capitalism moved into crisis. Neo-liberalist strategies to reconstruct the labor market became part of a broader strategy to confront this contradiction, but they have tended to reinforce the structural imbalances.

Neo-liberalism and Strategies for Economic Recovery

In the face of persistent economic problems, a new threat emerged in the latter part of the 1970s and the early 1980s in the form of increasing competition from Japan and the "Newly Industrializing Countries," which has tended to further entrench the liberal orientation of state policy, alongside, rather paradoxically, a rejuvenated neo-mercantilism. The international competitiveness of European industrial enterprise was placed in question by the emergence of the East Asian industrial powers. Europe feared an explosion of imports and the loss of export markets, which combined would exacerbate employment problems as well as the profitability of European enterprise. Governments responded with a new determination to protect European enterprise as well as to remove those barriers that were deemed to obstruct capital accumulation. States have been active in promoting more flexible modes of production in order to address the problem of excess productive capacity. Deregulating labor markets with a view to reducing direct labor costs has been a key strategy to enhance competitiveness and profitability. The deregulation of finance and capital markets has been promoted as a means of facilitating the mobility of capital to encourage investment in new equipment and industries as well as, it was hoped, discouraging speculative investments. This liberalization occurred simultaneously with more direct efforts by European states to stimulate investment. In varying degrees, states assisted in promoting investment by, for example, providing subsidies or research and development assistance to private capital, guaranteeing and protecting markets, or through state enterprises or directly taking the lead.

What is distinctive about this period is that alongside the liberalization of various arenas of the economy, the European states have tended to pursue policies that were introspective in character. Throughout the period, the focus of state management remained locked into national objectives; into encouraging capital accumulation within national boundaries as a means of promoting economic prosperity.

From the mid-1980s it was increasingly recognized that these particular neo-liberalist strategies had failed to arrest the slowdown in productivity growth and falling profitability, or to improve international competitiveness and reduce the high unemployment. But rather than bring about the demise of Europe's engagement with neo-liberalism, the failure to promote capital accumulation across Europe has underwritten another stage in neo-liberalism. This is evidenced in the more strident and dramatic moves to remove still more institutional barriers to the free movement of labor, capital, and commodities within and across Europe. The proposal to unify European market economies is merely one aspect of this shift in neo-liberalism, albeit politically one of the most significant.

The Single European Act provides the institutional framework for removing those remaining national barriers that stand in the way of the movement of goods and labor within the European Community. Yet, it is important to recognize that the agreement among the twelve members of the European Community to work toward the liberalization of the European market by 1992, is but one dimension of a development that has its origins in the economic crisis of the 1970s. The year 1992 needs to be situated in the context of a transformation of the forces promoting the liberalization of the European economy in general.

This transformation is evident in the shift in state policies. Most of the nation-states within Europe have, since the mid-1980s, downplayed the neo-mercantalist tendencies of state interventionism to adopt a more extroverted, or European, economic outlook. The failure of previous neo-liberalist strategies to boost productivity growth and the intensification of competition with Japan and the Newly Industrializing Countries, as well as with European enterprises in general, has prompted most of the European states to promote the international competitiveness of their respective economies. Policies that promote liberalization and deregulation have been integral to this shift in policy direction.

The most striking aspect of this shift has been the deregulation of finance and capital markets within national economies. In many respects deregulation was forced upon European nation-states because of the development of the unregulated financial system, and especially the Eurocurrency market, and also due to the internationalization of banks and other financial institutions and of financial markets generally.[3] But deregulation was also conceived as a means of enhancing the flow of funds with a view to encouraging productive investment. It was also envisaged that the removal of exchange rate controls would promote a more efficient competitive productive base. In the event that these liberalizations proved to be destabilizing and seemed to stimulate speculative investment, the agreement to establish the European Monetary System in 1979 – to provide an institutional framework to enhance monetary stability – has not necessarily meant that European states deviated from the

3. Committee on Financial Markets, *Trends in Banking in OECD Countries* (Paris, 1985).

neo-liberal path. While the establishment of the EMS has meant that member countries are required to peg their exchange rates within a given band, this has effectively meant the removal of many national controls on exchange rates. This has also served to reinforce and generalize the retreat from Keynesian-type expansionary policies.

The liberalization of financial and monetary affairs has, in effect, been institutionalized across the European Community, and perhaps is being consolidated by the continuing evolution of the EMS, especially in the recent moves for a European monetary union championed by the European Commission's president Jacques Delors, now more or less ratified by member countries. While monetary union will entail a degree of institutional intervention, which might not seem to sit comfortably with the push for liberalization insofar as union will involve greater currency alignment and the formal coordination of monetary and fiscal policies of member countries, and the eventual establishment of a European central bank and currency, the direction of institutional developments to date suggests that this is not greatly at odds with the continuing liberalization of the European economies. The development of the EMS will enable all European banks to conduct services throughout Europe. One of the conditions of Britain's late entry into the EMS was agreement on the British Prime Minister's demand that capital movements, exchange controls, and financial services all be liberalized.[4] Delors' program envisages a European central bank modeled on the Deutsche Bundesbank, which retains an autonomy from the state. (As will be argued below, however, this does not foreclose on the possibility of the central bank pursuing an expansionist monetary policy that would be at odds with the neo-liberalist strategy elements.)

1992: A Panacea for Europe's Economic Malaise?

The Single European Act has been held out as a necessary institutional development if the neo-liberal strategy for rejuvenating the European economy was to have any measure of success. In conjunction with the development of an integrated financial and monetary

4. *The Economist*, 24 June 1989, 1 July 1989; *Australian Financial Review*, 19 June 1989, 26 June 1989, 4 July 1989; European Commission, *A European financial area: the liberalization of capital movements*, June–July 1988.

system, the unification of European markets is reckoned to provide a guaranteed basis for the economic prosperity of Europe. Estimates of the extent to which unification will boost economic activity vary. Studies commissioned by the European Commission calculate that the removal of all those institutional obstacles in labor, capital, and commodity markets will reduce transport and a range of production costs and provide an immediate boost to economic activity right across Europe. The Cecchini Report has forecast that the direct effects of market unification will be a reduction in prices by as much as 6 percent and increase in economic growth by 4.5 per cent.[5] A truly European neo-liberalism is presented as the panacea for Europe's economic malaise.

There have been several major criticisms of the likely economic benefits of market integration. It is questionable whether the issuing of directives is a sufficient means of ensuring the removal of the large range of obstacles, including technical as well as institutional rigidities, to the free movement of goods and services and more generally to the unification of economic and production relations within Europe. The political commitment to the sentiments of the Single European Act is also a matter of concern. Europeanization will not necessarily diminish national loyalties and priorities. There is already some evidence to indicate that individual nation-states are somewhat reluctant to remove all obstacles to the free movement of goods and are unwilling to adopt policies that disadvantage particular sectors or enterprises. A degree of parochialism on the part of the nation-states will act as a fetter on any substantial liberalization.

There is a broader and more systematic critique of the notion that liberalization is a means of promoting economic recovery in Europe. Two recent studies contend that the neo-liberalist program does not address the essence of the problems confronting Europe and cannot, therefore, lay the foundations for a new regime of accumulation.[6] Market liberalization will not overcome the structural imbalances that exist within and across Europe. Liberalization will achieve at best a fairly superficial unification of the European economy, and one that is shaped by international links. It will not provide the material conditions for underwriting sustained increases

5. European Commission, *The big European market: a trump card for the economy and employment*, August–September 1988; *The Economist*, 14 May 1988.

6. John Grahl and Paul Teague, "The Cost of Neo-Liberal Europe," *New Left Review*, 174 (March/April 1989); Patrick Camiller, "Beyond 1992: The Left and Europe," *New Left Review*, 175 (May/June 1989).

in productivity and it will not address the lack of correspondence between the organization of production and patterns of consumption. Moreover, the ascendancy of the European Commission will not provide the institutional basis for a coherent state agenda for constructing an integrated European market, let alone for revitalizing Europe and laying the foundations for social cohesion generally. According to this argument, the reconstruction of a European regime of accumulation is unlikely because of the hegemony of neo-liberalism.

These analyses paint a bleak picture of the likelihood of any sustained rejuvenation of the European economy. Yet, this scenario is based largely on the argument that market liberalization is the key aspect of the institutional transformations in evidence within Europe at present. The focus tends to overemphasize the significance of 1992 as the pinnacle of the transformation of Europe, and there is a tendency, particularly within the more systematic critiques, not simply to argue that neo-liberalism has set the agenda for change, but to take the hegemonic ascendancy of neo-liberalism as unproblematic. A broader focus, and one that considers the wideranging reorganization of production across Europe and the implications this might have more capital accumulation, as well as the different politico-economic agendas that could be set in the context of the changing role of individual nation-states and with the emergence of suprastate forms in the shape of the European Commission, suggests a more promising prognosis: the possibility of a new regime of accumulation within Europe.

The Restructuring and Europeanization of Corporate Europe

The Single European Act signals a strategy to open up markets across Europe with a view to extending business opportunities and, thereby, hopefully to provide a fillip for investment. It is a measure to combat the effects of the way in which corporate capital and states responded to economic recession through the 1970s and early 1980s. By and large, capital reacted to the crisis by moving to protect and secure control over existing market shares or, through takeovers and mergers, to capture a share of other markets, but there was little consideration given to developing markets. In general, the focus of much corporate investment shifted away from expanding productive capacity and introducing new technologies, into takeovers and mergers, with a considerable proportion of investment funds being exported offshore and not in Europe.[7] The restriction of investment was also characteristic of many state-owned enterprises. Individual nation-states throughout much of Europe reacted by seeking to protect local markets for national manufacturers and to protect local producers from competition. State assistance with finance and the growing significance of the state as a purchaser reinforced this emphasis. What was distinctive about the reactions of both corporate capital in its approach to production and the state's policymaking with respect to industry, was that they tended to become more introspective and introverted in outlook. In general, the period was one of containment rather than expansion, and European industry concentrated on reducing productive capacity rather than improving productivity.[8]

This process ebbed and flowed, but from the mid-1980s a quite different pattern of restructuring of industrial capital became discernible. Several factors combined to bring about a concerted effort on the part of the corporate sector and a number of European states to strengthen the industrial base of Europe through the revitalization of industry and the adjustment of production structures.[9] The continuing profitability crisis and the failure of the private and publicly owned enterprises, as well as state industry plans, to reverse the slowdown in productivity gains, the persistence of recession, and above all increased competition with imports from Japan and the Newly Industrializing Countries, forced private companies and various states to embark on a broad-ranging and more radical program of adjustment.

From the mid-1980s a significant industrial transformation within Europe has become discernible. It has been associated with a renewed bout of takeovers and mergers, which has brought a greater degree of centralization and concentration of capital. This

7. Nigel Harris, *Of Bread and Guns: The World Economy in Crisis* (Harmondsworth, 1983), 125–29.

8. See, for example, Linda Hesselman, "Trends in European industrial intervention," *Cambridge Journal of Economics*, 7, 3 (1983); Christopher Wilkinson, "Trends in Industrial Policy in the EC: Theory and Practice," and Jacques Lesourne, "The Changing Context of Industrial Policy: External and Internal Developments," in *European Industry: Public Policy and Corporate Strategy*, ed. Alexis Jacquemin (Oxford, 1984).

9. Commission of the European Communities, *Improving Competitiveness and Industrial Structures in the Community* (Brussels, 1986).

has gathered considerable pace in the lead up to 1992, to such an extent that both the number and value of mergers and takeovers in the European Community has reached an all time high.[10] Unlike previous periods, however, when this takeover activity was associated with agglomeration, with some exceptions, from the mid-1980s takeover activity has been directly linked to a rationalization and concentration of activities by enterprises, with sell-offs of unwanted subsidiaries and/or incidental operations. The underlying objective in this transformation has been a new determination to construct a stronger competitive base for European-based industrial enterprise.

This takeover activity has a number of different dimensions, but the general consequence has been what can be described as a Europeanization of enterprise. First there have been the nation-based mergers of companies endeavoring to establish a larger base from which to build a competitive organization able to compete more openly within Europe. States have often played a crucial role in such rationalizations.[11] Another aspect of this has entailed states endeavoring to improve the competitive position of some nation-based enterprises through the merger of state enterprises with private companies. One of the striking features of Italy's industry policy has been the sale of several state enterprises to leading private companies engaged in similar activities, and this has served as the foundation for some major Italian corporations to develop a stronger European profile.[12]

A second path has been through the merger of enterprises from different European countries. The most dramatic instances of this are in the electronic and telecommunications industry, where there has been a dramatic surge in takeovers, mergers, and rationalizations.[13] But there are numerous instances of this sort of activity in other sectors of the European economy. European state enterprises have also entertained mergers with private companies domiciled elsewhere in Europe with a view to injecting a competitive spirit into the enterprise. The most notable example of such an arrangement is that of the French state enterprise *Compagnie Generale de Constructions Telephoniques*, which sold a 20 percent interest in the

10. *Australian Financial Review*, 11 August 1989.
11. For example, the 1988 merger between Spain's *Banco de Bilbao* and the *Banco de Vizcaya* to become the largest bank in Spain, assisted by generous tax concessions.
12. *The Economist*, 27 February 1988, 13 August 1988.
13. *The Economist*, 11 March 1989.

business to Ericssons in order to gain access to new technologies and management strategies.[14] A more conscious strategy to develop a more European orientation can be found in the growing number of joint ventures involving both state-owned and private enterprise. The Airbus project is perhaps the most well known project, but the fighter aircraft project involving Britain, Spain, France, and Germany is also another such example.

Smaller enterprises, less willing or able to become directly involved in "foreign" markets within Europe, have begun to extend their reach by entering into franchise and subcontracting arrangements and other forms of partnerships, to develop a more European orientation. The European Commission, through the passing of directives allowing the registration of such agreements, has been actively encouraging the formation of links between small and medium-sized enterprises across Europe. Such arrangements are complementing the development of a system of production engendered by the Europeanization of corporate and state enterprises.

The changed focus of industrial policy has also been crucial in this process. European states have played a central role in promoting the competitiveness of industrial enterprises. There have been a number of efforts made to assist in the modernization of state and private, nation-based enterprises to enable them to become more competitive and adopt a more European outlook, encouraging the adoption of new designs and technologies. Financial assistance from the European Commission has often been important to these programs.[15] The "corporatization" of state-owned enterprise, operating state enterprises along private sector lines, has been another strategy to promote the international competitiveness of enterprise. The most striking examples of this strategy can be found in France. This has frequently been the product of efforts to contain state expenditures or resulted from pressures within the European Commission to place all European enterprise on an equal footing, but the effect has been to promote the development of a more outward looking enterprise. Industrial policy has been transformed to promote the process of Europeanization of enterprise. What is noteworthy with this development is the general tendency for an increasing correspondence of state industrial policy across Europe.

14. *The Economist*, 23 April 1987.

15. Such as the Portuguese Government's opening of a new *Centro de Desenho Portuges*, S.M.H. 20 May 1989.

The increased authority of the European Commission has also been important in this transformation, directly through its own, albeit, small industrial programs, as well as through the Commission's promotion of Europeanwide research and development, particularly with projects such as the design of microchips. Indirectly, the European Commission is playing an increasingly important role in industrial transformation within Europe, insofar as it is assuming a substantial role in overseeing corporate affairs within Europe. Most significantly, the European Commissioner overseeing the EC's competition and antitrust policy has declared his support for the "creation of big European companies or joint ventures" and, in an attempt to assert the will of the Commission over national governments that continue to possess the power to obstruct mergers and takeovers, the Commission has directed "governments to be less nationalistic."[16] This is, more or less, an explicit endorsement of Europeanization.

Europeanization in and of itself has been important in a number of respects. It has prompted the rationalization of business enterprise across much of Europe. The bout of mergers and takeovers has been linked to European-organized and based enterprises shedding some superfluous or incidental business activities, a process that signifies a reversal of the trend of agglomeration. It has enabled the disposal of unwanted businesses and of obsolete plants. This has brought a greater degree of specialization of industrial and commercial enterprise, and with this, an improvement in productivity, greater utilization of productive capacity, and international competitiveness. This in turn is laying the foundations for a period of renewed and more sustained capital accumulation.

Another important consequence of the Europeanization of industrial enterprises has been the linking of the rationalization of productive activities with the geographic restructuring of enterprise. Mergers and takeovers have been important in facilitating the spatial reorganization of production across Europe. This tendency to relocate activities has also been evident in established enterprises, and this has been especially evident in the automobile industry. Ford and General Motors have transferred plants from West Germany to Britain where labor costs have proved to be substantially lower.[17] It is envisaged by both companies that production will

16. *The Economist*, 27 June 1987.
17. *The Economist*, 13 February 1988.

expand to meet local demand as well as to enable exports to mainland Europe. Volkswagen has relocated some production to Spain following the acquisition of a state-owned production plant. Citroen has relocated some production to Portugal.

What is increasingly significant about this redirection of investment and the spatial restructuring process is that the Europeanization of industrial and commercial enterprise has been directly linked to an emergent system of production that is organized on a Europeanwide basis. The relocation of industry to Britain, Ireland, Portugal, and Spain has occurred in the context of capital seeking to take advantage of wage and skill differentials across Europe. The restructuring of industrial Europe has been associated with the construction of a European division of labor. The regional development programs of the European Commission have also facilitated this development.[18] The consequence is that while European capital has internationalized, this does not simply mean that capital is now driven by an international dynamic, as some theorists have noted. Rather, it is clear that there is an emerging articulation of a European-based production system with its own dynamic.

The spatial restructuring of capital has enabled the location of enterprise to take advantage of disparities in the wages across Europe, as well as regional development programs, to improve their competitive position. This has been clearly demonstrated with the restructuring of the European automobile industry.

The Europeanization of business enterprise has also been linked to and provided capital with a greater capacity to not only reorganize the location of production but also to restructure the way in which production is organized. The restructuring of industrial, financial, and commercial enterprises across Europe has presented capital with a greater degree of flexibility and more opportunities to explore different modes and techniques of production. The spatial restructuring of capital has resulted in new technologies and management techniques being imported into regions that previously had next to no industrial base. This transformation in industrial organization is also in evidence in the major industrial centers of Europe. The net consequence of this can be observed in the 10 percent increase in nonresident gross capital formation in 1988 over the previous year.[19]

18. *The Economist*, 15 July 1989.
19. O.E.C.D., *Economic Outlook* (July 1989).

In general, this process of Europeanization has heralded an improvement in the competitive position of European enterprise. While the spatial restructuring of capital has enabled capital to relocate production to take advantage of lower real wage costs, it is also evident that there has been a noticeable reduction in real unit labor costs. Productivity has been enhanced and the net consequences of this can be evidenced in the noticeable recovery in corporate profitability since the mid-1980s. Average profits and rates of return were 10 percent higher in 1988 and 1989 than for the period 1973 to 1987, and this contrasts with patterns in North America and Japan.[20] British companies are now more profitable than at any time since the 1950s.[21]

While the recent recovery in corporate profitability does not make an economic recovery, there is increasing evidence that this is engendering an upswing in investment.[22] Private capital accumulation does appear to be being moved by a new dynamic in the European economy. There is increasing evidence pointing to a recovery in private capital accumulation in Europe. The enactment of the Single European Act has provided an impetus for this process. The further liberalization of trade, labor, and capital flows, as well as the standardization of technical and other aspects, should facilitate the further development of the Europeanization process. Production is being restructured across Europe and is laying the foundations for a more unified and articulated European economy. And production is being restructured in such a way as to provide a greater degree of flexibility so that the disparate and differentiated needs of the different markets within Europe are being catered to far more, and more from within Europe. The efforts of the European Commission, albeit not very substantial to date, to promote a degree of even development throughout the European Community, have tended to complement this process.

These developments have occurred alongside a marked shift in and redirection of investment flows. In general and in contrast with much of the 1970s and early 1980s, an increasing proportion of investible funds are remaining within Europe. While direct private investment beyond Europe, that is direct foreign investment, continues to be significant, there has been a noticeable decline in the

20. O.E.C.D., *Economic Outlook* (July 1989), 39, 113.
21. *The Australian*, 12–13 August 1989.
22. O.E.C.D., *Economic Outlook* (July 1989), 177.

exodus of investment funds. Although accurate estimates are not readily available, the consequences of Europeanization of European capital can be evidenced in substantial direct intro-European investment, and especially into Britain, Spain and Portugal.[23]

The development of the European oriented production system and the linking of this to market integration has also attracted an influx of non-European capital. There has been a substantial increase in foreign investment within Europe as non-EC enterprises endeavor to establish local subsidiaries to service the needs of the European market from within the Community. North American and Japanese companies have been at the forefront of this development, but companies from non-Community European countries have also demonstrated a lot of initiatives in this respect, as have a number of Australian companies. (Australian companies have been predominant in the Europeanization of transport systems in Europe.)[24]

This Europeanwide restructuring of production and the unification of markets should serve to promote some degree of correspondence between systems of production and consumption patterns across Europe rather than, as some have argued, reinforce the discontinuities. The evidence to date indicates that it is also fueling a new dynamic and promoting the foundations for sustained capital accumulation.

Furthermore, this stimulation should be enhanced by the ever-increasing incorporation of countries outside the EEC. In terms of the developing trade links and the organization and ownership of business enterprise in the region, the process of Europeanization that has been alluded to here has not been confined to the boundaries of the European Community. The restructuring and rationalization of economic activity in Europe has encompassed a broader base. There are two related aspects of this worthy of consideration.

23. Electrolux's takeover of several consumer durables enterprises in a number of Community countries and Nestles' acquisition of the British Rowntree as well as companies in Italy and France, are noted examples of non-Community European enterprises *Europeanizing*. T.N.T. Ltd. and Brambles Industries Ltd. dominate courier and special delivery services, express air freight, and rail freight.

24. Eurostat *Balance of Payments: Geographic breakdown 1981–1985* (Luxembourg), 1987; *The Economist*, 20 May 1989; Banco de Portugal *Report for the year 1988*, 119; *Report of the Deutsche Bundesbank for the year 1986*, 20; *De Nederlandische Bank Annual Report 1987*, 56; *Australian Financial Review*, 11 August 1989; *The Australian*, 12–13 August 1989. Still, half of British and German foreign investment is directed toward the United States.

The commercial links that have provided one of the forces making for unification are not restricted to the member countries. A number of those countries making up the European Free Trade Association clearly have strong commercial ties as well as financial links with the EC.[25] EFTA countries absorb 27 percent of the EC's exports. Indeed, each has a free trade agreement with Europe. The increased transport links, especially those associated with the Europeanization of private freight forwarding companies conducting services by road, rail, and air, and the future development of transport systems, especially highway systems and rail arterial networks, will consolidate commercial and industrial links. While the formal unification of Europe in 1992 will mean that the position of these countries is going to have to be renegotiated, commercial and financial relations are so intimately bound up with Europe, it is difficult to see how they cannot form an integral part of the process of unification.

The fact that the restructuring in the organization as well as ownership of capital has also not been restricted to the boundaries of the EC, should reinforce this. Swedish enterprises have, for instance, played a crucial role in the process of rationalization discussed above. In a wide range of industries, from autos to white goods to building materials and services, Swedish capital has taken over EC-based companies and assumed an active part in the restructuring and rationalization of enterprise throughout Europe.[26] This process has not been structured around the constraints of the European Community but around a more broadly organized European capital. If there is a European division of labor emerging, then it also necessarily encompasses the EFTA group of economies.

Moreover, the boundaries of this European system of production really extend beyond Western Europe. The signing of the joint declaration of mutual recognition by the European Community and COMECON in June 1988 opens the way to boost trade and economic ties as well as for the EC to open diplomatic relations with individual COMECON countries. But in many respects the significance of the declaration merely gives a political imprimatur to economic links that have been "normalized" for some time now. Trade between the EC and COMECON is quite substantial. The

25. The European Free Trade Association comprises Switzerland, Austria, Sweden, Norway, Finland, and Iceland.

26. *The Economist*, 9 April 1988.

EEC provides one-third of COMECON's imports, and the economic well-being of the Community is very much contingent upon imports of oil and natural gas. More interesting, however, has been the increase in direct investment in COMECON countries by European and other Western capital. This has in part been motivated by the desire of private capital to establish a presence in the Eastern bloc, but it is also evident that some of the COMECON countries represent cheap labor havens for establishing production bases for the manufacture of commodities for Western consumption.[27]

Toward a New European Order: New Regimes of Accumulation and Modes of Regulation

The industrial rejuvenation in evidence in Europe suggests that capital accumulation is gathering a new momentum. But this is a process that is going to be significantly shaped by the degree to which the new institutional forms of state management will effectively oversee economic recovery. The substantial critique of the neo-liberalist strategy for 1992 is that not only will the European Commission not provide sufficient impetus to promote economic recovery, but that it will not have the institutional force necessary to carry out this task anyway. While one can only speculate about the course of future developments concerning the role of European states and the European Commission, however, this conclusion appears to be unduly pessimistic; all the more so given the increasing support for proceeding with the development of the European Monetary System.

There is a growing acknowledgment among more and more states within Europe that a coordinated expansionist economic program is the most appropriate path to enhance the future of the European Community. Active efforts by individual states to promote a greater degree of coordination in the efforts to revitalize the European economy in general are a relatively recent phenomenon. It is only as recently as February 1977 that a Franco-German summit agreed on closer coordination of economic policies through regular meetings of their respective Ministers of Finance and Economics, and until quite recently there has been considerable resistance by Britain to any active involvement in this.[28]

27. *The Economist*, 30 April 1988.

28. Roger Morgan and Caroline Bray, *Partners and Rivals in Western Europe: Britain, France and Germany* (Hants, 1986).

The development of the European Monetary System has necessarily meant an expansion of this cooperation, and the European Commission is increasingly overseeing the implementation of a European economic program. What is distinctive about this is the ascendancy of an expansionist outlook. This is most clearly evidenced in terms of its policies with respect to promoting schemes to boost economic activity in depressed areas, including areas that have been subject to deindustrialization: it is evident in the Commission's social charter program to provide assistance for schemes to address the problems of long-term unemployed and youth unemployment; and, it is evident in the efforts of the European Commission to develop a stronger political presence throughout Europe. The recent successes of socialist and other progressive candidates in the elections for the European Parliament should give the Commission a stronger mandate to proceed with its expansionist programs.

Much of the force for sustaining capital accumulation will be generated by the policies emerging out of the European Commission, but even if the neo-liberalist philosophy diminishes the impetus provided by the Commission, the other major institutional development (of the European Monetary System) is likely to generate conditions for enhancing capital accumulation within Europe. The development of the European Monetary System has been an important fillip to the process of integrating the European economies and to developing a more stable financial and monetary system. The program for extending the monetary union has, over the course of the last twelve months, radically and quite dramatically propelled the responsibility for the determination of monetary and fiscal policy out of the realms of individual states into that of the European Commission. In many respects it has meant that the neo-liberal agenda has become a vehicle for promoting a state apparatus that is in a better and stronger position to oversee the more systematic aspects of financial and monetary affairs across Europe.

The immediate agenda of this program is not necessarily an endorsement of a state directed expansionist program, although it is much more Keynesian in orientation than the neo-liberal agenda would wish.[29] Indirectly, however, it would seem that the consequence of going further down the monetary union track being

29. Will Hutton, "They do things better in Europe," *The Guardian*, 10 September 1989.

advocated by Delors will be that a more developed European Monetary System will prove to be expansionary because of its indirect impact on European financial affairs. One of the objectives of union is to promote a greater degree of financial stability within Europe. The present EMS secures some degree of stability in exchange rates, and the extension of the System will enhance currency stability within Europe. Similarly, the present System provides for a degree of coordination of monetary policy, and the further development of the System, with the incorporation of new members as well as with the institutionalization of the requirements for policy coordination, will provide for a greater degree of stability and commonality in the direction of policies within individual countries. This will tend to have a significant impact on reducing opportunities for speculative investment of capital within Europe. It will tend to remove one of the major disincentives for productive investment within Europe. Furthermore, the development of the European Monetary System should mean that lifting of capital controls across Europe will result in a greater mobility of capital, which will feed into the process of Europeanizaton. In general, the development of the EMS will underwrite the economic expansion that is already being evidenced across Europe.[30]

The conditions seem to be set for a period of sustained capital accumulation within Europe. In terms of this heralding a new order, a new regime of accumulation, analysts have suggested that a number of major problems remain that will frustrate this possibility. In particular, it is argued that there are major discontinuities in the structure of the European economy as a direct result of the way in which production is increasingly being organized. The shift from Fordist to neo-Fordist production techniques, according to this argument, has seen a shift in the organization of production based on the employment of the great bulk of the labor force in a full-time capacity to a system of production in which a core of workers participate actively in the rejuvenation of industry, and enjoy the fruits of the industrial recovery, while a growing number of workers are marginalized into casual, part-time and low-paid positions, forced to eke out an existence on the periphery of the labor market. This is the consequence of a discontinuity in the structure of the economy, a lack of correspondence between the organization of production and the real material needs of European communities.

30. *The Economist*, 24 June 1989.

There is much in this argument, although it does tend to exaggerate the extent to which the respective systems of production have been generalized.[31] The conclusion, however, rests on the acceptance of the continuing hegemony of the neo-liberal strategy. The development of a "social charter" points to a significant challenge to the neo-liberal order. The European Commission's Social Affairs Commissioner has formulated a program for tackling a wide range of employment issues, including unemployment and job training, rights to a "decent wage," regulations on working hours and conditions, comparable employment contracts for part-time workers to those for full-time workers, employment contract rights, and equal rights for men and women, as well as some form of worker participation.[32] The "social charter" represents a striking challenge to the erosion of working conditions and material well-being of many of Europe's workers that has followed in the wake of state directed neo-liberalism.

There is little doubt that there is considerable opposition to this social charter. Grahl and Teague in particular argue that the present moves to implement almost any elements of the "social charter" are doomed. In some respects, implicit in this argument is an assumption that the emergence of the European Commission as a political force will not provide an arena for challenging Europe's neo-liberal path and remedying the divisions and the economic incongruities this has created. Yet, while there is substantive and effective opposition to the implementation of the "social charter," and especially from British Tories, it is evident that some elements of the charter will be accepted by the European Commission. Moreover, the proponents of the charter are exploring other avenues for pushing some of the charter's objectives. In particular, the Commission is proposing to link some elements of the charter to its proposed European Company Statute.[33]

There is some hope then that the "social charter" will provide some redress for those who have been disadvantaged by the way in which industry has restructured in Europe. Failing much advance through this institutional development, it must also be noted that

31. For a critique of this argument, see Michael Piore & Charles F. Sabel, *The Second Industrial Divide* (New York, 1985).

32. *Australian Financial Review*, 19 May 1989.

33. *The Economist*, 8 July 1989; Michael Emerson, "Regulation or Deregulation of the Labour Market. Policy Regimes for the Recruitment and Dismissal of Employees in the Industrialized Countries," *European Economic Review*, 32 (1988).

the regional development programs provide another avenue for the pursuit of these concerns. Increasingly, the EEC is developing a more significant role as a regional aid fund, with 15 percent of its budget now allocated toward specifically regional concerns.[34] In effect, regional aid may become a "social charter" by stealth.

The significance of this in terms of postulating the possibility of a new European regime of accumulation is that the promotion of the "social charter" is laying the foundations for a new mode of regulation in which a range of new institutional relations are being established. These will include institutional arrangements for improving the material well-being of most Europeans and constructing an order in which the deleterious consequences of working in the contemporary capitalist system are ameliorated, as well as establishing institutional organs that help to order work relations and contain possible conflicts involving labor and capital. Furthermore, this institutional order will necessarily involve promoting arrangements that not only ensure that some of the tensions between competing capitals are contained, but arrangements that help to secure capital accumulation.[35] The institutional development of the European Commission does seem to be addressing these concerns and, in effect, underwriting a new European regime of accumulation.

Conclusion

The Single European Act, together with the equally important development of the European Monetary System, on terms more or less advocated by the European Commission's President Jacques Delors, should remove some of the remaining institutional barriers to the integration of what will amount to a federation of European economies. In addition, the European Commission's gradual assumption of powers over the registration of companies, of both financial and non-financial institutions, as well as the authority to

34. *The Economist*, 15 July 1989.

35. There does appear to be a growing acknowledgment of the right of the European Commission to oversee merger policy. For instance, the Special House of Lords Committee on the European Community has urged the government to give control of the review of big mergers to the European Commission. This is an important breakthrough in efforts to dissolve tensions arising from competition between different national capitals. See *Australian Financial Review*, 10 April 1989.

veto mergers and takeovers, should further this development by facilitating the Europeanization of business enterprise. These developments will work toward consolidating the restructuring of not only both private and state-owned enterprise in Europe, but of the European economy as a whole. This restructuring should enhance the viability of business activity within Europe and, equally importantly, in conjunction with the European Commission assuming a more substantial hand in the coordination and administration of fiscal and monetary policies, and significantly policies that are likely to be expansionist in character, underwrite sustained economic expansion. Europeanization and the economic integration of Europe, along with the increased authority of the European Commission as an overseer of these processes, will tend to enhance capital accumulation within Europe, laying the basis for a new regime of accumulation.

–7–

Multinational Companies and the European Community

DANIEL VAN DEN BULCKE

Introduction

When the Treaty of Rome was signed in March 1957 and the European Economic Community (EEC) was launched in January 1958, little or no special attention was given to Multinational Enterprises (MNEs). Although foreign (American) direct investment (FDI) increased greatly during the 1960s, it was only in the 1970s that the term "Multinational Enterprise" became ubiquitous in political, economic, and social circles. At that time, the European Commission was very much concerned about countervailing measures to curb the growth of MNEs. Since the 1980s, however, the EEC has taken a more collaborative stance and even developed special forms of industrial collaboration with MNEs.

Early theory of international economic integration also neglected the influence of FDI and MNE. It was considered as evident that the elimination of customs duties among member countries would result in less FDI within the newly formed customs union. Unhindered by tariffs, companies from the partner countries would be able to sell abroad via exports, at least if transport costs or other location factors did not oblige them to produce abroad. Second, it was thought that the creation of a common external tariff toward third countries would be an important incentive for outside (mainly American) producers to leap over tariff barriers and start local production. With the gradual decrease in tariff protection as a result of the GATT-tariff-rounds, the common external tariff would have a declining attraction for outside MNEs. The first hypothesis especially was proved wrong.

According to L. Franko, international trade within the Common Market actually developed less rapidly than FDI among member states, even in those countries where important economies of scale would have resulted from the elimination of smaller enterprises.[1] Franko's analysis of sixty-nine large MNEs showed that European MNEs acquired more foreign subsidiaries after 1958 than before and that market penetration of other EEC member countries was mainly preceded by takeovers of existing companies.

This unexpected spread of foreign subsidiaries is due to the gradual switch by many EEC countries from internal customs duties to nontariff barriers. Thus, the great number of subsidiaries that belong to the ten largest MNEs in the pharmaceutical sector result from numerous national regulations. Government procurement policies are also highly discriminatory as regards investments goods; companies feel obliged to locate within particular countries in order to be awarded government orders.

Besides, there is the attitude of MNEs themselves. In line with oligopolistic theory, MNEs would take over local competitors in the partner countries in order not only to extend their market reach, but also to protect their market position in their home country. MNEs from small countries tend to do the opposite and establish foreign subsidiaries to function as export platforms for the parent company. Some foreign investors have even been inspired by considerations of the "fifth column"-type, i.e., to locate in the markets of the foreign competitors in order to retaliate quickly in case competitive pressure in their home market is increased. J. Pelkmans mentions that foreign production may not be a phenomenon encountered immediately after the formation of the union, but may become a regular feature once certain firms have become well established MNEs and have accumulated enough experience in the national market to spread out their technological advantages in order to achieve the optimal spatial distribution of plants within the economic union.[2]

Now that the EEC has thrown off its Euro-sclerosis-syndrome, which occurred immediately after the second oil shock and the Cockfield report announced the realization of the "internal market," it is striving to realize the full promise of its 1957 founding

1. L. Franko, *The European Multinationals. A Renewed Challenge to American and British Big Business* (London, 1976).

2. J. Pelkmans, *Market Integration in the European Community* (The Hague, 1984).

charter by establishing a genuine Communitywide market, free of restrictions over the movement of goods, services, persons, and capital and fostering common policies.

In order to complete the Common Market, the White Paper targeted the removal of the remaining physical, technical, and fiscal barriers.[3] Differing indirect tax rates and health regulations, for instance, still necessitate border controls, which cause significant delays and costs. Divergent product regulations and standards as well as protectionist public procurement policies are other examples of barriers, the removal of which should offer important gains of economies of scale and scope to companies located or locating in the EEC.

Because of the advantages of MNEs in organizing cross-border activities and coping with environmental uncertainty, it is reasonable to predict that they will be among the main beneficiaries of this removal of nontariff barriers and the ensuing benefits resulting from the rationalization of production, especially now that the European Commission also is relying on MNEs to achieve certain of its goals, e.g., through all kinds of collaboration projects.

Some Data about FDI and MNEs in the European Community

When MNEs from EEC countries are lumped together with the foreign-owned subsidiaries located in their territories, about 40 percent of industrial employment in these countries results from the activities of MNEs. While foreign MNEs in the mid-1970s were especially important in Belgium, the home MNEs had the largest employment impact in the Netherlands and the Federal Republic of Germany. In 1978, about two-fifths of employment in Belgian manufacturing resulted from foreign subsidiaries, as compared with about one-fourth to one-fifth in the United States, United Kingdom, the Federal Republic of Germany, and France, where the employment creation of their own MNEs is two to four times higher than the jobs they provide abroad.

The United States is the major foreign direct investor in the European Community. In Great Britain, American MNEs carried out 55 percent of all FDI. In other EEC countries, the Ameri-

3. EC-Commission, *Completing the Internal Market* (Brussels, 1985).

can share represents about 40 percent. Although there has not been a substantial withdrawal of American companies from Europe during the 1970s, American investment has been reoriented toward the Pacific Basin.[4] Between 1979 and 1983, American FDI in Japan and other countries of the Pacific Basin expanded at an annual growth rate of 20 percent, that is, three times as high as American FDI in Europe. From 1973 to 1977 the stock of American FDI in the European manufacturing sector increased by 52 percent, as compared with only 22 percent during the 1978 to 1982 period. Important new developments are on the one hand the rise of intra-EC investment and on the other hand the increase of Japanese investment within the European Community.

Foreign penetration differs greatly between the various industrial sectors, however. The chemical sector is the most multinationalized one, but the petroleum subsector largely accounts for this high share. Foreign MNEs are also quite important in metals, particularly in technically advanced branches such as machine construction, transport equipment, and electronics.

EEC Policy Toward Multinational Enterprises: General Considerations

It took the European Commission fifteen years after 1958 to become interested in the activities of MNEs. In 1973, a memorandum was published about the role of MNEs in the European Community.[5] After the proposals to the Council of Ministers had already been approved by the Economic and Social Committee and the European Parliament, however, the Commission in 1976 decided to withdraw its package of about thirty measures. This unexpected decision was undoubtedly based on tactical considerations, as the Commission had belatedly realized that a global acceptance by the Council had become illusory and that it would be more appropriate to introduce individual measures. Equally in 1976, all individual EEC countries signed the Code of Conduct of the Organization for Economic Cooperation and Development (OECD), and the European Parliament discussed the so-called

4. D. Van Den Bulcke, et al., *Investment and Divestment of Multinational Corporations in Europe* (London, 1979).
5. EC-Commission, *Les entreprises multinationales dans le contexte des règlements communautaires* (Brussels, 1973).

Lange-Gibbons code, which also proposed a general code of conduct. This latter proposal was only discussed in one of the committees, however.

Since then a number of specific measures have been taken and some proposals formulated, which, although of general scope, have a special bearing on MNEs. The relationship between the EEC and MNEs became extremely controversial when the Commission introduced in 1980 the "Vredeling" directive on "information and consultation of employees in MNEs." Before discussing in more detail the EEC measures in the fields of competition, industrial relations, tax policy, information, and consultation, the European Community policy will be evaluated in general terms.

In the early 1970s, the EEC Commission did not have a clear conception about its policies toward MNEs. On the one hand, the EEC Commission thought that Galbraithian countervailing powers should be developed to restrain the monopoly position of MNEs within the Common Market. On the other hand, the Commission wanted to support its own MNEs in external markets. Both to restrict and at the same time to favor the multinationalization process, gives rise to unavoidable contradictions. In recent years, however, the Commission has leaned more and more toward a supportive attitude and its attitude is no longer as ambivalent.

The "countervailing power" idea was already formulated in the EEC Commission's memorandum on industrial policy in 1970 (Don Colonna report), which listed a number of suggestions for increasing the size and competitive strength of European companies, thus enabling them to withstand better the pressure from American and Japanese MNEs, both in the EEC and in world markets. The Commission pointed out that many legal and fiscal barriers interfered with the intentions of enterprises from member countries to merge across borders. Too much time, however, was spent on the European Company Statute. The European Investment Bank received permission to specifically support initiatives that could lead to mergers among companies from different member countries. In 1973 the Business Cooperation Centre (the so-called Marriage Bureau) was set up as an intermediary for mergers and cooperation projects from small and medium-sized firms in different member countries. The EEC Commission also suggested measures to enhance the multinationalization of the EEC companies outside the Common Market; some kind of European insurance scheme for private direct investment abroad has been considered.

In its attempts to build up the trade unions into effective counterweights to MNEs, the EEC Commission attached much importance to transparency. Apart from information about global operations of MNEs, the Commission insisted upon the following: participation of employees in management decision making, measures to achieve industrial democracy, and advance notification of important decisions (e.g., in case of mergers, collective dismissals, and other decisions of importance to employees). Paritary committees per industrial sector, for the Community as a whole, and European collective agreements were also proposed. The vehemence with which the Vredeling proposal has been opposed by the employers, however, suggested that such measures upset one of the basic characteristics of MNEs, namely their flexibility. Also, the unofficial version of the ninth directive of company law has been regarded by international business circles as a straightforward attack on the legal duality of MNEs. While parent company and subsidiary are legally independent companies, economic reality has shown that MNEs often follow a global strategy based on centralized decision making: not only investment decisions, but also financing, export policy, research, production, and some other decisions are typically taken by headquarters.[6] According to Robinson, "the very existence of the multinational has undermined the notion of economic independence for supposedly legally independent subsidiaries."[7] Acceptance of the ninth directive would imply that the parent company is held legally responsible for the subsidiaries that belong to the group, for example, with respect to competition policy, participation of employees in management and environmental effects. The unofficial version of the ninth directive caused such an outcry from MNEs that any eventual proposal will undoubtedly look very different.

The Commission, as regards industrial policy, looks differently at MNEs headquartered within the EEC and those from third countries. This may cause conflicts with the United States and Japan. The OECD code of conduct (1976) states that discriminatory measures are only allowed with respect to newly established foreign companies. Special care may have to be taken to prevent some EEC interventions from burdening European MNEs more than foreign MNEs, which only have subsidiaries within the Common Market. In the proposed Vredeling directive it was accordingly stipulated that it

6. D. Van Den Bulcke and E. Halsberghe, *Employment Decision-Making in Multinational Enterprises: Survey Results from Belgium* (Geneva, 1984).

7. J. Robinson, *Multinationals and Political Control* (London, 1983), 66.

was the foreign parent's duty to ensure that the information and consultation procedure be respected. Such a point of view has extraterritorial implications. This is a major reason why American and Japanese MNEs strongly opposed the Vredeling proposal. Despite the major role performed by MNEs headquartered within EEC countries and foreign owned subsidiaries, the majority of companies operating in the European Community are uninational, as they only produce in a single EEC country. Like the OECD, the EEC subscribes to the principle of nondiscrimination between national and multinational firms. According to one critic, "the EEC's claim not to discriminate between MNEs and national companies may hold good in an abstract legal sense, but there is little doubt that policy measures are chosen by the EEC which have had the greatest, if not exclusive impact on MNEs."[8] Even the EEC measures to support small and medium-sized companies can to some extent be considered as a form of discrimination.

MNEs are now joining Europe's political leaders as leading actors in the attainment of the priorities of the EEC Commission. Especially relevant is the "Roundtable of European industrialists," which was launched in 1983 by chairmen of important MNEs and was instrumental in setting up the 1992 deadline for the achievement of an integrated internal market.

The EEC Competition Policy

Although the European Commission had received extensive powers in the field of competition, it first concentrated on the development of case law for article 85, which regulates cartels. At about the time that the European Commission became concerned about the impact of MNEs, it made use of article 86, concerning the abuse of dominant positions, to prohibit a takeover in the packaging sector by Continental Can, a large American MNE.

The European Commission invoked the Continental Can Case to propose, in 1973, a directive that would oblige enterprises to notify the Commission about intended mergers, more specifically about those that would involve joint sales of 1 billion ECU and would give control over twenty percent or more of a specific market. Although the European Council did not act on this proposal,

8. Robinson, *Multinationals*, 43.

another case, that of United Brands, strengthened the powers of the Commission, as the Court of Justice in 1978 equated a dominant position with 45 percent of a particular market; even lower percentages could be considered.

The Court's verdict about Hoffmann La Roche in 1979 further increased the scope for intervention by the EEC Commission, since practically any anticompetitive behavior could now be taken into account. As the above test cases have extended the antitrust powers of the European Commission, the proposed directive became less urgent.[9]

The IBM affair had been viewed by Americans as inspired by industrial policy considerations aimed at developing an independent European information processing sector. The EEC Commission, after an antitrust suit against IBM, which lasted from 1980 to 1984, suspended the case, and IBM agreed to make available more information about its computers to enable rival companies to design equipment that could be linked to the System/370. When announcing the agreement between the EEC and IBM (August 1984), the Commission accepted IBM as a full participant in ESPRIT, the research and development endeavor in the field of information technologies (see below).

Apart from the suspended IBM case the European Commission had until 1984 opened fifteen cases on the basis of article 86 of the Treaty of Rome. Eight were directed against MNEs, of which four were of U.S. origin.[10]

With regard to the cartel arrangements prohibited by article 85 of the Treaty of Rome, it must be stressed that parent company and majority-owned subsidiaries are considered as parts of the same economic unity, even when they have a different legal status. These agreements (e.g., about prices and distribution) within MNEs are not covered by article 85.[11] Besides, since 1983 the Commission has become more lenient and has invoked paragraph 3 of article 85 to allow the block exemption for intercompany arrangements about exclusive distribution, purchasing, specialization, research and development, and patent licensing.

The EEC Commission is also relying on the same paragraph 3 to allow franchising and joint venture agreements. In November 1985

9. Robinson, *Multinationals*.

10. E. White, "Abuses of dominant positions by TNCs: the EEC Experience," *CTC - Reporter* (Spring 1985), 43–45.

11. R. Jones, "Executive's Guide to Antitrust in Europe," *Harvard Business Review* (May–June 1976).

the Commissioner in charge of EEC's competition policies came out in favor of joint ventures, as they are instrumental in increasing competition and economic growth in the European Community. Although he rejected the conceivable anticompetitive effects of joint ventures (such as market sharing or price fixing between the parent companies), it was stated that a combined market share by the parent companies of 15 percent or less did not normally distort the competitive structure of the market; if the 15 percent ceiling was exceeded it might still be possible, after examining the particular case, to admit the joint venture. This undoubtedly would favor cooperation between European firms.

Since 1960 the Commission has been concerned with the need to enable European companies to merge across borders. Initially, however, the Commission devoted practically all its attention to the *European Company Status*, which would allow two or more interested companies from different member countries to merge and to create a new type of enterprise, with a parallel, specifically European legal statute. The provisions calling for the participation of the workers' representatives, however, were strongly opposed by MNEs and some national authorities.

The proposal for international mergers, whereby a company could acquire a company in a partner country, was rejected by West Germany and the Netherlands, which feared that their companies would seize the opportunity to change nationality and thus evade their more stringent social and fiscal obligations. Accordingly, companies that intend to merge across international borders are forced to devise complicated legal structures, which often consist of a holding company participating in the operating companies and allowing them to maintain their nationality. In any case, practically all such legal constructions set up in the sixties and seventies (e.g., Agfa-Gevaert, Fokker-FVW and Hoogovens-Hoesch) ended in failure.

An important new development is the European Economic Interest Grouping (EEIG) whereby firms, since 1 July 1989, have been able to join forces, transnationally, while retaining their legal and economic autonomy. The EEIG is the first legal entity based on Community law. "It will provide an appropriate structure for cross-frontier cooperation and will transcend some of the legal, fiscal and psychological barriers that currently prevent business from using the European dimension to the full."[12] The legal structure of the EEIG is very

12. S. Israel, "The European Economic Interest Grouping," *Commerce in Belgium* (January 1986), 7–9.

flexible. Companies are enabled to pool activities, resources, or skills, while remaining legally and economically independent. Consequently, it differs from the traditional joint venture, which involves the creation of a separate new unit. In the EEIG, profits will be apportioned among the members. It is expected that companies will make use of the EEIG structure, for activities such as common research and development initiatives, joint purchasing, manufacturing, or assembly, and sales or export promotion. As the EEIG, which was inspired by the French *groupement d'intérêt économique*, is limited, however, to companies with 500 employees or less, and is not empowered to centralize functions of the group, the new legal instrument is most appropriate for small and medium-sized companies. Its activities must also relate to those of the member companies. A more serious limitation is that third parties can lay claims on the unlimited financial liability of the members of the EEIG.

Sixteen years after the EEC Commission formulated its original proposal, the regulation on the control of concentrations between undertakings was finally approved in December 1989. This so-called merger control regulation entered into force in September 1990. As was already explained, the commission examined several mergers on the basis of articles 85 and 86. These articles, however, were not drafted with the control of mergers in mind, and the burdensome procedure did not allow *a priori* control. The new regulation gives the EC Commission the power to examine if concentrations with a "community dimension" are compatible with the Single Market whenever: (1) the aggregate worldwide turnover of the companies concerned is higher than 5 billion ECU; and (2) the communitywide turnover of each of at least two of the firms concerned is more than 250 million ECU. The regulation, however, is not applicable to concentrations where *each* of the companies derives two-thirds of its community turnover from the same member country. Although the thresholds have been set quite high, it is expected that they will be lowered later on and that the investigative powers of the Commission will be extended.

The EEC Social Policy toward Multinational Enterprises

The European Commission views trade unions as valuable counterweights to the activities of MNEs (EEC Commission memorandum, 1973). Of the twenty-nine measures initially envisaged, nine were related to the protection of employees within MNEs. Although some social directives have since become accepted by the Council – such as the harmonization of national legislations concerning mass dismissals (1975), the protection of employees' acquired rights in the case of mergers (1977), and the protection of employees in the case of insolvency by the employers (1978) – some controversial proposals are still pending before the Council of Ministers. While some of those proposals actually try to harmonize company law, they also have important social repercussions.

The directive to harmonize collective lay-offs assumes that MNEs, which carry out rationalizations, might be led by noneconomic criteria when deciding in which countries plants should be closed down. Consequently a harmonized definition of collective dismissals was introduced. It takes account of company size (based on the number of employees) and specifies a time period, during which the lay-offs are carried out. Besides, enterprises undertaking collective dismissals are obliged to inform representatives of the employees at least thirty days beforehand and must look for alternative solutions. Following important lay-offs by the Dutch multinationals Philips and AKZO and a debate in the European Parliament, it was concluded that the directive about collective dismissals lacked clout; among others, MNEs were not obliged to provide information about their worldwide operations. This discussion on collective dismissals set the stage for the Vredeling proposal of 1980.

The directive for the protection of acquired rights of employees in the case of mergers only concerns legal acquisitions, i.e., when one of the merging companies ceases to exist. Dismissals that result entirely from the merger itself are not allowed. Also, the rights of the workers must be subrogated by the new legal entity. The directive also provides for advance notice and consultation of workers about the measures resulting from the transfer that could affect them. Implementation by the member states of this directive does not seem to be satisfactory, while the restriction to an actual change of ownership leaves out other forms of acquiring control by MNEs that fall short of a complete merger.[13]

The proposed directive about a European Company Statute (already mentioned) carries important social provisions. In its revised 1975 proposal, the Commission intended to protect the interests of the employees by creating a supervisory board and establishing a Eu-

13. P. Lemaitre and C. Goybet, "Multinational Companies in the EEC," Part A and Part B, *IRM Multinational Reports* (July–September 1984).

ropean workers' council. The supervisory board would control the management board and would have to agree on decisions that are essential to the survival of the company (two-tier structure). One-third of the members of the supervisory board would be designated by the workers, one-third by the shareholders, while the remaining third would be co-opted by the two previous subgroups. In its newest revision of the European Company Statute, which the EEC Commission introduced in August 1989, an optional model for worker representatives is chosen. This would allow for a more flexible system based on three models, i.e., representatives of the workers on the supervisory board or the managing board; a separate body that would represent the employees; other models that could be agreed upon by negotiations with the workers' representatives. The regulation proposed in 1989 for the European Company Statute also tries to establish the position of the employees with respect to information and consultation with regard to important strategic decisions such as closure of subsidiaries, rationalizations, mergers, changes in the organizational set-up, and establishment of a subsidiary or holding company.

The fifth directive on company law about the structure of public liability companies is even more relevant to the issue of workers' participation than the draft for the European Company. Initially (1972), it covered public limited companies with more than 500 employees, and would have generalized the two-tier management structure (board of supervision and management board) and workers' involvement by having one-third of the seats on the supervisory board reserved for the workers' representatives. In the revised version, the EEC Commission increased the company ceiling from 500 to 1,000 employees or to parent companies or groups employing over 1,000 employees in the whole of the EEC; an exception was provided for holding companies. The Commission's new text (1983) is less strict and allows companies to choose among different formulas that are more in line with their national systems.

As a complement to the program for the Internal Market, the EC member countries signed in December 1989 the so-called Social Charter, which establishes the basic rights that EC citizens should enjoy with regard to: freedom of movement, employment and remuneration, improvement of living and working conditions, rights to social protection, freedom of association and collective bargaining, vocational training, equal treatment, information, consultation, and participation, etc.

In its 1973 memorandum the Commission urged member countries to exchange information about tax issues and to exercise stricter control. Transfer prices and royalties for licenses would have to be closely monitored. The Commission stated that the actual operations and transactions of legally independent companies were sometimes so closely linked that profits declared in individual countries might be rather arbitrary.

The directive for mutual cooperation and support among tax authorities of EEC countries (1977) in the field of direct taxes, was the first step in this direction. Fiscal authorities are obliged to spontaneously inform their colleagues in other member countries whenever they notice that, solely on fiscal grounds, transactions are artificially channeled over other countries. All information thus obtained has to be kept confidential, according to the rules in each country. Provision of such information, however, may be refused if it results in the disclosure of confidential trade information, or if the country to which the information is forwarded is not empowered on legal grounds to reciprocate with similar data. It would be most interesting to know more about how this intra-EEC exchange of information actually operates. One might expect that member countries will not be eager to exchange tax data about their home MNEs if this benefits the latter (if, for example, the transfer price manipulations increase tax revenues in that country).

In 1979 the principle of mutual assistance was extended to indirect taxes. The EEC Commission has also shown some interest in thwarting the (ab)use of tax havens and has even suggested the establishment of some kind of databank, to monitor intragroup trade and the transfer prices that are practiced.

The Commission also formulated three other fiscal proposed directives (1) a common fiscal system for mergers, hive-offs of companies, and the outlay of assets (1969); (2) a common tax system for parent companies and subsidiaries from different member countries (1969); and (3) the prevention of double taxation by one of the tax administrations in case of profit adjustments among related companies. So far none of these proposals has been accepted by the Council.

The EEC and Disclosure of Information by Multinational Enterprises

In 1973 the Commission promised to publish some kind of annual report with basic information about large national and multinational enterprises, so that an interested person could get an idea about the policies of those firms. More particularly, data about employment, investments, profits, taxes, research expenditures, and royalties, both about the parent company and foreign subsidiaries, would be made public. Although this promise was not kept, steps were taken by the fourth and seventh directives in the area of company law, toward the publication of information to the benefit of shareholders and creditors. The Vredeling proposal would oblige MNEs to provide information to employees in the subsidiaries, i.e., to the trade unions involved. Meanwhile, the proposed fifth directive of company law would allow employee representatives to be regularly informed, since they would be members of the supervisory or other boards.

The fourth directive (1978) is meant to harmonize the individual annual accounts of public liability companies in the European Community, but financial accounts that would have to be published made no reference to the possible group membership. Therefore, the seventh directive on consolidated accounts is specifically aimed at companies that belong to the same group "concerns."[14] Whenever a parent company exercises legal control (e.g., because it enjoys a majority position at the annual meeting of shareholders of another company or has the right to appoint or dismiss the majority of the members of the board of directors), consolidated accounts would have to be prepared. To make the directive applicable from 1990 onward, national governments are obliged to integrate the seventh directive into their national laws at least two years before this date. National governments are allowed to extend the concept of legal control to other situations of actual control.

The consolidation, which applies to all subsidiaries of the group, is only relevant to joint stock companies with important activities in the Common Market. Small groups can be exempted from these consolidation principles only if they do not exceed any two of the

14. J. Baillie, *Consolidated Accounts and the Seventh Directive* (Amsterdam, 1985) and Kredietbank, "De geconsolideerde jaarrekening in de Europese Gemeenschap," *Weekberichten* (11 October 1985).

following three minimum levels: a balance sheet total of 6.2 million ECUs; a net turnover of 12.8 million ECUs; and an average number of 250 employees during the year. As those criteria are quite low, the member states are empowered until the year 2000 to stretch these limits by multiplying the above floors by 2.5 and by exempting companies employing up to 500 people, except when the company's shares are traded on the stock exchange. National governments can also exempt holding companies whose activities are purely financial and that do not intervene in the decision making of the companies in which they participate. When subsidiaries of the EEC firms themselves participate in other companies, they would not be obliged to consolidate when they are themselves wholly owned (at least 90 percent) by the EEC parent company. When the shares of the subholdings belong for less than 90 percent to the EEC parent company, they may be exempted from consolidation. If the parent company does not have its headquarters within the European Community, the possible exemption of "subconsolidation" will be decided upon by the member government involved.

In 1980 the EEC Commission supported a proposed directive of its Dutch member, Henk Bredeling, concerning the information and consultation of employees in enterprises with a complex – in particular, with a transnational – structure. After discussions in the Economic and Social Committee and fierce debates in the European parliament, however, several key points of the original proposal were modified.

The second version (1983) stated that parent companies of industrial groups with 1,000 or more employees within the EEC have to inform the representatives of the workers in their subsidiaries at least once a year about the structure of the multinational group and its prospects in terms of production, sales, employment, and investment. In addition, the parent company should inform them about intended decisions that have serious consequences for employees, and it has to consult the workers' representatives (through the management of the local subsidiary) about the motives and effects of measures planned with respect to employment, such as: closure or transfer of an establishment or major parts thereof; restrictions or substantial modifications in the activities of the enterprise; major modifications with regard to the organization, working practices, or production methods, among them the introduction of new technologies; long-term cooperation with other enterprises, or its cessation; and measures relating to workers' health and to industrial safety.

An important aspect of the directive is the so-called "bypass," which would allow employee representatives in the subsidiary to have direct access to the "real decision makers" in the parent company. This bypass has been considerably toned down in the amended version of 1983; the direct contact in the original version was replaced by a written request and the answer from headquarters is to be transmitted through the local management.

The reformulated Vredeling proposal also stipulated that when the decision-making center of an "undertaking" is located in a nonmember country, its management may be represented by an authorized agent. In the absence of such an agent, the management of each subsidiary shall be held responsible. The "hostage concept" in the previous version, whereby the largest subsidiary of the non-EEC group located in the European Community would be responsible, has been abandoned. Elsewhere, we have argued that the assumption that all subsidiaries largely depend for all decisions upon the decision-making authority of the parent company is overdrawn and that some of the criteria used in the Vredeling proposal do not sufficiently reflect the findings of empirical studies on decisions about employment within MNEs. The assertions, however, by MNEs that their operations are completely decentralized, is also unsubstantiated.[15]

Although the chances for adoption of the Vredeling proposal may have vanished, since not only Great Britain but also Denmark and Ireland joined the opposition, the controversy about information and consultation of employees in multinational groups is unlikely to fade away. The trade unions invoke both the spread of "new technologies" and the recent merger movement for their claims to be informed and consulted. They tend to subordinate a positive attitude toward EEC policies of industrial renewal to Vredeling-type rules on information and consultation within MNEs. As the EEC Commission is itself launching several technology projects, the urge to win the support of the trade unions may take on an extra dimension. Meanwhile, the rights of workers on information, consultation, and participation have been recognized in the newest version of the optional European Company Statute and the declaration of the Social Charter.

15. D. Van Den Bulcke, "Decision Making in Multinational Enterprises and the Information and Consultation of Employees: the Proposed Vredeling Directive of the EC-Commission," *International Studies of Management and Organization* (Spring 1984), 36–60.

The EEC and Collaborative Ventures with Multinational Companies

Since the early 1980s, the EEC Commission has put new emphasis on the creation of transnational opportunities for European companies. Starting with ESPRIT (European Strategic Programme for R & D in Information Technology, February 1984) a number of projects have been launched that are jointly sponsored by the EEC Commission and private firms, mainly in the field of research (e.g., COMETT, Community in Education and Training for Technology; BRITE, Basic Research in Industrial Technologies for Europe; RACE, R & D in Advanced Communications Technology in Europe) but also with respect to production initiatives, such as EUREKA (European Research Coordination Action). The EEC Commission decided to play a more active role in the field of industrial integration that extends far beyond the preparation of harmonized legislation.

ESPRIT is "the clear manifestation of a new type of cooperation and the mark the Community can make on EEC industry, particularly the larger firms, through its existence and actions."[16] ESPRIT's program has been devised by the EEC Commission and twelve European multinational electronics firms. EUREKA attempts to bridge Europe's gap (including the EFTA group) in information technology. To induce cooperation, the EEC bears half the cost of joint projects by firms from several countries. Public funds, however, can be used only in a complementary fashion, and full use has to be made of private capital markets and the existing EEC financial instruments.

A novelty is that the projects are conceived not by public "research bureaucracies" but by the companies and research institutes themselves. The qualification of projects for the program does not depend on the approval of all partner countries (twelve EEC and five EFTA countries) but requires a consensus only among the parties involved in each particular case. Flexibility is further enhanced by the establishment of a small and flexible EUREKA secretariat, instead of a fully fledged agency.[17]

The signing of the European Single Act allowed the EC, from

16. P. Lemaitre and C. Goybet, "Multinational Companies in the EEC," *IRM Multinational Reports* (July–Sept. 1984).

17. K. Grewlich, "EUREKA - Eureka?," *Aussenpolitik* (March 1986), 1–9.

July 1987 onward, to carry out a number of actions to speed up and facilitate the integration process and explicitly permitted the Commission to intervene in the field of scientific research by launching long-term programs. The ESPRIT program was extended and its budget was doubled to 1.6 billion ECUs. Although R & D has been receiving much more attention by the European Commission, it should not be forgotten that the budget for all special programs only represented about 2.5 percent of the total EC budget in 1988. The increased tendency for European companies to prepare for the internal market of 1992 by entering into cross-border mergers and collaborative ventures will inevitably go together with larger scale production-oriented research and development initiatives.

–8–

Changes in EC Budgetary Funding

HEATHER FIELD

In February 1988 the European Council reached agreement on a package of measures designed to increase the amount of money available to the common budget of the European Community and to stabilize expenditure for the Common Agricultural Policy (CAP). The measures adopted included an agreement to allow members' contributions to EC funds to increase up to a ceiling of 1.3 percent of gross national product of each member; the extension of maximum guaranteed or threshold quantities of production to a much wider range of agricultural products, including cereals; and a projected increase in funding for structural programs of a regional, agricultural, and social nature to roughly a quarter of the EC budget in 1992.

The main budgetary aspects of the agreement included the incorporation of a measure based on gross national product in the budgetary formula, the introduction of a tighter monitoring system for agricultural support expenditure, and the creation of a more integrated system of EC funding. The Australian Bureau of Agricultural and Resource Economics examined the policy package in terms of the contribution it will make in solving EC budgetary problems and the extent to which it is a genuine move toward reforming present EC agricultural policies.[1] In this paper the relationship between the budget and agricultural price support is discussed and developments in the EC budgetary situation are examined.

1. H. Field, S. Hearn, and M. Kirby, *The 1988 EC Budget and Production Stabilisers: a means of containing the Common Agricultural Policy?*, ABARE Discussion Paper 89.3 (Canberra, 1989).

Background

A major feature of the common EC budget is that it has been mainly used to support a high level of protection for one industry, agriculture, through the Common Agricultural Policy. Agricultural price support accounts for some 60 percent of all EC budgetary expenditure.[2]

Support for agriculture in the Community is provided by taxpayers indirectly through the EC budget, more directly through national budgets of the individual member states, and from consumers. The EC budget provides both price support for agricultural products and funding for structural programs, such as farm modernization and adjustment, through the European Agricultural Guarantee and Guidance Fund (EAGGF). The remainder of the EC budget is used to support other EC policies, including regional policy, social policy, assistance to less developed countries, and research. Member states' national budgets for agriculture also provide assistance for structural programs, as well as for research, education, and training, and other purposes.

In 1980 it was estimated that consumers met over half the costs of agricultural support, and the EC budget about a quarter, with national budgets making up the remainder.[3] More recent estimates by the OECD, cited in a recent International Monetary Fund study, suggest that a somewhat higher proportion of total costs has been met by consumers — 63 percent for the period 1979 to 1981 and 62 percent for 1984 to 1986.[4]

In addition to support for agricultural prices and funding for the agricultural structural program, since 1988 the EC budget has provided funding for a special stock disposal fund and for the set-aside and income assistance schemes. In 1988 the appropriations for the guidance (that is, structural support) section of EAGGF amounted to 1203m ECU, and those for the stock disposal fund 1240m, with the appropriations for the set-aside and income assistance schemes amounting to less than 100m ECU.[5]

2. See Appendix, Table 8.1.

3. Bureau of Agricultural Economics, *Agricultural Policies in the European Community*, Policy Monograph 2 (Canberra, 1985), 69.

4. M. Kelly, N. Kirmani, M. Xafa, C. Boonekamp, and P. Winglee, *Issues and Developments in International Trade Policy*, Occasional Paper 63 (Washington, December 1988), 140.

5. Commission of the European Communities, *The Agricultural Situation in the Community* (Brussels, 1989).

The assistance provided through the EC and national budgets and through transfers from consumers has resulted in sectors covered by the CAP receiving high levels of assistance, details of which are given in terms of producer subsidy equivalent levels in Appendix.[6]

Developments in Budgetary and Agricultural Support Expenditure

The CAP support system varies in detail between commodities, but typically consists of target or guide prices being set for supported products, from which intervention or support purchasing prices (threshold prices at which goods may enter the EC) and import levies are derived. In effect, commodities that cannot be sold at the intervention price on the domestic market are purchased at the effective support price (intervention or buying-in price) and stored for later export, domestic consumption, or denaturing. Some production is exported directly with the aid of subsidies known as export refunds, which are designed to match the difference between the domestic support and world market prices. Although the CAP system was intended to some extent to be a price stabilization system, (with commodities being released from stocks onto the domestic market when market prices rose above support prices) in practice, support prices have been set so as to generally rule out the possibility of such an occurrence, except through a limited number of special subsidized domestic disposal schemes.

The availability of CAP price support, together with direct production subsidies under national support schemes, has led to increases in production and in the degree of self-sufficiency in agricultural products.[7] This, combined with the expansion of the Community in 1973 to include the United Kingdom, Denmark, and Ireland, resulted in the European Community becoming a major source of disturbance for world markets, due to increasing subsidized exports of agricultural products. The further enlargement of the Community to include Greece, in 1981, and Spain and Portugal, in 1986, greatly added to potential agricultural production in the Community and to the structural problems in agricultural and other

6. See Appendix, Table 8.2.

7. F. Duchêne, E. Szczepanik, and W. Legg, *New Limits on European Agriculture: Politics and the Common Agricultural Policy* (London, 1985).

sectors without increasing actual and potential Community funds to an equivalent extent.

Around half of expenditure on agricultural price support goes to intervention costs such as purchasing, storage, and, in some cases, destruction or denaturing of surplus products, the remainder being used for export refunds on surplus products. In 1987 export refunds cost the Community 9642m ECU.[8] This factor makes CAP budget expenditures to some extent responsive to changes in international commodity prices.

CAP support prices in ECU terms have been frozen or held constant for major commodities in recent years, but this has had only a limited impact on prices to producers, and hence on production levels and budgetary expenditure, because of manipulations to the green currency system.[9] This system is essentially a set of special exchange rates used to convert support prices for farm goods in ECU terms into national currencies. Modifications to the "green rates" have the capacity to achieve the same price raising result as an increase in the support price, since it is receipts in national currency that are the effective incentive to farmers.

Changes made to the green currency system in 1984, which introduced a "green ECU" based on the Deutschmark, have effectively tied agricultural support prices in the national currencies of member states, other than the Federal Republic of Germany, to the Deutschmark.[10] The appreciation of the Deutschmark against the ECU has the eventual effect of raising farm prices in the rest of the community by three-quarters of the appreciation. The effect of the 1984 changes has been to increase agricultural prices in national currencies.[11]

The nature of the EC decision-making process has been a major factor in the growth of CAP expenditure and EC surpluses. The requirement to achieve unanimity in Council decisions on major changes, which has now been partially modified by the adoption of

8. Commission of the European Communities, *The Agricultural Situation* (Brussels 1989), T/86.

9. See Appendix, Table 8.3.

10. C. Tanner, *An Analysis of the Commission's Proposed Changes to the Agrimonetary System*, Report prepared for the Department of Trade, Sydney, 28 May 1987.

11. Agra Europe, *Lack of Guidance on 1992 Agrimonetary Policy*, P/1-P/2, London, 16 September 1988; *Abolition of MCAs Dependent on Monetary Union, Say EC Auditors*, E/7-E/8, London, 26 May 1989.

the Single European Act, tended to result in the adoption of measures that increased expenditure and support, and acted as a barrier to effective reforms. National governments have tried to externalize the costs and internalize the benefits for their own member states of the decisions being taken.[12] Governments of those member states most likely to benefit have pressed for increased support measures in the knowledge that they would have to meet only a proportion of the cost.[13] Runge and von Witzke describe the budgetary outcome of this system as the "restaurant table effect:" the collective financial responsibility results in individual member states spending more than if they had been individually responsible.[14]

The decision-making process, and the increases in support that result from it, have created substantial transfers between the EC members states, with small states being major net beneficiaries, and Germany and the United Kingdom major net contributors.[15] Since 1980, a rebate has been given to the United Kingdom to lessen its net budgetary contribution.

Prior to 1971 the EC budget was financed by contributions from national budgets. On 1 January 1971 a system of "own resources" for the Community was adopted. These "own resources" included agricultural levies such as that on sugar, revenue from the common customs tariff, and up to 1 percent of values added tax (VAT) applied on consumption of goods and services throughout the Community. The revenue from customs duties and levies was transferred to the Community over the four-year period to 1 January 1975, and the VAT levy was in place by 1979. A deduction of 10 percent from the amounts collected is retained by member states to cover the costs of collection.[16]

The combination of high guaranteed support prices and increases in yields and subsidies on exports resulted in Community agricultural support expenditure growing rapidly and exceeding available

12. D. Bergmann, "Plaidoyer pour une réorientation des politiques agricoles d'une Europe élargie" in *Prospective Evolution of EEC CAP: Its Relevance for Mediterranean Members*, ed. F.B. Soares (Lisbon, 1985), 95–108.

13. S. Tangermann, "Special features and ongoing reforms of the CAP," in *Confrontation or Negotiation: United States Policy and European Agriculture*, ed. Curry Foundation (New York, 1985), 84–115.

14. C.F. Runge and H. von Witzke, "Institutional change in the Common Agricultural Policy of the European Community," *American Journal of Agricultural Economics*, 70, 2 (1987), 213-22.

15. See Appendix, Table 8.4.

16. Commission of the European Communities, *The European Community's Budget*, European Documentation Periodical, Brussels, 1 (1986).

budgetary funds in the 1980s. Spending under the European Agricultural Guarantee and Guidance Fund (EAGGF) rose from 11,300m ECU in 1980 to an estimated 18,099m ECU in 1984 and 26,400m ECU in 1988 (see Appendix, Table 8.1). The percentage of VAT receipts that each member state was required to contribute to Community funds reached the agreed limit of 1 percent in 1984. The immediate budgetary crisis, which the reaching of this limit caused to the Community at that time, was temporarily overcome by agreement that the VAT percentage going to the Community's "own resources" would be increased to 1.4 percent from 1 January 1986, with the possibility of a further increase to 1.6 percent on 1 January 1988, subject to unanimous agreement. Agreement was also reached on a permanent system of rebates for the United Kingdom to cut that country's net budgetary payment.[17] These changes were the major points of the 1984 Fontainebleau Agreement reached between the member states.

The financial crisis of the European Community in 1987 and early 1988 was the most serious in EC history. Major contributory factors to the crisis included increased pressures on the budget from the third enlargement of the Community to include Spain and Portugal, the inability of the Community to restrain the growth in agricultural support expenditure, and the lack of agreement among the member states to raise their financial contributions or moderate their demands on the system. Low world prices for key temperate commodities during the mid-1980s accentuated this pressure by increasing the level of the subsidy payments required to continue the dumping of surplus EC products on world markets.

A further factor increasing payments of export subsidies was the fall in the U.S. dollar relative to the ECU. In 1985 the average ECU to U.S. dollar rate stood at 1.32 ECU to U.S. $1.00. The value of the U.S. dollar in ECU terms declined by 39 percent over the next two years, to stand at 0.81 ECU on 29 April 1988. A 10 percent drop in the value of the U.S. dollar relative to the ECU is estimated to lead to an increase of 1000m ECU in EC budgetary expenditure; thus, the fall in the U.S. dollar led to a significant increase, perhaps on the order of 4000m ECU, in Community budgetary expenditure over this period.[18]

17. Commission of the European Communities, *The European Community's Budget*, Brussels, 1 (1986), 20–21.

18. Commission of the European Communities, *The European Community Budget: The Facts*, Brussels, 1986, 12.

A rational economic response to lower world prices and the fall in the U.S. dollar would have been to reduce the level of support for agricultural products; hence reducing total output, the surpluses to be exported, and the increase in budgetary costs. EC institutional and decision-making arrangements, however, prevented the effective adoption of such a strategy.

At its December 1987 summit meeting, the European Council failed to agree on measures for the balancing of the Community's 1988 budget. Fall-back budgetary provisions were applied from 1 January 1988, whereby budgetary expenditure each month was limited to one-twelfth of that in the 1987 budget. Under these arrangements, support expenditure could only have been maintained until mid-year, when funds would have begun to run out.

To balance EC income and expenditure, supply control measures, cuts in price support, or increases in budgetary funds were needed. The issue was resolved in February 1988, when the European Council reached agreement on a system of supply controls in the form of production stabilizers and land set-aside arrangements, as part of a package of measures that included the major changes to EC budgetary funding and substantial increases in structural funding. This package was primarily designed to constrain the growth of agricultural expenditures and limit the rate of expansion in agricultural production.

The 1988 EC Summit Agreement on Budget and Production Stabilizers

Budgetary Funding

Budget Contributions The changes made at the February 1988 EC summit meeting allowed for significant increases in EC budgetary funding. Details of funding for the total 1988, 1989, and 1992 budgets are given in the Appendix.[19] EC funding was increased through the enlargement of the existing financial resource base to include a proportion of the gross national product of each of the member states.

The effect of these changes was to add a "fourth resource" to the existing "own resources" from which the European Community finances itself, so that these are now as follows:

19. See Appendix, Table 8.5.

- agricultural levies (variable levies on agricultural imports from non-member countries, and sugar and isoglucose production levies);
- customs duties;
- 1.4 percent of the assessment basis for VAT in each member state (if the U.K. rebate is taken into account, the effective rate of VAT over the Community as a whole is 1.25 percent); and
- the difference between the 1.4 percent nominal rate of VAT and 1.3 percent of gross national product (with qualifications for member states such as Portugal and Luxembourg that have a disproportionately high level of consumption relative to income).[20]

Member states will continue to be reimbursed by the European Community for 10 percent of the VAT and the levy and duty proceeds that they collect and pass on to the Community, but they will not be reimbursed for any of the collection costs of the new gross national product contribution to Community funds. The reimbursement that member states receive for their intervention expenditures on behalf of the CAP will be paid two and a half months, instead of two months, in arrears.

Agricultural Support Expenditure The base for EAGGF guarantee section expenditure (that is, agricultural price support expenditure) was set at 27,500m ECU in 1988, with its growth rate for the four years from 1988 being limited to 80 percent of the rate of growth in gross national product in an attempt to limit the proportion of total budget funds used for agricultural support purposes. The budgetary limit for agricultural price support expenditure, based on this formula, is 28,624m ECU for 1989 and, on the basis of provisional estimates, 30,000m ECU for 1990.[21] The Community's contribution to the cost of the land set-aside scheme will also come within the total agricultural price support expenditure growth limit of 80 percent of gross national product growth, effectively reducing the growth rate for price support expenditure to 74 percent of growth in gross national product.

There are several exceptions to the overall limit. Depreciation of existing surplus stocks is being financed separately, with 1200m

20. Council of the European Communities, *Document S461/88*, Brussels, 1988.
21. Commission of the European Communities, *Commission Proposals on the Prices of Agricultural Products and on Related Measures*, COM (89) 40 final, II (Financial Implications), Brussels, 1989, 3.

ECU provided for this in 1988 and 1400m ECU in each year 1989 to 1992. Expenditure by the national governments of the member states on land set-aside and other jointly financed schemes is not included in EC accounts. A monetary reserve fund of 1000m ECU has been set up to cover extra expenditure resulting from fluctuations in the ECU to U.S. dollar rate, with the money committed to the fund being called upon from the member states if it is actually required. In theory, savings resulting from exchange rate fluctuations may be used to supplement the fund up to a limit of 1000m ECU.

The agreement also made an important change to the EC system of agricultural support financing by setting up an "early warning system" to monitor expenditure growth for each commodity sector on a month by month basis and compare its growth with the average for the preceding three years. If the rate of growth is found to be above the previous trend, then it is to be reduced, first through the Commission using the means at its disposal, such as manipulation of intervention purchasing, and, if this proves ineffective, by policy changes being proposed to the Council. A major difficulty with the new arrangements is that action is only taken once budgetary problems in a sector have become evident, and the "previous trend" test locks the system into a pattern of established budgetary growth.

The Commission is to put forward only proposals for expenditure appropriations that are consistent with the overall budget ceilings and the subceilings, which are to be agreed upon for different commodity sectors. Under the terms of the stabilizers agreement, the European Council bound itself to adhere to the budgetary ceilings and growth formula determined in fulfillment of the terms of the agreement.[22] In the event of the Agricultural Council taking decisions that would lead to expenditure in excess of the guidelines, the finance ministers of the Community are to become involved in the decision-making process, with the final decisions being made by a joint council meeting of both agricultural and finance ministers.[23] The commitment on the part of the Council to respect the budgetary ceilings must be seen within the context of the essential requirement arising from the Treaty of Rome, that

22. Council of the European Communities, *Document S461/88*, Brussels, 1988, 3.

23. S. Tangermann, "Evaluation of current CAP developments." A University of Göttingen paper presented to the European Agricultural Outlook Conference, London, 22–23 February 1989, 8.

agricultural price support expenditure arising from the decisions of the Council of Ministers must be undertaken and may therefore be regarded as compulsory.

Structural Funding – General Meeting demands made by the southern European member states and Ireland, the 1988 budget agreement also included provisions for increased structural funding in real terms by 1992. The amount available will increase from 7800m ECU in 1988 to 13,000m ECU (1988 prices) in 1992, a significant increase when compared with total expenditure of just under 6000m ECU on the combined regional and social funds and the guidance (structural support) section of the EAGGF in 1987.[24]

This structural funding will be used to finance assistance measures and projects deemed to meet the new regional, social, or agricultural criteria. Projects eligible for support include a wide range of farm modernization schemes and agricultural processing facilities, as well as manufacturing and tourist industry enterprises, and selected infrastructure programs. The new structural funds could be used to assist in the development of a more diverse regional economic structure, with scope for greater non-farm or part time off-farm employment, which will in turn affect the incomes and occupational mobility of farmers.

Some of this structural funding will be used to fund or subsidize improvements in agricultural production and infrastructure. The requirements and guidelines for the application of structural funding suggest that, especially in southern Europe, which will receive most of the expenditure, much of the 1200m ECU structural aid earmarked for agriculture in 1988 and 1500m ECU in 1989 will be targeted at smaller scale low income producers, and at the improvement of processing, storage, and transport facilities in areas that lack modern facilities.

The move to increase structural funding was in response to pressures largely from the new Mediterranean member states. Agriculture in the new member states is characterized by a large proportion of small farms, many of which are subdivided into as many as thirty small plots, and by low productivity.[25] Most producers in

24. Commission of the European Communities, *EAGGF: The European Community's Expenditure on the Common Agricultural Policy*, Green Europe Newsflash 42 (Brussels, 1987).

25. A.R. Jones, "Agriculture, organization, reform and the EC," in *Southern Europe Transformed*, ed. A. Williams (Harper and Row, London, 1984), 236–65.

these countries operate small holdings and lack the capital and technology to benefit fully from increases in support prices by increasing their output. In some regions landless laborers make up a third or more of the workforce.[26] Any increase in prices and profitability from which the landowners are able to benefit, may well lead to a loss of jobs as capital is substituted for labor in order to increase output, thereby aggravating already high unemployment rates. The new structural funding scheme can be better targeted at small producers and landless laborers than general price supports can be, providing them with a greater proportion of CAP benefits, than can CAP price guarantees of which large scale producers are the major beneficiaries.[27]

A further factor behind the pressure for increased structural funding is the greater internal competition that the industries of the new member states will face when the integrated European market commences in 1992. The increased overall level of structural funds will allow these countries to improve their infrastructure and modernize their industries, so that they will be more able to compete in the integrated European market.

Production Stabilizer Arrangements

The package of budget and production stabilizers agreed upon by the Council contained a number of major policy elements, in addition to the increase in overall EC budgetary funding. These elements included:

- production thresholds or maximum guaranteed quantities, with price or co-responsibility penalties, or both, being applied if these are exceeded;
- the continuation of existing quota mechanisms;
- the adoption of land set-aside payments as a means of reducing production while maintaining producers' incomes; and
- sociostructural measures including early retirement and direct income supports.

The most important change resulting from the production stabil-

26. Duchêne, et al., *New Limits.*
27. Bureau of Agricultural Economics, *Agricultural Policies*, Canberra, 1985.

izers was the adoption of a maximum guaranteed quantity of 160T for cereals. Other developments included the extension of stabilizer measures, or tightening of existing arrangements, to the oilseeds, sheep meat, fruit and vegetables, dairy, wine, and tobacco sectors. The principle behind the operation of the production stabilizers is that a threshold or maximum guaranteed quantity of production is set. When this quantity is exceeded, producer returns are reduced at predetermined rates by changes in support levels. The details of the stabilizers vary considerably between products, with use being made of price reductions, co-responsibility levy increases, decreases in production subsidies, and quota buy-back arrangements.

The stabilizers adopted vary considerably in the magnitude of price penalties and production growth restraints. Perhaps the weakest in terms of impact is that for rapeseed, in spite of an overshoot of 18 percent in the maximum guaranteed quantity; the stabilization arrangements resulted in an increase of 2 percent in the support price for rapeseed for the 1988 to 1989 marketing year.[28]

Assessment of the Stabilizers

The projected budgets given in the Appendix Table 8.5 allow for an estimated limit to growth of 7.6 percent in real expenditure on agricultural price support over the whole of the period between 1988 and 1992, or just under 10 percent if expenditure on stock disposal measures, set-aside, and income assistance schemes is included. This is lower than the increase in real terms of 12.4 percent for the four years between 1983 and 1987.

The budgetary system is now operated with a monitoring system aimed at containing the aggregate cost of support on a product by product basis, similar to the system of segmented budgets suggested by Spaventa, et al.[29] The limit to growth in expenditure on real agricultural price support of some 7.6 percent for the four years to 1992, could be difficult to adhere to in more difficult world market conditions than at present, unless binding controls can be applied when limits are exceeded. Improvements in international commodity prices eased budget pressures in 1988, as lower export subsidy

28. Field, et al., *The 1988 EC Budget*, 21.

29. L. Spaventa, L. Koopmans, P. Salmon, B. Spahn, and S. Smith, *The Future of Community Finance*, C.E.P.S. Papers 30 (Brussels, 1986), 3.

outlays were needed to bridge the gap between EC support and external market prices. In fact, the favorable world market prices allowed agricultural price support expenditure to be 4 percent less than the budgeted amount in 1988. As a result of these and other savings, unused funds amounting to some 2000m ECU were transferred from the 1988 to the 1989 EC budget, effectively increasing the funds available for 1989.[30]

The budgetary arrangements allow scope for future budget expansion, and for the transfer of funds from one commodity sector to another, and, though less easily, from one category of expenditure to another. Transfers from the oils and fats and fruit and vegetable sectors to sheep meat and other sectors with budgetary deficits, were necessary to keep expenditure within the 1988 budget guidelines.[31] This potential weakness in budgetary discipline is compounded by the availability of the 1000m ECU fund for additional CAP expenditures in the event of further declines in the U.S. dollar, or any assessed breach of international commitments by other exporting countries that causes repercussions on world markets.[32]

If, however, increased budget pressures have strengthened the Community's commitment to adhere to the new threshold formulae, over-threshold penalties could have an impact if set at adequate levels. The chosen production ceilings will consolidate production and exports for major commodities (dairy quotas excepted) at close to current levels. In the short term, the price and co-responsibility penalties are unlikely to have more than a marginal impact, although longer term adjustments could be more marked in the event that production stabilizers (maximum guaranteed quantities) are reduced and threshold penalties increased. Cuts in prices in ECU terms due to the effect of the stabilizers, however, may well be neutralized or overridden by green currency changes. The price review and green currency changes in both the 1988 to 1989 and 1989 to 1990 marketing years illustrate how the green currency system of agricultural exchange rates can frustrate price restraint. On both occasions, changes in the "green currency" agricultural exchange rates of countries with currencies depreciating relative to the Deutschmark resulted in increases in support prices in national currency terms, even though support prices in ECU terms were to remain the same or be reduced in

30. Agra Europe, *Commission Makes 1.1 BN ECU Savings on 1988 Farm Spending*, E/3-E/4, London, 9 December 1988.

31. Agra Europe, *Commission Makes Saving*, London, 9 December 1988.

32. Council of the European Communities, *Document S461/88*, Brussels, 1988.

most cases. There is no indication that such currency adjustments will cease in the near future, particularly in view of the Commission's expressed objective of eliminating the "green ECU" and the negative monetary compensatory amounts (MCAs), which operate as a system of taxes and subsidies on trade in agricultural products, by 1992. No change has been made in the prices set for most commodities for 1989 to 1990 in ECU terms.[33] The operation of the green currency system, however, resulted in an immediate increase in the prices of many commodities in national currency terms in most of the EC countries, increasing producer prices for milk and livestock products in national currency terms.[34]

Conclusions

The major budgetary outcome of the February 1988 EC Council agreement was the increase in EC funding through the adoption of a wider revenue base, to incorporate a ceiling of 1.3 percent of gross national product for member states' contributions and other modifications that will increase the funds available. These measures allowed the Community to overcome its immediate budgetary crisis by increasing the funds available for agricultural support and other expenditures. Potential agricultural support payments will be limited by being tied, at least in principle, to the growth in gross national product.

While, however, the budget and production stabilizers agreement represents a temporary solution to EC budgetary problems, the new system of funding will permit growth in expenditure on agricultural assistance, unless the production stabilizers that accompany it are closely adhered to and tightened when they fail to stabilize production. The assertion that the Community has taken a decisive step toward bringing production more in line with market demand, is not borne out by an analysis of the potential effect of the stabilizers agreement.[35]

One aspect of the agreement is the provision of a higher proportion of expenditure associated with agricultural support from outside the EAGGF budget. This is evidenced by the creation of a

33. Agra Europe, *Community Operating Two-tier ECU Prices*, AE1336, London, 5 May 1989.

34. Australian Agricultural Counsellor Brussels, personal communication, 27 April 1989.

35. F. Andriessen, Address to World Food Conference, Brussels, 7–9 April 1988. Field, et al., *The 1988 EC Budget*.

stock disposal fund outside EAGGF, the financing of set-aside arrangements from outside EAGGF, and the increase in funding for the combined agricultural, regional, and social structural adjustment budget. The result of these moves is that the level of overall agricultural assistance may increase, even if the production stabilizers are successful in preventing further increases in output.

Appendix

Table 8.1 The EC Budget and EAGGF Guarantee Section (Price Support) Expenditure

Year	EC budget expenditure	EAGGF guarantee section expenditure	Guarantee section share of total EC budget	EAGGF guarantee section index	Real index
	'000m ECU	'000m ECU	%	%	%
1980	16 290	11 315	69	100	100
1981 (a)	17 792	11 141	63	98	90
1982	20 012	12 406	62	110	94
1983	24 871	16 006	64	141	113
1984	27 249	18 099	66	160	119
1985	28 085	19 728	70	174	116
1986 (b)	35 174	22 112	63	195	126
1987	35 789	22 950	64	203	127
1988 (c)	44 100	26 395	60	233	140
1989 (d)	44 800	26 741	60	236	na

(a) EC enlarged to include Greece; (b) EC enlarged to include Spain and Portugal; (c) estimate; (d) budgetary appropriation. na: Not available.

Note: European Agricultural Guarantee and Guidance Fund expenditure totals for 1988 and 1989 do not include stock disposal funding of 1240m ECU and 1450m ECU, respectively, in those years.

Source: Calculated from data in Commission of the European Communities. *EAGGF: The European Community's Expenditure on the Common Agricultural Policy*, Green Europe Newsflash 42 (Brussels, 1987a); *Act 89/.40 of the European Parliament*, L26/32, Brussels, 30 January 1989a.

Table 8.2 EC Producer Subsidy Equivalents as a Percentage of Total Producer Receipts (a)

Commodity	1982	1983	1984	1985	1986	Average 1982–86
	%	%	%	%	%	%
Wheat	27.93	12.46	8.25	33.50	57.75	27.97
Other grains	9.48	14.30	4.40	20.87	48.93	19.60
Oilseeds	49.74	35.90	17.73	53.72	62.40	43.90
Meat	27.26	32.86	33.57	36.05	34.47	32.84
Sugar	43.17	24.31	56.02	52.29	49.17	44.99
Dairy	34.19	34.01	40.35	43.80	65.52	43.57

(a) The producer subsidy equivalent is a measure of the payment or subsidy that would be required to compensate producers (in terms of current income) for the removal of certain support programs.

Source: M.A. Normile "The EC oilseeds sector: recent developments and reform proposals," *Western Europe Agriculture and Trade Report*, June 1988, 59, Table 2.

Table 8.3 Average Increase in CAP Support Prices, 1984–85 – 1987–88

	1984–85		1985–86		1986–87		1987–88	
	ECUs	National currency	ECUs	National currency	ECUs	National currency	ECUs	National currency
	%	%	%	%	%	%	%	%
Germany, FR	–0.6	–0.6	0.3	0.3	–0.2	–0.2	0	0
France	–0.6	5.0	–0.1	1.7	–0.3	2.0	–0.2	4.1
Italy	–0.4	6.4	–0.2	3.3	–0.6	4.2	–0.6	3.3
Netherlands	–0.5	–0.5	0.5	0.5	0	0	0	–0.5
Belgium	–0.6	3.9	0.2	0.2	–0.1	1.7	0	1.7
Luxembourg	–0.5	4.0	0.6	0.6	–0.1	1.7	0	1.6
UK	–0.6	–0.6	0.2	0.2	–0.5	1.9	0	6.3
Ireland	–0.6	3.9	0.4	0.4	–0.3	2.5	0	8.5
Denmark	–0.7	1.5	0.1	0.1	–0.7	1.2	0	2.3
Greece (a)	0.4	17.6	0.4	13.6	–0.5	13.5	–0.4	3.3
Spain (b)					1.8	3.3	1.8	7.2
Portugal (b)					0.3	1.7	'0.5	6.1
Average (c)	–0.3	3.3	0.1	1.8	–0.3	2.2	0.2	3.3

(a) Including adjustments to Greek prices resulting from membership agreements. (b) The prices for 1987 to 1988 include the impact of the alignment of common prices resulting from the accession agreements. (c) Average of EC-10 only for all years.

Source: Kelly, et al., *Issues and Developments*, 146.

Table 8.4 EC Budget Transfers 1985

Country	Gross domestic product per person as a proportion of EC-12 average	Transfers before U.K. rebate	Transfers after U.K. rebate
	%	m ECU	m ECU
Denmark	153	400	300
Luxembourg	142	300	300
Germany, Federal Republic	138	–3 100	–3 500
France	126	500	0
Netherlands	112	500	400
Belgium	108	600	500
United Kingdom	91	–3 000	–1 000
Italy	86	1 200	800
Ireland	66	1 200	1 100
Greece	38	1 400	1 300

Source: *Economist*, London, 20 June 1987, 25.

Table 8.5 EC Budgetary Funding Appropriations and Estimates

Budget item	1988	1989	1992 (a)
	'000m ECU	'000m ECU	'000m ECU
EAGGF guarantee section (b)	27.5	26.7	29.6
Financing of stock disposal	1.2	1.5	1.4
Set-aside payments and aids to income	0	0.1	0.5
Structural funds (c)	7.8	9.3	13.0
Policies with multiannual allocations: research, integrated Mediterranean programs	1.4	1.5	2.4
Other Policies	1.7	1.4	2.8
Reimbursements and administration	3.5	3.3	2.0
Monetary reserve	1.0	1.0	1.0
Total	44.1	44.8	52.7

(a) In 1988 prices. These estimates are based on an assumed growth rate of 2.5 percent a year in real gross national product for 1988 to 1992. (b) Agricultural price support expenditure. (c) The new combined structural funds include agricultural, regional, and social policy expenditures.

Source: Council of the European Communities, *Act 88/41 of the European Parliament*, L226/32, Brussels, 16 August 1988; *Act 89/40*, L26/32, Brussels, 30 January 1989.

–9–

Europe 1992: The Organization of Production and the Challenge to the Educational and Training Systems

CORRADO PARACONE

At the beginning of the 1980s, when a wave of technological innovation based on electronics and computer science spread all over Europe, discussion about technology and even fear of technology was related above all to its impact on employment. Over the last few years, however, people have come to realize that the reduction in the number of jobs caused by new technologies has been less significant than expected, and has, in fact, been offset by the development of new job opportunities in both traditional and new sectors. As a result, attention is now turning to the type of culture and professional skills necessary to work in a drastically changed productive system and to support the new course of economic development.

If the present international competition is to be won, technical innovations in products and in the working process alone are not sufficient. It is also necessary to educate workers to share the objectives of the firm – be it an industry or a service company – by means of a wider professional background. First, it should be wider from the point of view of technical and specialist knowledge and working capacity. Second, the ability of the worker to participate in activities and specialized functions of the firm that are different from his own is essential. Indeed, the activity of a modern firm requires a systematic approach to optimize results. Third, professional knowledge needs to be more dynamic because all workers, at all levels, should be able to bring about continuous improvements and continuously learn something new.

If we do not want to create a bleak society of robots, we must respond to the challenge of technological innovation: the challenge, involving managers, engineers, and professional workers, of avoiding mechanical routines. The capacity to bring about continuous improvements means, on the one hand, eliminating routine jobs that transform the worker into a passive assistant of machines, who might easily be replaced by a machine and therefore lose his job. On the other hand, it means the opportunity to make one's own firm more competitive. Indeed, the more advanced a firm is in the use of technology, thus approaching "productive perfection," the more the competitive drive of the firm depends upon the ability of those writing in it to make continuing improvements.

More responsibility and autonomy, however, must be exercised by workers if they are to bring about improvements. At present, the more advanced systems of production organization, particularly developed in Japan and the U.S., and now gaining ground also in some EC countries, are moving in this direction. Their aim is total quality and total flexibility.

The situation outlined above already characterizes particularly advanced firms, which focus their attention on future development and are sensitive to changes concerning technology, organization, and professional skills. The productive system of EC countries is quite segmented, and firms very different in size and degree of innovation coexist within it. Borrowing an expression used for supersonic airplanes, it can be said that the productive system of EC countries is a "variable geometry" system, which will evolve at different speeds in the next few years. Traditional and strongly innovative firms will continue to coexist. Thus, within Computer Integrated Manufacturing (CIM) many traditional workers and machines may still be employed: it depends on economic and organizing convenience.

If we are to understand the dynamics of change and the trends according to which professions will change, however, we need to turn to those firms that have attained the greatest success. Indeed, their present development is of paramount importance for understanding all the changes that the whole productive system will undergo in the next few years. In advanced firms, the professional worker using new technologies will need to be able to combine the practice of using logical and mathematical models, as well as the engineers' methodology in the use of automatized systems and computer controlled procedures, with the ability to implement ideas and intuitions. Therefore, the highly skilled professional worker will be a person capable of acquiring, in addition to the precision typical of engineers and the speculative ability of physicists, the creativity typical of persons who have followed social and humanistic studies.

When we turn from highly skilled professionals and advanced firms to the wider aspect of concrete professional changes, some fundamental observations can be made. In the next few years labor, synthetically speaking, will be divided into three groups. The first group, which is comparatively narrow, will include highly skilled professionals who will bring about not only technological but also financial and organizational innovation: innovations in management, industries, services, and public administration. They will need a cultural background based on school and university education, perhaps also integrated with further specializations in specific professional fields. The second large group will be formed by average-skilled professionals who will work in complex systems and will have to shoulder responsibilities in order to fulfill their tasks. They will need higher education integrated with higher professional education. These first two groups will form the labor nucleus; therefore, professional training and courses to help these people to remain up-to-date in their professions will be necessary throughout their career. The third group – again a large one – will be formed by people engaged in those activities that do not require particular professional skills or advanced studies. This sector will offer many job opportunities that will often be temporary and will not help the worker to improve his social status.

This new situation reflects the opportunity for workers to climb from the lowest to the highest group, which is opened up by education and professional training. In other words, the professional skill of a worker will depend more and more on the knowledge and ability he acquired through school and vocational training. This does not mean that experience is no longer important. Up to the 1970s it was an essential element of professional skill (especially in industry); today, however, the influence it exerts is remarkably lower.

The 1980s are thus a turning point. In the age of mechanical technologies the best way to learn a craft was to observe workers carrying out their tasks. Nowadays, where electronic technology and computer science have been introduced, this method is losing ground, because these types of technology are abstract: their logic, symbols, and basic concepts must be known and understood.

Two fundamental trends influence the changes in professions. Society is more and more based on technology, and even those activities that seem to be distant from technology will somehow have to come to grips with it. Sometimes the acquisition of new abilities will not be remarkable. For instance, a solicitor may have to use a computer to look up a decision on law included in a wide collection of legal acts; this requires only modest confidence with a personal computer. In other cases, the impact is stronger. Philosophy is a discipline normally considered totally distant from technology, but in fact, this is not always true. In systems marked by greater experience, especially in the United States, data banks are being replaced more and more by "knowledge banks," where data are gathered in order to provide systematic information and knowledge that can be used by "expert systems" of artificial intelligence. For this reason, people employed to work in the setting up of knowledge banks are very often philosophy graduates, especially if they have studied logic, because of their ability to make analyses and syntheses. Of course, they must have acquired a profound knowledge of computer science.

The second fundamental trend concerns the fact that professions are becoming less rigidly confined within the limits of one specialization; they need to be increasingly polyvalent in order to perform different functions. Therefore, a basic specialization, which is necessary, must be combined with the ability to cope with other fields of knowledge and operate in sectors different from one's own.

Over the last few years much has been said about new professions for the 1990s in Western Europe. In the first half of the present decade, it was thought that a revolution would take place in the field of professional skills and that the 1980s would be marked by the overwhelming presence of experts in high-tech, new materials; "neuro-scientists" working in the field of artificial intelligence. All these predictions proved wrong and new jobs certainly exist. For example, in manufacturing industries that have abandoned the traditional Tayloristic organization of labor, shop-floor workers perform various functions once divided among different people, with the aid of a computer. The assessment of their professional ability no longer depends on the number of manual operations performed, but on how careful they are in running a machine, interpreting symbols, and preventing accidents; however, there will be very few totally new jobs in the future. In the great majority of cases, the professions will be the result of the development and renewal of present ones, not only because of technologies but also because of changes in organization. There may also be complex professions, combining two or more different specializations. The future professional may be an engineer-economist, a doctor-engineer, a graduate in chemistry expert in biotechnologies, or an expert in environment. It is not a matter of new jobs, but of new job opportunities resulting from the different organization of traditional professions.

What are the repercussions of this transformation of the professions on the educational and professional training systems? How can young people entering the labor market in the next few years be trained? And how can already employed adults gain further qualifications?

Changes occurring in the wake of the large number of innovations brought about in the last ten to fifteen years have shattered the educational and vocational system of economically developed societies in the capitalist world. The only exception to this trend is Japan, a country whose educational system is the strictest and most embracing in the capitalist world. Criticism can certainly be leveled at the Japanese educational system, the content of which has been renewed but whose strictness in making citizens aware of the fact that nothing can be attained without effort and sacrifice is old-fashioned. Education is certainly one of the most important factors in Japanese social integration and, at the same time, it plays a fundamental role in the development of the productive system.

The crisis in the educational and vocational systems of nearly all Western developed countries, together with a widespread awareness that their efficiency is of paramount importance in coping with the competition of the 1990s, is leading to renewed efforts to reorganize, in a modern way, education and professional training. The decline of the American educational system is well known. One of the priorities set by the Bush administration is reorganization of the system through the extensive use of technology to foster education. Many Western European countries are also taking steps in this direction, even though the decline of their educational systems is much less marked. They are aiming at:

- improving the educational background not by increasing the number of students taught at school, but by improving the students' way of learning;

- offering the opportunity to choose from many different professional channels especially set up to help young people entering the labor market for the first time; and
- creating a flexible system to provide updated information and continuous training for those who are already employed or want further qualifications.

Here a fundamental aspect, which simplifies the solutions that must be found through the vocational system, must be borne in mind: whereas in the past the development of hundreds of different crafts required hundreds of different qualifications, it is now possible to distinguish a comparatively small number of general, basic professional qualifications for industry, factories, offices, banks, agriculture, etc. – a number of "macroprofiles" or professional archetypes. These general qualifications will then become more specific according to the individual industry, firm, agricultural enterprise, or service company. The knowledge of a person employed in a highly automated chemical industry will differ by 20 to 30 percent from that of a person working in a highly automated mechanical industry; however, the basis of their knowledge is the same for both.

Our research has indicated that no more than eight to twelve professional archetypes (or macroprofiles) can be identified in a factory. Some firms are taking even bolder steps: for instance, General Motors Europe is passing from the 187 professional qualifications previously present in its factories, to four macroprofiles only. In other words, the whole situation might be compared to a volcano: the thousands of professional qualifications that once existed, have been reduced to a small number of professional archetypes concentrated at the top of the volcano. And just like the lava that erupts from the volcano, these archetypes spread in different directions, indeed, they acquire different features in each firm.

The path to a complete professional training is marked by three steps. First, a basic education, providing extensive knowledge and scientific and technical culture; second, training to the level of a professional archetype; and last, workers must be enabled to meet the needs of any particular type of job. The first two tasks must be fulfilled by the educational and vocational systems, including university education; the third can only be fulfilled by the worker's firm or industry.

The educational and vocational systems naturally differ from country to country. School, more than any other institution, has its roots in the history and traditions of each state. Beyond the different features of the educational system of each country, however, the three steps toward the acquisition of a modern and complete professional training must be taken and they must be clear-cut. Otherwise, it will not be possible to resolve the dilemma of whether to establish an educational system that provides a broad cultural background or one that provides training for future jobs. This is a false alternative, because both are needed. They must not, however, be confused; they must remain conceptually independent, otherwise both general and technical education will fall into decay.

Over the last seven years, in Italy, the Agnelli Foundation has carried out a program, unique in Western Europe, aimed at providing Italian state-school teachers with courses on the changes in the productive system, the challenges it will have to meet, and the reasons why education must play a key role in a society that wants to become advanced. The participation of teachers from all over Italy in this training initiative was unprecedented.

At a time when complex professional skills and people able to integrate their competence into various sectors are more and more necessary, technical education must also become, at least partially, managerial training, since an engineer also needs managerial capability and vice versa. There is more to it than this as training becomes the main means of fostering the participation of workers and their involvement in the goals and culture of a firm.

Some may think that this aim of providing more people with technical and managerial training is unnecessary, since many are still engaged in traditional jobs, carrying out purely executive tasks. The opposite is true, however. Indeed, training "in excess" means the elimination of future expenditure for requalification and contributes powerfully to the drive toward modernization. The challenge of the changing professions must be met on this ground. It is the best protection provided to the citizen worker against the risk of being overwhelmed by the great changes taking place in the economic system. This holds true for Italy, for Australia, and for any modern country committed to development.

–10–

Is Science Going European? A German Perspective

MARTIN L. MRUCK

In this essay I wish to discuss the following aspects of research policy in the Federal Republic of Germany: science, research and technology today; promotion of basic research; promotion of market oriented technologies; improvement in basic conditions, for innovation in small and medium-sized companies; strengthening of research with long-term and international prospects; key technologies; research and development (R & D) expenditure; internationalization of production and utilization of technological knowledge; and European cooperation.

Science, Research, and Technology Today

For a number of years now, science, research, and technology have continued to gain in topical importance and impact and today dominate an ever-increasing proportion of economic and political debate in the Federal Republic of Germany (FRG). The question of international competitiveness in areas of high technology is always an essential aspect of this discussion and invariably provokes thoughts on the relative futures of Europe, Japan, and the United States. Expenditure on R & D in these countries is presently approaching 3 percent of GDP (gross domestic product), while in the early 1970s this proportion was 1.9 percent and 2 percent in Japan and the FRG respectively. Structural innovations developing from the three research-intensive key technologies (i.e., information technology, biotechnology, and new engineering materials) are extending to ever-increasing areas as a result of the discovery of more and more new applications and combinations. At the same time, these technologies have lost nothing of their fascination and continue to be at the very heart of innovatory efforts worldwide. Corporate strategies across the globe are marked by the declared goal of technological expertise, to be achieved by increasing international cooperation and integration in R & D and by rapidly increasing expenditure on research.

The more recent developments in basic or fundamental research force us to rethink our ideas on universal laws and "orders" and on human thought in general. The study of nonlinear phenomena in mathematics with applications in physics and biology, or the progress made in neurosciences, are good examples of this. Genetic engineering is an example of an area of research that questions established ethical and moral positions. At the same time, the scientific breakthrough in superconductors, representative of similar leaps in knowledge in other fields, shows us that this same research can open up surprising avenues for further new technological applications. And finally, there are those topics connected with research and technology that dominate discussions on the future: ecological risks; conceivable changes in climate; possibilities in genetic engineering and medicine; the future safeguarding of the energy supply; safety aspects (particularly of large-scale and complex technological systems); and prospects for new jobs. Last but not least, there must be research in the sense of an assessment of the impact and the implications of (new) technology.

Promotion of Basic Research

One of the advantages of the system of promoting scientific research in Germany is that the importance of basic research is undisputed and that its financing has been kept at a high level and has even been increased in recent years. Under this system, the main emphasis is placed on the joint financing of research by the Federal and Länder governments. The two key areas of support are:

- the promotion of priority areas of research in universities through the DFG (*Deutsche Forschungsgemeinschaft*/German Research Foundation) and special research departments;
- the promotion of the Max-Planck-Gesellschaft and the financing of the National Research Centres (90 percent by the government

of the Federal Republic of Germany) with their high requirement for large-scale equipment for basic research and the devotion of a high proportion of their activities to such research.

In addition, there are the contributions made by the Federal government to international institutions for basic research, such as CERN (European Council for Nuclear Research) and ILL in Grenoble, France.

Promotion of Market-oriented Technologies

Here, a concentration of funds on the development of civil aircraft, on cross-industry key technologies, as well as on selected areas of energy and transport technology and marine engineering, has been achieved over the years. More specifically, funds were concentrated on the completion of the Airbus project, information technology, materials research, biotechnology with applications in genetic engineering, molecular biology, and regeneration of raw materials. Certain selected physical technologies (including laser technology and thin film technology) that offer substantial synergy effects for the above-mentioned areas were also targeted.

Improvement in Basic Conditions for Innovation in Small and Medium-sized Companies

In recent years, with the declared aim of "helping those who help themselves," the government has provided substantial support to small and medium-sized companies in the area of research and development. Funds earmarked for these measures rose from DM 116 million in 1982 to just under DM 300 million in 1987. The combined financing of these types of projects by the BMFT (*Bundesministerium für Forschung and Technologie*/Federal Ministry for Research and Technology) and BMWi (Bundesministerium für Wirtschaft/Federal Ministry of Economics) amounted to some DM 763 million. Obviously, small and medium-sized companies received higher subsidies than larger companies for every deutsche mark they spent on research.

Such programs were of a temporary nature from the outset. Some of them were aimed specifically at small and medium-sized companies, in particular the pilot scheme for the setting up of technology-oriented companies, the personnel costs subsidy program of BMWi, and the research personnel growth promotion program of the BMFT.

Strengthening of Research with Long-term and International Prospects

Apart from the promotion of basic research, the government also helps in the opening up of long-term prospects and opportunities in many diverse areas. These include strategic programs, such as nuclear fusion research, marine and polar research, and, only recently, space research.

In addition to the pure research oriented aspects, a further important factor in such programs is the aim of greater integration within Europe and closer cooperation within the Western world as a whole in this area. In view of the ongoing discussion on the advantages and disadvantages of the free flow of technological know-how, and in view also of increasingly tough technological competition and rising protectionist sentiments, more cooperation is needed. This must necessarily have an adverse effect on healthy competition between companies in the marketplace and also in research. Both ideas – extensive European independence from the United States as a research policy option and European and Atlantic cooperation as elements of integration – have been keynotes of a number of recent international conferences. In the context of broad agreement between the European countries, a ministerial meeting in November 1987 agreed to far-reaching, basic decisions on an independent European space travel program and also on transatlantic cooperation, with the possibility of necessary corrections and adjustments.

Next to cooperation in space research, the continuing political integration of Europe is, of course, very much at the center of considerations regarding the expansion of joint European research promotion. There have been several irreversible steps in this direction, beginning with the adoption of the Single European Act, which stresses the strengthening of the scientific and technological basis of industry in the European Community as well as the promotion of its international competitiveness. The adoption of the new framework research program of the European Community and the implementation of the Franco-German EUREKA (European

Research Co-ordinating Agency) idea, represent further steps of this kind. EUREKA in particular has, to an extent not anticipated, stimulated research and development cooperation between companies and research institutes in Europe. It is noteworthy that the EUREKA program extends far beyond the member countries of the EC and embraces in particular the technologically advanced member countries of EFTA (the European Free Trade Association).

Opportunities for achieving open European markets in areas of high technology have thus improved considerably.

Key Technologies

Emerging ever more strongly worldwide since the end of the 1970s, a number of key technologies have advanced still further in their scientific and technological development. Their increasing application is breathtaking. Information technology (with microelectronics), advanced information processing and communications technology, modern biology (with its advances in genetic engineering, molecular biology and biotechnology), new materials technologies (with improved ceramic materials through composites, new polymers), the various means of laser application, surface technology, and the scientific breakthrough in superconductors serve as just a few examples.

Such innovations can revolutionize the process of development, production engineering, and obviously the end products. Furthermore, these technologies themselves spur the process of technological development and scientific research. A good example of this is the computer stimulation of technical designs replacing elaborate individual design work and extensive testing. The interlinking of an extremely wide range of different demands on technological design, particularly in the case of modern sophisticated aircraft design, is thus greatly simplified. Other examples include: high-power computers as tools for scientific research, particularly for complex model and simulations calculations ranging from modern nonlinear mathematics through physics, meteorology and climate research, to genetic engineering.

But there is also the economic significance to be considered. The above-average economic growth potential of the high-technology sectors is proven. According to the OECD (Organisation for Economic Cooperation and Development) the demand for high-technology goods (electrical and electronic equipment, information technology, chemical and pharmaceutical products) in the OECD countries rose in real terms between 1972 and 1982 by 6.7 percent per annum, whereas the demand for products from manufacturing industry registered an overall increase of only 3.1 percent per annum. In addition, the integration of high-technology components into the classical industrial range of products, has at the same time permitted cost reductions necessary for structural changes and has also led to a new quality of products that in turn has stimulated demand. OECD estimates assume that in 1985 microelectronics and electronic equipment had already reached a production value of almost 4.7 percent of the world gross national product ($500 billion), and that a figure of 8 percent could be reached by the year 2000.

At present, the principal areas of technological development are: even higher integration density in components in the submicron range in the direction of 4- and 16-megabyte memories (chips); parallel computers; further interlinking, especially in production engineering; artificial intelligence (AT); and software development in general. New areas of biotechnological research, such as neurobiology and biosensors, are also opening up new opportunities for miniaturization in computer technology and communication engineering and also in the monitoring of production processes.

With regard to new materials, the focus of attention is on high-tech applications for ceramics, composites such as carbon- and aramide-fiber-reinforced plastics, special purpose polymers, new surface technologies, and superconductors. OECD projections assume that the demand for new, highly specialized materials will increase at two-figure growth rates, while conventional materials will average growth rates of only approximately 3 percent per annum.

The combination of complementary areas of knowledge, necessary in all these fields and scarcely feasible to its full extent within the research program of one single country, is one of the other reasons for the currently noticeable internationalization – even globalization – of research. This trend adds a new element to international cooperation besides the desire for access to international markets as well as the need for cost sharing (even in large companies) in view of rising R & D expenditures accompanied by shorter innovation cycles.

R & D Expenditure

A quick glance at the worldwide increase in expenditure on R & D and the rising share of R & D in overall investment is instructive. The more clearly emerging economic potential of research and development in key areas has accelerated the growth in expenditure, noticeably in the second half of the 1970s and even more so after the economic crisis of 1980 to 1982 had been overcome. Apart from the rapid rise in expenditure, it is important to note the growing share of industry in the financing of the national R & D budgets in the majority of countries, and the rising share of expenditure on R & D in comparison with the total investments made by companies.

Looking at the major industrialized countries in the West, one can detect a number of developments. Since 1970, there has been a considerable rise in all leading industrialized countries, most noticeably in Japan and the FRG, in the proportion of gross domestic product accounted for by expenditure on R & D. Whereas in 1970 this share was still only about 2 percent in the FRG, and slightly lower in Japan, it is today at the level of approximately 2.8 percent and 2.9 percent respectively. One expects a figure of 3 percent to be reached by both countries and also by the U.S. at the beginning of 1990. It should be remembered, however, that in the United States R & D already accounted for some 2.5 percent of GDP at the beginning of the 1970s, this figure declining in the course of the decade before accelerating again in the 1980s to exceed the previously achieved level. In the meantime, Japan and the FRG have been able to draw level; however, because economic growth in Japan was particularly high during the 1970s, it managed to achieve a particularly dynamic expansion in R & D. Between 1971 and 1985 Japan achieved approximately a sixfold increase in its R & D expenditure, with the FRG and the United States recording approximately a fourfold increase.

It is interesting to note that in these three countries the growth in R & D expenditure is supported by industry to a constantly increasing extent. On the whole, this trend has in recent years also applied to the United Kingdom. Only in France and Italy has R & D expenditure continued to be financed in approximately equal proportions by government and industry.

Also of interest is the fact that in the majority of western countries the rate of capital expenditure on R & D is considerably higher than expenditure on plant and equipment. According to the OECD, the

"R & D intensity" (i.e., R & D expenditure in relation to production value) in Japanese and German industry rose by 75 percent and 63 percent respectively between the early 1970s and the 1980s. Over the same period, the corresponding "plant and equipment intensity" fell by 20 percent and 24 percent respectively. However, this must not become an excuse for complacency. National and European research policy must watch the volume and international distribution of R & D resources.

If one takes the R & D expenditures of the six economically strongest OECD countries (the United States, Japan, the FRG, France, the United Kingdom and Italy), then, at the levels of 1985, the United States has approximately 53 percent of combined R & D expenditure, Japan over 19 percent, the FRG just under 10 percent, and the other three countries together just over 17 percent. In other words, the United States was spending more than five times, and Japan twice, as much on R & D as Germany; the big western European countries together were spending about half as much as the United States but more than Japan. This can only mean that cooperation in Europe and also worldwide must become even stronger. Yet, it also means that in order to keep up internationally in research and technology, the efforts undertaken in Germany must not slacken.

Internationalization of Production and Utilization of Technological Knowledge

Hardly any significant development in research policy in recent years has shown dynamism comparable to the rapid rate at which the development and utilization of technology has become internationalized, even globalized. Together with the worldwide advance in key technologies, there had been signs of this new trend for some time. Indications were provided by increased foreign investment, joint ventures and company takeovers, and especially by cross border cooperation agreements. The steady rise in international R & D cooperation agreements between companies and universities gave a further hint. As an example, international cooperation agreements between large companies in the semiconductor industry in Europe increased from two agreements in 1978 to more than forty agreements in 1984. Or consider that in only two years, from 1984 to 1986, over thirty joint enterprises were founded between American and Japanese companies in the field of biotechnology. These moves all have the aim of broadening a company's technological base as well as extending its market access.

A consequence of the hitherto unknown degree of both competition and cooperation at national and international levels in the field of research and technology is that it has become very difficult for small and medium-sized economies to hold their own against the stronger economies. The growing problems of the Third World present a further challenge to international science policy. Since these problems are beyond the scope of this essay, let it suffice to say that certain Asian countries have moved with unimagined speed toward industrialization, in particular South Korea, Taiwan, and Singapore. Other countries, like India, Brazil, China, and Indonesia, are on the verge of achieving this state too. For these countries, scientific and technological cooperation is of the greatest importance. By contrast, the situation of the remaining developing countries is much more difficult, especially in Africa and in the poorer countries of Asia and South America.

European Cooperation

In Europe, EUREKA, the Franco-German initiative, is becoming highly successful. The total volume of projects sponsored hitherto amount to DM 9 billion. EUREKA has already exceeded all expectations in its broad-based impact and in its success in attracting interest even from small countries. German companies are involved in fifty projects worth over DM 3 billion. Newly announced projects also include a fair share of German companies.

EUREKA is an example of how joint action on the part of European governments can remove barriers to cooperation between companies. It is open to integrated European projects in near-market research and in areas of long term government programs and "preventative research" (Vorsorgeforschung). It represents an important instrument for the realization of closer cooperation in research and technology at a European level. The German government intends to continue its active support for this initiative and to give priority to the promotion of EUREKA proposals.

Another major program aimed at strengthening European cohesion is the new framework research program for 1987 to 1991. Its objective is primarily to promote those regions in Europe insufficiently developed from the technological point of view. It focuses on the speedy realization of a common international market for high-technology goods, where standardization is a matter of some urgency. This standardization of norms should not be achieved by "compulsory harmonization," it should rather develop from joint work in technology.

European cooperation in basic research has a long history. Decisions by the German government to participate in the building of a European synchroton-radiation source in Grenoble and to support the new DM 1.2 billion high-energy accelerator LEP at CERN, emphasize the high priority attached to European cooperation at the basic research level. While giving its clear support, the German government expects that other European countries will also make appropriate contributions toward large-scale research projects in Europe. Clearly this constitutes a strong signal that it is the intention of the German government to help establish a European community of technology within the framework of the common international market, and thus represents a further decisive step toward the political unification of Europe.

Part III

Foreign Policy and Defense

–11–

EC-Europe: An Actor *Sui Generis* in the International System

WOLFGANG WESSELS

1992: The Lively Debate About the International Role of EC-Europe

The debate about the international role of EC-Europe has become quite lively.[1] The Single European Act (1987) and the "Delors Package," passed by the special Summit of Brussels 1988, opened the way to achieving the "Internal Market" by 1992. This process created worries among many partners in the international trade system, leading to the unfortunate and unfair term of "Fortress Europe." The Community responded to this reproach with the pledge to remain and to develop further its role as "Partner Europe."[2] Not only the internal success story of recent years, however, but also changes in the international economic system, led to speculation about what EC-Europe could and should do in the near future. In particular, the "(r)evolution" in Eastern Europe and in general East-West relations have provoked a major debate on the Community's possible contribution to the creation of a "New European Peace System" (as NATO formulates it), or a "Common European Home" (to use Gorbachev's term). Additionally, in the international economic system, the relations of the EC to the two other major poles – the United States and Canada, Japan and the Southeast Asian nations – have been the subject of academic and political discussions.

1. The term EC-Europe is used both to indicate some coherence among the different procedures and instruments that the EC and EC members apply, and to indicate that the EC is not the whole of Europe.
2. Declaration of the European Council of Rhodes, December 1988.

With these challenges ahead, the present state of the EC's international role is difficult to grasp. Although the basic features of EC international policies – the commercial policies, the association policies with Third World countries, and the building up of a "European Foreign Policy" – can be described, the exact forms, instruments, and procedures are quite often Byzantine, but not, as we will show, by pure accident.[3] When facing new challenges ahead on a ground that is only partly solid, it is not surprising that many suggestions reflect elements of wishful thinking, that exaggerated fears are expressed and that quite often unfounded speculation arises as to the possibilities and limits of the role of EC-Europe in the international system. Research is quite often limited to specific aspects, especially to the Lomé Agreement with sixty-six countries of Africa, the Caribbean, and the Pacific (ACP), or to the specific features of European Political Cooperation. An overall picture outlining general patterns is normally not drawn, or only in a rather superficial style.

This paper aims to elaborate some basic growth patterns of EC-Europe in the international system, and to suggest certain general explanations of how and why the Community and European Political Cooperation have developed and differentiated their instruments and procedures. Using this analysis, we shall look at future priorities of EC-Europe in the international system.

The Growth and Differentiation of the European Actor

Three Phases

Looking back at postwar history, one can identify three periods in the growth of the European actor in the international system. The first phase was characterized by a modest beginning in the 1950s and early 1960s with some Association Agreements (essentially, with Greece and Turkey) and an entry of the Community as a single actor in General Agreement on Tariffs and Trade (GATT) during the Kennedy Round.

The second phase began with the Hague Summit of 1969, which enlarged the scope of policy areas and led to the entry of the United Kingdom, which must be seen as a major factor in the emergence of EC-Europe. The Hague Summit also set up the Political Coopera-

3. Article 30 of "The Single European Act."

tion Procedures (EPC). In the 1970s and the first half of the 1980s, the scope of activity and the range of instruments applied were constantly extended. New forms of economic and foreign policy cooperation were developed, some of them quite original contributions to the procedures and instruments of the international game.

The third phase is linked to the passing of the Single European Act. New institutional features, as well as the Act's impact on the process toward 1992, have created new expectations and opened up new possibilities. From the middle of the 1980s, one may also note the rather dramatic developments in Eastern European countries, which afford new challenges to EC-Europe.

Basic Trends in the Role of EC-Europe

Extension of Scope The basic elements of the international role of the EEC have been the Common Commercial Policy (Article 113 of the EEC-Treaty and following), the policy of Agreements with third countries or organizations (Article 228), and Association Agreements (Article 238).

The Community has, most significantly from the early 1970s onward, made extensive use of these articles. EC bodies have concluded special preferential agreements with the ACP countries, offering them free access to all Community markets and creating specific forms of technical cooperation and financial assistance, such as the STABEX and the SYSMIN systems (to stabilize export earnings of the least developed countries). Within this framework, the EC has also tried to support the ACP states in the South Pacific (Fiji, Kiribati, Papua New Guinea, Solomon Islands, Tonga, Tuvalu, Vanuatu, and Western Samoa).

The EC has concluded twelve association or cooperation agreements with the (Maghreb and Mashreq) Arabic countries of the Mediterranean, and with Israel, providing free access for industrial exports to the EC, some concessions for agricultural trade, grants, and loans by the European Investment Bank.

The EC has also formed free trade areas with the countries of the European Free Trade Area.

There are also nonpreferential trade and cooperation agreements with countries like Bangladesh, India, China, Canada, Brazil, Pakistan, and Sri Lanka. The Community has also developed additional instruments such as food aid and a generalized system of preferences (GSP) to developing countries, a first in this area. While

Table 11.1 Overview of use of Anti-Dumping/Anti-Subvention Controls by the EC against OECD States

	1981	1982	1983	1984	1985	1986
Australia	–	1	–	–	–	–
Austria	–	1	–	–	1	–
Canada	1	1	1	1	–	–
Finland	–	–	–	–	–	–
Iceland	–	1	–	–	–	–
Japan	1	3	4	4	2	1
New Zealand	–	–	–	–	–	–
Sweden	–	1	–	1	1	–
Switzerland	–	–	–	–	1	–
Turkey	–	1	1	–	2	1
U.S.	6	7	1	1	–	–
Yugoslavia (associated)	2	2	3	4	5	4
OECD Total	10	18	10	11	12	6
Total (all third countries)	48	58	38	49	36	24

the list of these schemes looks impressive, the real effects are, however, disputed, especially since the Community has developed some ingenious ways to limit competitive imports like the Multi-Fibre Agreement for textiles by agreements of "voluntary" self-restraint.

The EC has also become a major actor within GATT: from the Kennedy Round via the Tokyo Round to the present Uruguay Round, the ability of the EC to come to an agreement with the United States was and is crucial for the success of the GATT rounds.

There are also autonomous trade decisions of the EC. Specific instruments are Anti-Dumping rulings (see Table 11.1), which have lately been extended to cover foreign "Screwdriver" plants.[4]

4. Annual Report of the Commission to the European Parliament on the Anti-dumping and Antisubvention measures of the Community, Doc. Nr. COM (84)21, (86)308, (87)178, (88)92. Quoted in Christian Siebert and Eirik Svindland, "Nationalstaat und Interdependenz – kooperative Interaktionsmuster in der EG-Handelspolitik," Berlin, December 1988, 104.

EC-Europe has also applied economic sanctions for political purposes. These were directed against Iran during the seizure of the U.S. hostages, against the Soviet Union during the Polish crisis, against Argentina during the Falklands War, against Libya, against South Africa, and most recently against the People's Republic of China. Except for Iran and Argentina, these sanctions were limited to certain products, and it is difficult to judge their real impact.

The EC activities have not, however, been confined to the traditional commercial fields. According to rulings of the European Court of Justice, the "external competence" of the EC is as broad as its "internal competence." Thus, the EC negotiates with third countries about access to fishing grounds (especially with Canada and Morocco), and in the area of transport policies, with neighboring countries (especially Switzerland and Austria); it also represents EC member states in environmental conferences.

When looking at the EC Treaty, one will not find any mention of the classic foreign policies. There was, however, already in 1959 a general feeling that the EC Ministers for Foreign Affairs needed also to deal with related foreign policy issues. As a consequence, however, of the failure of the De Gaulle-inspired Fouchet Plan, it was only from 1969 onward that the Foreign Ministers were able to create a highly differentiated system for coordinating their Foreign Policy positions.

With the EPC, the Community countries have taken positions on practically all international developments and crises (see Table 11.2).[5]

The EC Ministers thus deal with questions of terrorism, human rights, and, in some limited aspects, with security, especially with disarmament questions.

The Differentiation of Institutions and Procedures The simple question of "who makes the decisions," is difficult to answer. The complexity of decision-making and decision-implementing procedures has constantly been increased, most recently by the Single European Act. For third countries to lobby or influence EC decision making is a difficult task, as it is necessary to make contacts both with Commission officials in Brussels and with the Ministers of member countries (quite often even with two – the Foreign

5. Elfriede Regelsberger, "Die Europäische Zusammenarbeit," in *Jahrbuch der Europäischen Integration 1988/89*, ed. Werner Weidenfeld, Wolfgang Wessels (Bonn 1989).

Table 11.2 Declarations of the EPC 1988

(including Conclusions of the European Council, published statements and Joint declarations in the framework of political dialogue with regional groups)

SUBJECT	Number of texts
Afghanistan	5
ASEAN, Cambodia	2
Arab-Israeli Conflict (inc. PLO, Occ. Territories)	7
Argentina	1
Burma	2
Central America	5
Chile	3
Cyprus	1
East-West Relations and CSCE	4
Ethiopia	2
Euro-Arab Dialogue	1
Gulf Cooperation Council	1
Guatemala	1
Haiti	3
Honduras	1
Horn of Africa	1
International Role of EC/Twelve	1
Iran/Iraq	2
Korea	2
The situation of the Kurds	1
Latin America	1
Lebanon	5
Memorandum on Human Rights	1
Morocco/Algeria	1
Nicaragua	1
Organization for African Unity	2
Panama	1
Poland	1
7th Report on Code of Conduct for businesses in S. Africa	1
Press statement on the above	1
Refusal of U.S. to grant a visa to Yasser Arafat	1
West Sahara	1
Terrorism	1
Shooting down of Iranian Airbus by U.S. Navy	1
South Africa (inc. N. Mandela)	8
Southern Africa/Namibia	5

Office, and the Economic or Trade ministry), and in certain cases also with the European Parliament. External representation of the EC is sometimes quite bizarre, leading to the famous formula of "bicephalous troika," a representation wherein both the EC Commission and the Presidency of the EC Council represent EC-Europe (bicephalous). The Presidency itself is supported by its predecessor and its eventual successor (the troika) so as to increase the continuity of the EC Council Presidency, since it rotates every six months.

By taking into account different patterns we can perceive the following general trends.

The EC Commission plays a crucial role in all trade negotiations as it prepares the EC mandate and heads the EC delegation in trade negotiations and environmental conferences. In crisis situations during negotiations, the Commission officials are quite often able to act at the same time as "brokers" inside the Community and in the bargaining process with third partners. The EC Commission is now also active in all other undertakings of EC-Europe. It is accepted as something like an expert guest at all EPC meetings and it participates at the Western Summits.

The decision-making body is the Council of Ministers, which both passes the mandate and legitimates the outcome of the Treaty: the civil servants of member countries scrutinize carefully all activities of the Commission in negotiations. In particular, the Article 113 Committee is present at negotiations, which means that the Commission, although quite important, does not play an independent role.

The European Parliament had, up until the Single European Act, practically no direct powers with regard to the external policies of the Community. The SEA has given the European Parliament the power of co-decision in the Association Agreements and in Membership Treaties. To the surprise of the Council, the Parliament used this power last year to block the adoption of an Association Agreement with Israel in order to indicate its opposition to Israel's policies in the Occupied Territories. In the classical Commercial Policy area, however, the European Parliament's role is still limited to informal procedures of information – the so-called Luns-Westerterp procedure.

The European Parliament has, however, tried to develop a role of its own in the international system. It has established delegations to parliaments of many third countries, including the U.S. Congress and the Knesset; together with parliamentarians of the ACP countries it even has a so-called Joint Assembly, and it has mixed Association Committees with other countries. Through its policies on human rights, it tries to make the moral voice of EC-Europe heard in the world. By inviting politicians of great international importance such as Sadat, parliamentarians provide an open forum for international political debate, though the impact of these activities on the policies of the European Community itself or on third partners concerned is difficult to assess.

One should also mention the Court of Justice of the EC, whose rulings are of high importance for defining the competences of EC external policies and the powers of each of the institutions.

The Secretariat for the European Political Cooperation, which was established following the Single European Act, is so far of only minor importance. It is designed to serve the Presidents of the European Political Cooperation, primarily by taking up administrative and logistical functions.

Multiplying Regular Contact Channels An additional indicator can be used to demonstrate the growth of EC-Europe as an international actor. Looking at the channels of contact with other partners outside the EC, one can also notice a considerable increase in activities. Since East European countries formally recognized the Community in 1988, more than 140 countries now have diplomatic relations with the European Community. The EC Commission itself has increased its delegations in third countries, and the European Political Cooperation has considerably increased its pattern of regular contacts with such countries. The EC and the EPC both have a high intensity of contacts in the framework of international organizations, like the U.N. General Assembly, the OECD, and GATT, as well as in special international conferences – most noteworthy is the "Conference on Security Cooperation in Europe." EC-Europe is here recognized as a major partner and actor.

The EC and EPC have also developed specific kinds of relationships with other regional groups, which show quite original elements in international affairs. Table 11.3 shows the meetings that the EC had in the German Presidency in the first half of 1988 with representatives of other regional groupings.[6]

6. Elfriede Regelsberger, "The Dialogue of the EC/Twelve with other Groups of States," *The International Spectator*, 23, 4 (Oct.–Dec. 1988), 253–54.

Table 11.3 Ministerial Meetings organized during the German Presidency (January–June 1988)

- EC and EFTA Economic Ministers on 2 February, the second in the history of this relationship.
- "San José IV ": fourth conference (since 1984) of Foreign Ministers of the EC countries and those of the Contadora Group and the five Central American states on 29 February/1 March.
- First meeting between the Twelve (ministerial Troika) and 12 representatives from the ACP group — discussion devoted to South Africa on 26 April.
- Informal exchange of views between the Twelve and "The Group of Eight" (i.e., the Contadora Group plus Argentina, Brazil, Uruguay) to discuss political developments in the region — the second meeting since its inception in 1987.
- The 7th meeting since 1978 between the Twelve and ASEAN at the level of Foreign Ministers on 2/3 May.
- Annual Council of Ministers' session accorded to the Lomé Convention on 10 May.
- Meeting between the President of the Council and the Commissioner in charge of North-South relations with representatives from the Gulf Cooperation Council on the occasion of the signing of a Cooperation Agreement and a joint (political) Declaration on 15 June.
- Participation of W. de Clerq (Commissioner for EC External Relations) at the Economics Ministers' meeting of EFTA on 15 June.
- Meeting between the Foreign Ministers ("Troika") and representatives from the Arab League, the first in the history of the Euro-Arab Dialogue, on 24 June.
- Meeting between the President of the Commission and Commissioner de Clerq and the Secretary General of COMECON on the occasion of the signing of the Joint Declaration, the starting point of mutual recognition and future cooperation in Europe, on 25 June.

The Imperfections of EC-Europe

Whereas these partly quantitative figures look quite impressive, there are certain blank pages where EC-Europe is not, or not fully, present. One major area is the security field: although the EPC deals with "political and economic aspects of security" (Article 30 of the Single European Act), and may even extend this brief in the context of international conferences like the CSCE, there is no standard place for common debates (not to mention position-taking) on crucial security issues. There is no forum in which, for example, the reaction of West European countries to the SDI initiative of President Reagan or the stances adopted regarding the latest Gorbachev initiatives may be tackled on a real Community-wide basis. The revitalization of the Western European Union (WEU) (from 1984 onward), in which nine of the twelve EC members are endeavoring to coordinate their security policy positions, has so far not really been successful, although some progress has been reported in out-of-area issues, such as the cooperation of some West European countries in sending warships to the Gulf region.

A second lacuna is the rather weak position concerning global macroeconomic and monetary policies. Although nine of the twelve EC members have linked their currency in the fixed exchange rate system of the European Monetary System (EMS), a common or coordinated external monetary policy has not been developed. The President of the Commission is present at the Western Summit, although the Commission is not represented at "G7" meetings.

A third lacuna is the external Cultural Policy. Although the impact of the individual cultural activities of EC members in third countries have clearly diminished in importance, there are still few coordinating efforts.

Some General Lines for Analysis and Assessment

When looking at the growth and differentiation of these activities, certain patterns, sometimes of a surprising nature, come into view. The West European State has not been replaced by a European Federal Superstate, and while there are more and more forms of Community, common, or coordinated activities, the role of the Member States' governments has not been downgraded. We might even argue the other way around, since they enjoy enhanced possibilities to shape events in the international system. Thus, we cannot talk about a zero-sum game between common activities on one side and national activities on the other. Member states' governments have had to give up autonomy of action, but have gained access and influence. Indeed, some authors argue that the EC has led to a renaissance of the nation-state.[7] My argument, however, would be that it is not the renaissance of the state in its traditional characteris-

7. Stanley Hoffman, "Reflections on the National State in Western Europe Today," *Journal of Common Market Studies*, 21 (1982), 21–37.

tics, but the evolution of the units into a new state system that may be characterized by the phrases "pooling of resources," "power sharing," and even "Cooperative Federalism."[8]

Thus there is a mixture of continuing national policies, coordinated and common activities, as well as of Community policies. The Community has not become a unitary actor, with policies consistent over time and coherent over different sectors. States thus continue traditional foreign policy approaches, including some kind of limited power games within EC-Europe and across the borders. For some, this gap between the potential power of EC-Europe as a whole and its inability to organize its resources effectively, is negative, as the weight of European interest is not being felt in a way that seems possible and necessary. Others might argue: (a) that differentiated approaches might sometimes be even more effective than common policies, which might then be too rigid, and (b) that EC-Europe has simply not developed a consensus strong enough for a stronger international role.

Future Priorities

If we assume that the progress toward the internal market continues up until 1993, the EC will be a different creature than during the time of the "Euro-sclerosis" of the early 1980s. By achieving at least some of the effects that the EC countries hope for with the implementation of the Internal Market program, the possible list of conflicts with other countries will increase considerably. Even if this progress toward the Internal Market were not to lead to more protectionism by the Community, major priorities for the EC are the establishment of GATT rules and its relationships with the United States and Japan, as well as the relations with the "rest of Europe," especially with the EFTA countries. Within the groups of neighbors, the process of 1992 has led to basic rethinking of their respective relations to the Community. Austria has applied for EC membership, Norway might like to wait for a certain time, and Switzerland, Sweden, and Finland are at the moment not interested in joining the Community but in establishing closer links between EFTA and the Community.

8. On this last notion see Simon Bulmer and Wolfgang Wessels, *The European Council: Decision-Making in European Politics* (London, 1987), 13, et seq.

Following the changes in Eastern Europe and in the East-West relationship, the European *Ost- und Deutschlandpolitik* has reversed the list of priorities and will constitute a major challenge for the 1990s. Consequent to the general declaration of the EC and COMECON countries in 1988, agreements were concluded between individual COMECON countries and the EC. While overall trade so far is not very important for the EC, the political overtones are, of course, of eminent importance. Although the wishful thinking of some East Europeans about joining the Community is certainly premature, forms of association agreements as proposed by Messrs. Kissinger, Giscard D'Estaing, and Nakasone in their latest report for the "Trilateral Commission" might be a concrete option to be pursued. The internal and external "digestion" of the GDR into the Community will be a major issue on the EC agenda. Regional problems are certain to increase in Eastern Europe and the Balkans, with the internal dissolution of Yugoslavia and the increase in tension between Eastern European countries becoming a major preoccupation.

As to other regions, there will be a specific concentration on the Mediterranean: for Turkey, constructive solutions have to be found. There is also growing concern about the demographic gap between the Arab and European countries. Around this region the overall interest in ACP countries will remain, although it is evident that Africa is economically not a very promising partner for the industries of the Community.

With the Falklands War and the entry of Spain and Portugal into the Community, Latin America has been placed higher on the agenda. While there is not yet much substance to the rhetoric, the activity of EC-Europe in Central America has shown the interest of the EC in assuming responsibilities outside its own "backyard."

The Pacific will certainly constitute a major challenge. The contacts with Japan are intensive, although the level of conflict will increase in the near future, and relations with ASEAN have developed diplomatically rather well, although there has not been the expected follow-up in terms of business contacts. Politically, one could say that EC-Europe has not really invested in this area.

And what about the OECD countries in the Pacific? New Zealand and Australia are clearly perceived as part of the western democratic world, and as stable factors in the international economic and security picture. They seem far away, however, and, aside from certain trade problems and some French activities outside the EC framework, the mutual relationship looks stable and undramatic.

In the near future, governments and political forces within EC-Europe will be absorbed in the internal process of achieving an "Internal Market," and an Economic and Monetary Union as well as with the *Ost- und Deutschlandpolitik*. The risk of a "provincial," or purely European, insular orientation of EC-Europe cannot be ruled out, while on the other hand some rhetoric reflects the danger of entering a phase of "imperial overstretch." The debate about the role of EC-Europe in the international system will be sure to continue.

–12–

European Defense Integration: Prospects and Problems

JOANNE WRIGHT

The issue of European integration and especially the future of European defense arrangements were brought into sharp focus by the momentous events of 1989. In the first half of the year, NATO celebrated its fortieth birthday amidst an apparent loss of public confidence in its future roles and directions. There is no doubt that this loss of public confidence was largely due to NATO's seeming inability to respond positively and imaginatively to President Gorbachev's arms control initiatives. It must also be said, however, that Gorbachev's initiatives accentuated a number of pressures on NATO that had been compounding for the past twenty years or so. The most important of these are weaknesses in NATO's flexible response strategy and arguments about burden sharing within the alliance. It can certainly be argued that both these pressures are pushing toward greater West European defense integration and cooperation.

Toward the end of 1989, the future of Europe was again at the forefront of international politics as a wave of reform swept over Eastern Europe. This can also be seen as a continuation of the breakup of the bipolar international system established in the wake of World War II. The new detente between the superpowers will undoubtedly bring benefits to Europe, but there is no guarantee that a multipolar world will be any freer of conflict and competition than a bipolar one. So how do these pressures affect NATO, the concept of an integrated European defense, and the major players in European defense? Are these additional pressures also pushing toward greater integration? Certainly, one person who appears to think so is President Mitterrand of France. On several occasions he has argued that the best way for the West Europeans to respond to changes in Eastern Europe is through a strengthening of the European Community's structures.[1]

While all these pressures within and without NATO are bringing the future of European defense to a crossroads, they are also more than ever revealing the ambiguities in French defense policy, especially in relation to Germany. After examining the pressures conducive to greater European defense integration, this paper will move on to discuss the ambiguities in French defense policy and conclude that for European defense integration, and ultimately full European Community integration to proceed, these ambiguities must be resolved.[2]

Flexible Response

Perhaps an appropriate place to begin an examination of the pressures pushing toward greater Western European defense integration is European dissatisfaction with NATO's flexible response strategy. It is certainly ironic that the compromises made to flexible response doctrine to appease the Europeans now appear to be the source of European discontent. When Robert McNamara first outlined his flexible response strategy in 1962, it was an attempt to respond to Soviet nuclear parity and resolve the clearly incredible mutually assured destruction that parity had brought about. It envisaged NATO developing a range of options to be able to respond to different levels of Soviet aggression. In terms of making strategy credible, the crucial component was a significant build up of conventional forces and abilities. But as far as the Europeans were concerned, this was also the most controversial component, and after five years of wrangling, a considerably modified flexible response strategy was adopted.

The European members of NATO, especially the United Kingdom, France, and West Germany, had both financial and strategic reasons for opposing flexible response as it was proposed by

1. See, for example, *Le Monde*, 24 November 1989; *Christian Science Monitor*, 30 November 1989; *The Guardian Weekly*, 19 November 1989; and *Die Welt*, 30 October 1989.

2. This is not to suggest, however, that French defense policy is the only obstacle to European integration. British attitudes and Ireland's nonaligned status also present considerable obstacles.

McNamara. In many respects the Europeans had come to think of nuclear weapons as a "cheap" form of defense and were immediately reluctant to commit the necessary resources to fulfill McNamara's plan. But the Europeans were also very reluctant to accept any strategy that they felt weakened nuclear deterrence, thereby making conventional war more likely. Their preference was for a strategy that emphasized the possibility of any conflict going nuclear. And accordingly, flexible response mutated into "flexible escalation," flexible *escalation* rather than flexible response because with its consistent failure to upgrade conventional forces to the required level, NATO was heavily reliant on nuclear weapons to offset the Warsaw Pact's conventional advantage, and on a strategy that emphasized a linkage between tactical, theater, and strategic nuclear weapons.[3] It was to bolster this linkage that the Europeans initially supported the deployment of Cruise and Pershing missiles. But it was the proposed deployment of these missiles that really sparked off an acute crisis of public confidence in flexible response and the growing peace movements.

Criticisms of flexible response centered not only on its incredibility, but also on its inherent dangerous qualities.[4] Flexible response is incredible because threatening to initiate a process that would lead to national suicide is bluff and would be seen as such by the Soviet Union. Arguments that flexible response is dangerous focus on two factors. First, that NATO's undue reliance on nuclear weapons means that the decision to use them would have to be made very early in the conflict. This pressure to bring nuclear weapons into play very early is accentuated by the possibility of losing forwardly deployed tactical nuclear weapons to advancing Warsaw Pact forces. Second, the framework of flexible response encourages military planners to incorporate nuclear weapons into a war fighting plan, to conceive of them as weapons with which it is possible to fight and "win." While of course it is exceptionally doubtful that any war fought with nuclear weapons can be won, it is also exceptionally doubtful that the process of nuclear escalation can be controlled amid the fog of war. So whereas in the 1950s and 1960s the Europeans resisted a build-up of conventional forces because they preferred a strategy of escalation, the experiences of

3. J. Baylis, "NATO Strategy: the case for a new strategic concept," *International Affairs*, 64, 1 (Winter 1987/88), 44.
4. J. Baylis, "NATO Strategy," 44–45.

the 1980s have certainly shaken, if not reversed, this belief. (Although it should perhaps be pointed out that there are still many people in Europe who strongly believe in the nuclear emphasis of NATO.) The INF agreement signed by the United States and the Soviet Union at the end of 1987 has, to a certain extent, already "de-emphasized" nuclear weapons by weakening the link between strategic and theater nuclear weapons even if the latter, as Richard Betts argues, were "largely symbolic."[5] Continuing this "de-emphasis" of nuclear weapons could provide a basis for greater European defense integration and a means by which NATO can capitalize on the opportunity presented by the INF agreement to reassess its strategy.

John Baylis has argued for a reassessment of NATO strategy on the basis of what he has called an "extended firebreak."[6] Instead of fuzzing the line between conventional and nuclear war, as current NATO strategy does, Baylis argues for a strategy that emphasizes the threshold between nuclear and conventional war in a "no-early-use" posture. The aim of such a strategy:

> would be to allow the Alliance to say to the Soviet Union, if you invade conventionally, we have the capability to defend conventionally for a considerable period of time. But we are not ruling out the possibility that we just might use nuclear weapons first, especially to demonstrate our resolve to resist. And if you use nuclear weapons first against us, don't forget that we have a devastating retaliatory capability.[7]

Once again, however, like the original flexible response, the key seems to be conventional forces.

Calls for additional resources to be devoted to conventional weapons are not new, and, given NATO's track record, is there any reason to suppose that it will be prepared to assign more resources to defense in an overall climate possibly even more unfavorable to defense expenditure than the 1950s and 1960s? Both economic and political arguments can be advanced to support the concept of a primarily European conventional defense. There are obviously immense savings to be made from greater defense cooperation, which would, in turn, help resolve arguments about burden-sharing within

5. R.K. Betts, "NATO's Mid-Life Crisis," *Foreign Affairs*, 68, 2 (Spring 1989), 46.
6. Baylis, "NATO Strategy," 49.
7. Ibid.

NATO. Greater European defense integration would also create the political framework within which the Europeans could be much more autonomous and less reliant on their American "big brother," something that is likely to find favor among European electorates.

Economic Integration

Arguments about burden-sharing within NATO have been simmering for two decades, with periodic flare-ups. Calculating each nation's contribution to the alliance is almost as difficult as trying to measure the military balance, for like the military balance it includes both quantitative and qualitative factors. In response to congressional grumblings about the Europeans' contribution to the alliance, NATO defense ministers produced a report late in 1988 entitled *Enhancing Alliance Collective Security*. It pointed out that while European defense spending has not been as high as the United States would like, some European countries have had to shoulder additional burdens, such as the opportunity cost of conscription and the financial and political costs of hosting NATO exercises. Nonetheless, it did recognize an urgent need for European members to enhance resources and improve efficiency, and it did show that several European states have consistently failed to reach NATO's recommended 3 percent of GDP. This may appease Congress for a while, but it has to be admitted that the Americans do have a point. Nearly two-thirds of the United States defense budget is spent on NATO. This is approximately equal to the sum that the Europeans spend collectively, and the American argument is strengthened further by the fact that materially, the Europeans are quite capable of defending themselves. It seems certain that financial pressure, coupled with arms control agreements, will reduce the U.S. defense commitment to Europe.

Certainly over the past few years there has been a measure of European defense collaboration. Both the Europeans within NATO and the West European Union have in the past year advocated greater European cooperation in research, development, and joint procurement. The United Kingdom, West Germany, Italy, and Spain have decided to proceed with the development of the European Fighter Aircraft. And at the end of 1988, the United Kingdom and France signed a reciprocal defense deal under which France will buy communications equipment from Britain, and

Britain will buy mortar rounds from France. But so far these instances of cooperation, while not insignificant, have been hodgepodge. Current Director of the International Institute for Strategic Studies, François Heisburg, advocates that the next step should be to coordinate the next defense reviews of France, the United Kingdom and West Germany. All three countries, he argues, have sound reasons for much greater financial coordination: France because it is overburdened trying to maintain a complete defense complement; Britain because of additional expenses caused by the Falklands War; and West Germany because of demographic constraints.[8] For such a radical step to occur, however, there would need to be a very strong political framework, and this is where the real obstacle to European integration currently lies.

Political Integration

There is no doubt that the political dynamics within alliances are as crucial to their stability and credibility as any piece of military hardware. It is certainly plausible to argue that American insensitivity to internal alliance problems contributed greatly to NATO's problems.[9] Many analysts on both sides of the Atlantic have argued that SDI and INF revealed a fundamental breach in the credibility of the American nuclear guarantee to Europe, leading to divergent United States and European security needs.[10] The heightened tension between the two superpowers in the early 1980s, and the sentiments expressed by the European peace movements, revealed large-scale public unease about America's role in Western Europe. Indeed several European countries did not follow America's lead in reacting to the Soviet invasion of Afghanistan or the suppression of Solidarity in Poland.[11] The West European reaction to the changes in Eastern Europe has also tended to be more positive than the American. The apparent break-up of the European postwar order provides the European Community with an opportunity to create an

8. *The Times*, 5 October 1988.

9. See, for example, W. Hanrieder, "Strategic Defence and the German-American Security Connection," *Journal of International Affairs*, 41, 2 (1988).

10. See, for example, C. Bertram, "Strategic Defence and the Atlantic Alliance," *Daedalus*, 114, 3 (1985).

11. Britain, for example, attended the Moscow Olympics, and Britain, France, and West Germany continued to trade with the Soviet Union after the United States called for sanctions.

integrated political framework that would include much stronger defense and security arrangements. The most crucial nexus in any such arrangement will obviously be between Paris and Bonn.

Arguing that the Europeans should have a defense capability independent of the Americans is, of course, nothing new to the French, but its acceptance by others, especially the West Germans, may be forcing the French to face up to the ambiguities and contradictions of their own defense position. Furthermore, German reunification is now making life even more difficult for the French.

French Defense

The 1980s have certainly provoked some very dramatic moves from the French, including President Mitterrand's 1983 visit to the Bundestag to declare his support for the Christian Democratic Union's stance on the deployment of Cruise and Pershing missiles. And in March 1988, for the first time in two decades, a French head of state, accompanied by the Prime Minister, attended a NATO summit. Both moves were prompted by two fears: that the withdrawal of American theater nuclear weapons would leave Western Europe facing a Soviet conventional superiority alone; and a fear that West Germany was drifting toward neutralism.

These fears provoked a concerted effort by the French to "anchor" West Germany more firmly within the Western Alliance. Included in this effort have been the establishment of a Franco-German brigade of 4,000 stationed in Stuttgart. In addition to increased contact between French and German military and defense personnel, French forces have begun to exercise further forward in West Germany. But does this all signify a radical departure in French defense policy? Has France finally committed itself to a defense of Western Europe, rather than just a defense of France? Unfortunately, from a West European, and particularly a West German point of view, they do not. The notion of France as a self-reliant "sanctuary" still seems to dominate French defense thinking.

Most significantly, French doctrine remains vague as to the exact timing, extent, and circumstances of any French participation in the defense of Western Europe. The withdrawal of American Cruise and Pershing missiles has left the decidedly ambiguous role of France's own tactical nuclear weapons totally exposed. In an attempt to cover their position, the French have recently renamed these weapons "pre-strategic," but that does not hide the limited range of even the new generation Hades missile. Furthermore, the French have a much greater number of these missiles than would be required to fulfill either of the roles envisaged for them: to test an enemy's intentions, or to serve as warning shots. This then leads to the question of where these weapons are targeted – a question the West Germans would undoubtedly like answered.

Some analysts, politicians, and indeed up to 40 percent of the French people are reportedly in favor of giving the West Germans an answer in the form of unambiguously extending the French nuclear umbrella over West Germany.[12] Regardless of whether or not West German public opinion would be any more tolerant of French as opposed to American nuclear weapons, there remains a fundamental uncertainty in French attitudes toward West Germany. In a speech to the Institute of Advanced Defence Studies, just after his reelection in 1988, Mitterrand declared that France's principal mission was to "maintain our own identity and independence" and that the defense of other countries in Western Europe was the responsibility of the Atlantic Alliance, which France would not rejoin.[13] Another analyst is perhaps more forthright when he declares:

> [t]he Federal Republic is at the same time our ally and our glacis, our friend and a former defeated enemy that must be controlled, in agreement with the USSR, if necessary. There is no question therefore of 'dying for Germany', but let her beware if she obstinately casts a skeptical glance at the less and less credible American umbrella. There is no question of extending east of the Rhine the French nuclear guarantee, but the West German pacifists had better pay attention when the President of the Republic goes to the Bundestag to encourage them to accept American Euromissiles on their soil . . .[14]

Since Mitterrand's 1988 reelection, events in Europe, and particularly in Germany, have taken everyone by surprise. *West* German neutralism is no longer really the issue. France, like the other countries of Europe and the United States and Soviet Union, is having to come to terms with German reunification (despite early

12. P. Lellouche, *L'Avenir de la guerre*, Paris, 1985, and *Le Monde*, 28 June 1985.
13. *The Times*, 12 October 1988.
14. *Le Monde*, 22 May 1985.

denials of such a prospect by both Germanies).[15] *German* neutralism, however, is a prospect even more unappealing to the French, as it is to the British, Americans, and, it seems, the Polish and the Czechoslovakians as well.

Mitterrand has quite clearly stated that neither he nor France have any ideological or political objections to German reunification, but at the same time, he has stressed that no national will for reunification can be imposed without reference to Britain, France, the United States, and the Soviet Union.[16] As French political scientist Alfred Grosser suggests, this French attitude

> consists of saying the whole world must practice self-determination – everyone, that is, but the East Germans. Why? Because we are afraid that there would be too many of them? That is not a sensible attitude.[17]

As stated earlier, President Mitterrand believes that a "sensible attitude" would involve strengthening the integration mechanisms of the European Community. He also believes that this is the most appropriate arena in which to pursue German reunification. But without an integrated European defense, the French-German nexus, central to any real European integration, will remain inadequate.

In conclusion, it must be restated that French defense policy is not the only obstacle to European integration. In fact, it would seem that there are two almost completely contradictory trends running in parallel in contemporary Europe: the integration of the States of Western Europe and a renaissance of the nation-state in Eastern Europe and within the Soviet Union. Chancellor Kohl's refusal to clarify the boundaries of a united Germany may help tilt the balance in favor of the latter trend. But whatever happens in Germany over the next few months, and despite the impetus given to European integration from changes in the world order, public dissatisfaction with NATO's flexible response strategy, and economic imperatives, it seems that history, emotion, and nationalism still stand in the way of a full integration process.

15. See *The Guardian*, 10 December 1989; *The Guardian Weekly*, 9 November 1989 and *Le Monde*, 24 November 1989.

16. *Christian Science Monitor*, 30 November 1989.

17. *Die Welt*, 30 November 1989.

–13–

The West Europeans and NATO

MAGNUS CLARKE

> In politics, a community of hatred is almost always the foundation of friendships.
>
> — de Tocqueville

In 1989 the North Atlantic Treaty Organization observed its fortieth anniversary, but by the end of that year found itself in quiet crisis. The deluge of events that culminated in the opening of the Berlin wall on 10 November represented a cause for celebration in the effective capitulation of the ideology of communism but, in that momentous change, lay also a challenge to the very existence of the Alliance.

But "crisis" has ever been a word liberally applied to the condition of NATO, and throughout these forty years, the Alliance has been more often deemed in danger of imminent dissolution than it has been reported strong and vigorous. Thus, even in the first half of 1989, *The Australian* was able to head a report of 29 April with the words "NATO in Crisis" and another of 1 June as "Cracks behind NATOs facade." These were but characteristic of the whole of NATO's forty-year history. To take a few examples from the 1980s alone and from one source only, *Time* magazine in May 1983 used "The Alliance, trying to heal the rift," in 1981 used "The Shaky State of NATO," and a year earlier had opted for "Storm over the Alliance."[1]

Although more positive headlines had also appeared, it may nonetheless be a matter of surprise that NATO had survived that long.[2] In reality, NATO had learned, as an institution, not merely

1. *Time*, 9 May 1983; *Time*, 10 August 1981; *Time*, 28 April 1980.
2. Such as that of *The Age* (Melbourne) of 22 December 1979: "NATO gets it together."

to cope with the frictions that must be involved between the sixteen sovereign nations that comprised it in 1989, but had accepted that friction as a part of its character and hence, finally, its strength. It has ever been said within the British Royal Navy that it is "going to the dogs," but it is also said of the Royal Navy that if it ever stopped saying that it was "going to the dogs," then it really would be. In short, if there had been "cracks" in NATO, then it was only because large alliances cannot be conducted without them.

The two questions that arose at the beginning of 1990, however, were whether the European political earthquake would enlarge these traditional cracks to the point of ruin, or if acquired skills in crisis management within the organization were sufficient to adapt NATO to survive in the new environment. In short, if NATO had been held together by external threat, then as that threat apparently receded, would the centrifugal forces grow to overcome the centripetal? And if it did not, what, then, would be the form of the new NATO, one deprived of defending the West against the "menace" of Communism?

This paper takes the fortieth anniversary of the Alliance as the opportunity to review NATO's problems, and the events of 1989 as an inadequate base on which to project its future in the next one or two decades, and even to speculate quite wildly about its fate in the twenty-first century. Such speculation was the compulsory content of the fortieth anniversary edition of the customarily bland *NATO Review* published in February 1989. It was predictable that George Bush would state: "One of the foremost objectives of my Administration will be to strengthen the Alliance further in all its aspects," since that was his known preference, but the review did contain some fundamental truths on NATO.[3] First, Bush stated, "The Alliance has been central to U.S. Foreign policy since the days of Harry Truman," and second, "We know that NATO works, it works because we're a community of great diversity but fundamentally one of shared interests."[4]

In the first, it can be observed that the United States has remained committed to NATO because of the centrality of the Alliance in American Foreign Policy; because, in itself, a permanent alliance represented a revolutionary departure for U.S. policy in 1949; because it has been useful, if costly, in providing moral support for

3. President Bush, "US Administration to seek strengthened Alliance," NATO Review, 37, 1 (Feb. 1989), 1.
4. President Bush, "US Administration."

U.S. actions, and because it has been unable to think of anything better. In the second observation, Bush underscored the essence of NATO as an alliance whose vigor has derived as much from its own conflicts as from the threat from outside. In other words, the *challenge* of keeping NATO alive was one of its main reasons for existence. In this it must be remembered that NATO was established to counter a threat from the East, rather than, as others have argued, to *create* a threat *to* the East (thereby establishing a long term adversary relationship, which resolved political ambiguities in postwar Europe); until 1989 the threat receded without huge damage to NATO cohesion.

The threat is still the centerpiece of the NATO edifice and the value of the Alliance in having acted as a deterrent to *possible* Soviet adventurism in that forty-year period cannot be discounted. As Manfred Wörner has stated, however, the Alliance has "also given our societies the basis of security which has enabled us to make tremendous economic and social progress, allowing human rights to prosper in a way never seen before."[5] Much of that economic advance must be ascribed to the growth of the European Community; but to rephrase Wörner, NATO had acted as the *screen* behind which the development could take place and, especially in its early years, allowed the West Europeans to avoid otherwise certain commitment to much greater levels of expenditure on defense, diverting precious investment funds. Moreover, the Treaty of Rome excludes the issue of joint defense, a responsibility that must then be allocated elsewhere, and the fortuitous existence of NATO offered the venue for that necessary cooperation without the need for the writing of a comprehensive defense contract between the West European states. The occasional acrimonies of NATO must be less than the acrimony potential to evolving a Common Defence Policy, at least judging by the difficulties that have been involved in the Common Agricultural Policy, and defense, as some have said, is a "thorny subject." Finally, NATO is the only vehicle that directly links Western Europe and the United States, if the OECD is excluded, and of course Canada. NATO is then the "tie" between the European peoples, both resident and nonresident in Europe, and the only large European communities that are then excluded from participation in Europe are Israel, Australia, and New Zealand.

5. Secretary General of NATO, Manfred Wörner, "Building a New East West Relationship," NATO Review, 37, 1 (Feb. 1989), 3.

Therefore, the issue of threat as the glue of NATO may be considered a matter of almost peripheral interest, despite media fixation on that aspect. If threat in the age of Glasnost and Perestroika has declined, then it is for the leadership of NATO to publicize these greater, and positive, purposes of the Alliance beyond those original purposes for which it was ostensibly established; namely, deterrence of the threat from the East and joint defense against it should that deterrence fail. In reality, even those original purposes are still valid. Threat is the product of capability and intention and, as Manfred Wörner pointed out, by February 1989 only the level of intention had thus far declined: "The formidable Warsaw Pact military potential is still there."[6] Moreover, as events in China of May and June of that year indicated, it is always possible for the political climate to alter rapidly.

Early in 1990, in the USSR, neither Glasnost nor Perestroika had yet become immutable, irreversible, or even clear as to their intended destinations and consequences. Similarly, the rapidity of change in Eastern Europe and within the non-Russian Soviet Republics offered myriad opportunities for new political confrontations between East and West, any of which might come to rival the crises of 1948, 1956, 1961, or 1968. The demands of the Baltic republics for the return of their independence and the resistance of Moscow to these demands are one example. The only change that could convince NATO of the impossibility of the event of a new East-West war in Europe would be reductions in the military capabilities of the Warsaw Pact to the point where such confrontation had become a physical impossibility. What had been learned over forty years could not be easily forgotten.

Yet, even the event of effective conventional and nuclear disarmament in Europe might not be sufficient cause for the dissolution of NATO. Insofar as NATO represents a valuable and *existing* mechanism for bonding of the European peoples across the Atlantic, it is more probable that the Alliance would shift its ground to a union that placed greater emphasis on cultural links, rather than a shared threat. It would thus partly replicate the Commonwealth, which can never replace it given the exclusion of the United States from the Organisation and the more varied membership of the latter body. If NATO and the Commonwealth may both be described as akin to family trusts, then it must be observed that there is family and

6. Wörner, "Building a New East West Relationship," 5.

"family": the first is the real family – especially in the case of North America with its mélange of citizens from diverse European stock – while the second, for all its practical aspects, must ever remain an ideology, in the mold of the "brotherhood of man" based upon the historical accident of the British Empire. If blood is thicker than water, then NATO is blood and the Commonwealth only water.

Nevertheless, despite the logic of continuing NATO into the future, purely in terms of its cultural advantages to the members, two developments will clearly place the Alliance under strain in the decades ahead, and they are only partly related to developments in the East: namely, European integration and the economically enforced U.S. retreat from its self-appointed role of "global policeman."

NATO has, at the insistence of its European founders, been traditionally described as the "Twin Pillars," the one being Europe, the other North America. But it has been led in all of its forty years by the United States, a matter made obvious by the traditional appointment of U.S. generals as SACEUR (Supreme Allied Commander, Europe). The present difficulty is that those pillars, given the process of European integration, have actually become equal, to an extent where leadership of the Alliance by the United States can no longer be the reality. Until the events of 1989, European integration had been accelerating, with the goal of full economic union within the EC being set for 1992, a significant milestone on the road to full political union, which must be followed by military integration of some form or another. One pattern existed in the establishment of a Franco-German brigade, but this was not without opposition from some NATO members.

The possible difficulties involved for NATO in advancing European integration, which included an expanded role for the exclusively European military cooperative body – the Western European Union (but which still excludes five of the European members of NATO) – have not been ignored by NATO's leadership. Manfred Wörner, again, accepted the inevitability of this trend and accorded the growing strength of Western Europe the status of benefit to the Alliance. At the same time, he has spoken against "Efforts at European co-operation which tend towards exclusivity – and could be seen as creating clubs within the club – or activities which cut across Alliance efforts . . .," drawing attention instead toward the cultural benefits of the Alliance (which this paper has highlighted) and to the practical advantages of retaining North America as the

European reserve and guarantee in the long run and, in the short run, of its importance in "the defence of the flanks," for which we may read the North Atlantic.[7] In this, however, the strains should not be underestimated. Paradoxically, although NATO was intended to act as the shield behind which European economic resuscitation could take place, its success in doing so now acts as a problem for the Alliance. In the first two decades, as Robert Hunter stated in 1988, "US and West European interests were clearly complementary," but in the decade of the 1980s, especially, European economic success accelerated to a point where it detracted from the U.S. economy, and economic competition replaced economic cooperation. As Hunter described it, "For the first time in the Alliance's history, economic tensions risk[ed] corroding political understandings."[8] Should that success continue, and there is no reason to suppose that it will not, the new markets in Eastern Europe being viewed as an "opportunity," rather than a potential burden, there will be even greater pressure on U.S. decision makers to reduce support to this "thankless child."

Overall, in the 1980s, up until 1989, the United States endured an increasing element of exclusion. The Western European members of NATO needed the United States less, both in that the military guarantee provided by the Americans was no longer deemed vital, and also in that the progress of integration and the strength of their economies would render the U.S. occupation inappropriate in the relatively near future. The net effect was an incentive for the United States to devote greater attention, politically, to Central and South America and, economically, to the Pacific Rim.

After mid-1989, however, the scale of change in Eastern Europe and in the Soviet Union began to negate some of the developments of Western Europe as they affected NATO. With a growing number of Eastern European states abandoning communism, the achievement of full economic union in the EC by 1992 had to become a lesser priority than the creation of mechanisms by which the West European economy could be expanded to absorb potential newcomers. Further, the enunciation by Gennady Garasimov in October 1989 of the so-called "Sinatra Doctrine," which determined that Eastern bloc states could now "do things their way,"

7. Ibid., 6.

8. Robert E. Hunter, "Will the United States remain a European Power?" in *Survival* (May/June 1988), 219.

specifically included the option of leaving the Warsaw Treaty Organisation after due period of notice. Hence, the directions that dominated the future of NATO at the beginning of 1989 were no longer obvious at its close. Above all, the impending reunification of Germany clouded all three issues: the future of the EC (including full economic union in 1992), the leadership of the Alliance, and the possibility of its replacement with an expanded Western European Union (WEU). We will return to the issue of Germany later.

If, however, it has been the tradition that the United States "leads" the Alliance, then it has been the almost equal tradition of the United States to complain of the costs of support to NATO in men, material, and "treasure," a matter which has increased with the passing years. As Nicholas Rothwell has expressed it, "In the early post-war decades, American economic predominance was assured, American culture exerted a hypnotic sway over each Western European Society [and] American troops served as the bulwark against the looming Soviet forces across the Iron Curtain."[9] Clearly the United States can no longer find itself the easy role of "postwar rescuer," since Western Europe has grown up, but it is also the case that the United States has "grown down."[10] In April 1989, the projected U.S. budget deficit for 1990 was $166 billion, and steps were taken to reduce this to a mere $100 billion, with the objective of a zero deficit by 1993.[11] That cannot be achieved without very large cuts in defense expenditure, in which the "National Defense Function" as a whole for 1989 was estimated at about $295 billion of a total government expenditure of $1,055 billion. Since social welfare programs (not defense) consume up to 75 percent of the total federal budget, cuts in defense threaten votes less directly than cuts in social welfare. Alliance commitments have already been reduced in the case of ANZUS, with a 20 percent reduction over five years in the strength of the Pacific fleet (about fifty ships) being announced in June of 1989, this being "made possible" by Soviet decisions to reduce its Pacific fleet, based in Vladivostock, by fifty-seven surface vessels.[12]

Much larger cuts in the U.S. commitment to the defense of Europe were also a U.S. objective, although they were equally

9. Nicholas Rothwell, *The Australian*, 1 June 1989.
10. Ibid.
11. *The Australian*, 17 April 1989.
12. *The Australian*, 9 June 1989.

dependent on Soviet reductions, more as a matter of "face saving" to the United States than strategic necessity. Given the new nature of the superpower relationships, the initial reductions were agreed with almost embarrassing rapidity and announced in mid February 1990. Under the agreement made between Soviet Foreign Minister Edward Shevardnadze and U.S. Secretary of State James Baker, the USSR would withdraw 380,000 troops from East Germany, Poland, Czechoslavakia, and Hungary, while the United States would withdraw 80,000 from West Germany by 1992. The agreement was to be signed at the superpower summit in Washington, scheduled for June 1990.[13]

Such reductions may be judged a beginning rather than the conclusion, since the United States still retained 225,000 troops in Europe as a whole, and it was a major objective of the 1991 U.S. defense budget to reduce the costs of overseas garrisons by reducing those garrisons, and in that it was estimated at the end of 1988 that each 100,000 demobilization of the U.S. commitment to Europe would save $5.2 billion.[14] In this it was not lost on the administration of George Bush that, at the end of 1988, the United States was still spending 6.8 percent of GDP on defense, while Britain, West Germany, and Denmark were spending 4.9 percent, 3.8 percent, and 2.1 percent respectively.

If further reductions take place, and it is the argument of this paper that they must, then taken together with the possible denuclearization of Europe, NATO must find itself in a period of fundamental change. The latter must not be underestimated as a factor of change, not merely in terms of the overall security of Western Europe but also in that the United States's position as nuclear armorer to Western Europe has allowed it a particular influence in NATO affairs, which will be lost should that eventuate.

The possibility of very large scale U.S. troop withdrawals from Europe relates back to the nuclear issue. Although, as Robert Hunter has observed, U.S. nuclear weapons in Europe "have become a shorthand, a symbol for a broader and deeper US engagement," their use in military crisis is linked to U.S. personnel stationed in Europe.[15] As Hunter further states, "Even if a U.S. President decided to sacrifice [the 305,000 U.S. military personnel

13. *The Australian*, 15 February 1990.
14. *The Australian*, 14 November 1988.
15. Hunter, "Will the United States remain a European Power?," 215.

in Europe] rather than begin using nuclear weapons, their fate would surely have more of an impact on his judgement than would nuclear theory or abstruse notions about using nuclear weapons based in Western Europe before they could be overrun by advancing Warsaw Pact troops."[16] In short, Triple-Zero is something of a red herring. The real guarantee to Europe of U.S. involvement in European war is the stationing of significant numbers of U.S. personnel; their withdrawal would thus pose a significant problem for NATO, always supposing of course that it still desires to retain the link to the U.S. strategic nuclear force. This argument does not require total withdrawal for effect: as U.S. numbers decline, so must presidential concern. A token U.S. presence of say 25,000 might well be sacrificed, where one of 305,000 could not be.

Beyond these factors for change in NATO (the process of European integration, the global withdrawal of the United States and the reduction of the threat from the East), political changes within what used to be the Communist bloc need also to be assessed for their possible impact on NATO, and in the longer run may prove the most dramatic. Glasnost and perestroika do not act merely in terms of reducing the threat to the Western Alliance, but appear to demand complete restructuring in the future.

Thus, if the Eastern European states were in 1989 abandoning communism in favor of multiparty democracy and moving toward free-market economies, then they were ceasing to be enemies and were transforming themselves into natural allies. More dramatically, republics of the Soviet Union itself were seeking escape. The Baltic republics of Lithuania, Latvia, and Estonia demand direct attention by NATO, while, further to the East, disturbances in several republics, from Georgia to Azerbaijan, herald future difficulties for Moscow as great as those experienced by London and Paris in maintaining control of Ireland and of Algeria in decades past. The processes may be summarized as the move back into Europe by those states west of the Urals and a resurgence of nationalist sentiment against Europe, and the reemergence of Islam in particular, by those to the east and southeast of the Urals.

NATO Secretary General Manfred Wörner observed on these changes as early as April 1989 that, "I see a change towards a new order in which the Soviet Union reduces its military power and opens itself up to western ideas and influence. If Gorbachev con-

16. Hunter, "Will the United States remain a European Power?," 215.

tinues to open up the society, to improve the relations, to improve the human rights situation, he may become *a partner*, not only a rival."[17]

Therefore, where NATO is concerned, there is a possible future in which the former enemies of the Alliance become new members and a parallel future in which states such as Poland, Hungary, and those on the Baltic, after an interim period, become members of the EC. This is, of course, simplistic, but it also appears a not improbable future.

In this the position of the two Germanies has resisted speculation but must prove the most problematic for NATO. Once East Germany had determined in November 1989 that "the wall" must be opened, in order to preserve what remained of its fragile economy, then reunification became an inevitability. The difficulty was then to decide the place of the new Germany in the European alliance structure. There were only two options. First that Germany should become neutral, or simply nonaligned, or that Germany should, as a whole, become a member of NATO. The solution favored by the East was not merely that of a neutral Germany, but of a neutral Europe, a concept clearly ahead of its time.[18]

The West German answer was that a unified Germany must remain in NATO, a concept supported by the United States. As a compromise, however, NATO forces would not be positioned east of the former boundary, a solution of equal impracticability to that proposed by the then Communist East, since it was accompanied by the suggestion that even if the new Germany was to be a member of NATO, Soviet troops would continue to occupy the eastern zone for at least ten years.[19] The reunification of Germany, with respect to its position in NATO, represented the greatest challenge faced by the Alliance in its forty-year history; one even exceeding that of the rearmament of Germany, which had led to the creation of the Warsaw Pact.

Radical change of direction by the traditional enemies of NATO, however, still does not necessarily spell the end of the Alliance, since these trends toward the end of all animosities in Europe to the Urals may be balanced by the emergence of new threats from beyond the Urals. Islam is in no sense united, yet it must not be

17. *The Daily Telegraph*, 4 April 1989.
18. *The Australian*, 8 January 1990.
19. *The Australian*, 25 February 1990.

forgotten that in 1945 the Arab nationalism which we now accept as a permanent factor in Middle East politics had not yet emerged. Therefore, one not impossible prospect for NATO in the twenty-first century, if it survives, is that it will incorporate states formerly in the Eastern bloc (and not necessarily excluding Russia itself) and command all that territory of Europe from the Atlantic to the Urals, an achievement that eluded both Napoleon and Adolf Hitler. It is possible that the United States and Canada would be excluded from that new structure, although it could not be their preference to be separated from this new grouping of more than 1,000 million people, with whom they would continue to share a fundamentally convergent culture.

In its editorial on the fortieth anniversary of the formation of NATO, the London *Times* drew attention to the belief among NATO's 600 million voters that the alliance was no longer required. Stated the *Times*: " . . . the familiar picture of Russian armour pouring across the North German plain towards the Rhine now looks like an implausible scenario to many electorates." It noted strains, "misgivings," which were "palpably obvious throughout the alliance," which arose "from the paradox that just as the ideological certainties which underpinned Communist assertion in the post-war years are dissolving, so is the ability of western nations to find a coherent response at a time of rapid change in the international system." However, went on *The Times* (with its usual good sense), "Senior figures who know that a problem exists must stop confusing the re-thinking of NATO with its dismembering . . . . The idea of defending the values which Europe and the United States stand for in 1990s, just as they did in the different world of the 1940s, is well understood by a huge majority. The idea of NATO needs to be reconnected to the ideals of freedom, peace and prosperity."[20]

Certainly those were the concepts for which NATO was created and *in that* nothing has changed, except that its goals had been achieved by 1990. Radical change is required only in more rapid reappraisals of friends and enemies in a rapidly changing international environment, and in those reappraisals there will be new strains for the Alliance and new headlines rumoring dissolution. Nevertheless, the demise of NATO remains improbable, even should no new threat emerge. What may be forecast is a change of

20. *The Times*, 3 April 1989.

name from NATO to NACO, the North Atlantic *Cultural* Organization, for that is what it really is and has always been.

Such change had already been proposed, in concept, early in 1990. Thus, meeting in Washington in February, President Bush and Manfred Wörner discussed the possibility that NATO should "partially shed its role as a military alliance." Rather, NATO would play a political role in "guiding Western policy toward the emerging democracies of Eastern Europe . . . [and] developing Western policy for regional and trans-national issues."[21] In this, as cultural "brothers," the United States and Canada would still have a role and, hence, retain a voice in Europe. To end where I began, "NATO has had about as many crises as birthdays" and in coping with the crises of the past, it has, as an institution, probably learned how to cope with those of the present and of the future.[22] The question then *for the future* is not "will the Alliance survive," but rather "who will be its members and what will be its role?"

21. *The Australian*, 13 February 1990.
22. Hunter, "Will the United States remain a European Power?," 210.

–14–

European Security in the Aftermath of the INF Treaty

JOSEPH CAMILLERI

The astonishing upheaval that swept Eastern Europe in the latter part of 1989 unleashed a powerful dynamic that is not only transforming the political life of these countries, but radically modifying the geopolitical equation established at the end of World War II. The implications for NATO are especially striking, although a fully-fledged public debate on the future of the Atlantic Alliance has yet to emerge. Events in Eastern Europe, however, are only one variable in a complex and increasingly fluid equation. Other factors likely to influence the outcome include the future of perestroika in the Soviet Union, the thaw in Soviet-American relations, and the gradual evolution of the Atlantic partnership. Repeated claims by the United States over the years that it stands by its commitments and that NATO's strategy of flexible response remains unchanged, cannot obscure the far-reaching changes that are under way, or dispel European fears that Moscow and Washington may be tempted to negotiate additional compromises that may not adequately reflect European interests. With German reunification now complete, it is generally agreed that the security system associated with the Cold War division of Europe is rapidly nearing the end of its life. Much less clear is the particular form that a new security system will take, and especially its implications for NATO. It may therefore be useful to begin by developing an analytical framework that can place recent events in their proper historical context.

Joseph Camilleri

The Atlantic Alliance under Stress

The long-standing ambivalence, verging at times on schizophrenia, of NATO allies toward American protection, has been strikingly captured by Jane Sharp's notion of the "abandonment-entrapment cycle."[1] NATO's security dilemma is described as a "cycle of anxiety," comprising eight stages. Any improvement in Soviet-American relations (stage 1), we are told, tends to undermine West European confidence in U.S. guarantees (stage 2), provoking fears that the United States might abandon Europe (stage 3). Allied governments inevitably seek reassurance (stage 4) to which the United States responds with renewed commitments to NATO and a firmer stand against the Soviet Union (stage 5). The ensuing deterioration in Soviet-American relations (stage 6), arouses the fears of NATO allies who, painfully conscious of the consequences of a superpower confrontation fought on European soil (stage 7), find it necessary to press for a return to the politics of moderation and détente (stage 8).

This cyclical pattern has been a distinguishing feature of the NATO alliance since its inception in 1949; yet, the abandonment-entrapment cycle does not fully capture the complex reality of the European security system. To begin with, not all European governments think alike. There are, as Sharp herself acknowledges, significant regional variations in both domestic and external influences arising from historical and geographical differences.[2] Moreover, the perceptions of policymakers are not necessarily reflected in public attitudes, which are seldom monolithic and often subject to considerable fluctuations over time. In any case, the policies of West European governments are only one of a complex set of factors that shapes and sustains the oscillation between cold war and détente. Nor are American objectives and strategies always coherent or internally consistent. American administrations have often conveyed signals that are either contradictory or open to varying interpretations, by both friends and enemies. What, for example, were America's allies to make of the Carter Administration's numerous, and no doubt genuine, arms control initiatives, which

1. Jane M.D. Sharp, "After Reykjavik: Arms Control and the Allies," *International Affairs*, 63, 2 (Spring 1987), 239–57.

2. Jane M.D. Sharp, "NATO's Security Dilemma," *Bulletin of the Atomic Scientists* (hereafter referred to as *BAS*), 43, 2 (March 1987), 44.

nevertheless coincided with a substantial modernization of strategic forces?

Finally, the security dilemma facing NATO allies, central though it is to the policymaking process, cannot be treated in isolation. Many considerations, not least economic ones, are bound to intrude and, at times, exert a decisive influence over both interbloc and intrabloc relations. In interpreting the European security debate, as it has evolved since the INF agreement, this paper makes use of the abandonment-entrapment model but by situating it in the larger and rapidly changing context of domestic and international politics.

The analysis begins with the INF treaty itself, since the withdrawal of intermediate-range missiles has been widely regarded as the early phase of an enduring trend that might see the nuclear, and perhaps conventional, "decoupling" of the United States from Europe. Traditionally, the more extreme versions of this scenario have envisaged a naked Europe, defenseless in the face of Soviet conventional superiority.[3] This view is now hardly credible, given the drastic loosening of the Warsaw Pact structure and the imminent reduction of the Soviet military presence in Eastern Europe. On the other hand, it is worth remembering that not long ago, NATO nuclear planners saw the deployment of Cruise and Pershing II missiles as an indispensable link in NATO's flexible response strategy. As Mary Kaldor has aptly put it, the missiles "were supposed to be the glue that would bring Europe and the United States together again. . . . They were the symbol of Atlantic unity – the vital rung on the ladder of escalation that linked threats to Europe to the U.S. strategic arsenal."[4] Placed in this context, NATO's double-track decision in December 1979 cannot be explained simply as an attempt to ease European fears of abandonment (by promising deployment of Cruise and Pershing II missiles) and preempt new fears of entrapment (by promising new negotiations to restrict this category of intermediate-range nuclear weapons).

The NATO decision was not so much a counter to the deployment of Soviet SS-20s as a logical consequence of the U.S. policy of extended deterrence. It reflected the implicit need to devise strategies that, in the event of war breaking out in Europe, would lessen the risk of automatic U.S. involvement in an all-out nuclear

3. This argument is canvassed in Georges Fricaud-Chignand, "The French Foundation for European Security," *BAS*, 44, 2 (March 1988), 24.

4. Mary Kaldor, "End the Cold War in Europe," *BAS*, 44, 2 (March 1988), 26.

exchange with the Soviet Union, while at the same time leaving the United States the option for controlled escalation of the conflict.

The new European fears of entrapment, fueled by the revival of Cold War rhetoric in the early 1980s and the almost complete breakdown of superpower dialogue on arms control, no doubt played an important part in the U.S. decision to negotiate the reduction of INF missiles. But here again, it is worth drawing a distinction between governments and public opinion, for it is the rising tide of anti-nuclear sentiment that largely conditioned the political debate on nuclear issues.[5] NATO policies, including the "zero option," were in part a response, however grudging or hesitant, to events they had not fully anticipated. Even Reagan's announcement of the Strategic Defense Initiative in March 1983, though it greatly complicated the arms control process and added fuel to the fire of anti-nuclear protest, may be understood as a reaction to the declining legitimacy of nuclear deterrence. It was in part an attempt to salvage something of the wreckage of American nuclear policy by demoting the priority hitherto assigned to deterrence and extolling the virtues of strategic defense.

No survey of the fortunes of INF negotiations would be complete without careful scrutiny of the Soviet role. A string of Soviet concessions, particularly during the Gorbachev years, was perhaps the critical factor that sustained the momentum that eventually paved the way for agreement. In November 1981 the Soviet Union refused to negotiate unless NATO renounced its plans for missile deployments, and in November 1983 withdrew from the Geneva talks. But by March 1985, having returned to the negotiating table, it embarked on a conciliatory strategy that stole the initiative from the United States. It offered to reduce SS-20 deployments, agreed to the exclusion of British and French nuclear forces from the INF treaty, and allowed the INF negotiations to proceed without direct linkage with strategic offensive and space weapon systems. In due course, it would accept the global elimination of longer-range INF missiles and, in a radical departure from previously stated policy, consent to intrusive on-site inspection. The combined effect of these concessions was to put a radically new complexion on the arms

5. See F. Barnaby, "Europe Aroused," *BAS*, 38, 2 (February 1982), 8–9; N. Mott, "European Opinion and NATO Policy," *BAS*, 38, 6 (June 1982), 4–5; K. Salomon, "The Peace Movement: An Anti-Establishment Movement," *Journal of Peace Research*, 23, 2 (1986); Nigel Young, "The Peace Movement: A Comparative and Analytical Survey," *Alternatives*, 11, 2 (April 1986), 185–218.

control agenda and significantly enhance the prospects of reducing Soviet and American strategic arsenals, as well as conventional forces, in Europe.

Several closely related questions had now become central to the European security debate: Would nuclear weapons continue to feature as prominently in NATO strategy? Was modernization of NATO's nuclear forces likely to unite or divide the Alliance? What would be an appropriate balance of conventional forces in Europe? What were the necessary conditions for a less divisive and more stable European security framework, particularly in light of the gradual decoupling of Eastern Europe from the Soviet Union? To what extent did movement in this direction presuppose structural changes in the relationship between the United States and Western Europe?[6] NATO's two-track decision had made it seem as if two diametrically opposed policies, disarmament and military build-up, could co-exist. The Reykjavik summit and INF agreement helped to dispel that illusion and, in the process, set the stage for a more sharply focused reassessment of European security.

The dismantling of the Euromissiles is but the first dramatic manifestation of several trends – some more recent than others – the net effect of which is to call into question the long-term viability of European dependence on the American nuclear umbrella. For, as Pierre Lellouche has rightly observed, the INF agreement has introduced a new phase in the "systematic crisis underlying the doctrine of flexible response."[7] True enough, Europe did manage to survive the ambiguities, not to say contradictions, inherent in the NATO doctrine without the benefit of Euromissiles for more than twelve years, but the decision to deploy them in 1979 was very much an attempt to lessen the effect of these ambiguities; in a word, to paper over the cracks.

The subsequent decision to dismantle them could not but reactivate those tensions, for the INF agreement was in part a symbol of Europe's diminishing role in American global strategy and diplomacy. It was also an indication that the Soviet Union has achieved strategic parity with the United States, which might help to explain the latter's newly found interest in denuclearization. It would be a gross overstatement to suggest that the INF accord had paved the

6. Several, though not all, of these questions are raised by Lewis H. Dunn, "Considerations after the INF Treaty," *Survival*, 30, 3 (May/June 1988), 195–209.

7. Pierre Lellouche, "L'après-Washington," *Politique étrangère*, 53, 1 (Spring 1988), 155.

way for an abrogation of the American nuclear guarantee. On the other hand, it is a fact that the United States has for many years pressed Western Europe to shoulder a bigger share of the defense burden. The possible reduction of American forces (nuclear and conventional) on European soil may be a calculated bid to achieve this seemingly elusive objective.

The European Pillar

The European continent is experiencing a period of considerable ferment, which may best be described as the tension between two competing yet intricately interwoven options. The first – close to the outlook of the recent past – envisages a prosperous Western Europe that remains firmly integrated within the Atlantic Alliance, obliged to keep a watchful eye on Soviet intentions and capabilities, reconciled to the continuing division of Europe, and ultimately dependent for its security on the U.S. nuclear umbrella. The second option is premised on the vision of a united, prosperous, culturally resurgent Western Europe, able to build bridges with Eastern Europe, break down the divisions of the Cold War, and substantially erode the rationale for militarization and the superpower military presence in Europe. Much of present-day European politics may be understood as the attempted transition from the first to the second option.

The possibility of bridging these two seemingly incompatible scenarios has provoked increasing interest in a European security community; an idea with a long history but one that has gained considerable currency in the last few years. The Franco-British Dunkirk Treaty of 1947 and the Brussels Treaty of 1948, which later formed the basis for the West European Union (WEU), were the first expressions of the desire for a common system of defense. But the onset of the Cold War, the formation of NATO, and national rivalries and suspicions frustrated intermittent efforts to develop a European defense identity. The concept has regained impetus partly as a result of progress made in economic and, to a lesser extent, political integration. With the current emphasis on removing trade barriers and establishing a single currency by 1992, attention is focusing more sharply on the international implications of European unification. Until now, one of the main difficulties has been to find an appropriate forum for such a project. Out of the plethora of existing institutions, which is the most likely to promote the desired level of cooperation? In the last few years, the inclination of West European governments has been to opt for a multifaceted, institutional framework that combines bilateral and multilateral approaches.

An interesting initiative has been the decision of the seven member states of the WEU to revive what had become a moribund organization.[8] The Platform on European Security Interests adopted by the WEU in October 1987 emphasized the need for a collective system of West European defense, specifically commended the contribution of British and French nuclear forces, and called for coordinated policies to deal with security interests outside Europe. The decision to send Dutch, Italian, and Belgian minesweepers to the Persian Gulf and West German ships to the Mediterranean was the first concrete manifestation of the desire to create a West European bloc or "pillar." But the latter term is itself an indication of the ambiguity of the concept. For as the WEU Platform itself stated, "Western European security cannot be assured without close links with our North American allies. The security of the Alliance is indivisible. . . . The presence of quantitatively significant US conventional and nuclear forces plays an irreplaceable role in the defense of Europe." Here European security is conceived very much in the context of a continuing trans-Atlantic arrangement premised on the perception of a sizable Soviet threat.

At the bilateral level, the emphasis has been on Franco-German and Franco-British cooperation, although Anglo-German dialogue has also gathered momentum. The British and French saw their nuclear deterrents – a view shared by some other European governments – as a backstop should the United States fail to use its own nuclear forces on Europe's behalf. These deterrents could be used either in their own right or as a trigger for the much larger U.S. arsenal. Either way, they could serve European, rather than just British or French, interests. Here, one detects a striking shift in French nuclear policy. Whereas in the Gaullist period attention was directed almost exclusively on French territory, there is now much greater stress on European solidarity, and on providing a security shield for Germany. For Bonn, the independent European deterrents serve a useful function in Europe, but their usefulness would

8. See Phil Williams, "West European Security and American Troop Withdrawals," *The Political Quarterly*, 59, 3 (July–Sept. 1988), 329.

be greatly enhanced if they assumed a more genuinely European character.

The French approach, particularly since the Reykjavik Summit, has been to canvass prospects for expanded bilateral defense cooperation with several NATO countries, including Spain and Italy, as well as Britain and Germany. The aim is to demonstrate France's European credentials but also to establish France as the center in the wheel of European security. Paradoxically, President Mitterrand had several years earlier endorsed the installation of Cruise and Pershing II missiles in Europe.[9] The influential speech he made in the Bundestag in January 1983 in support of missile deployment was a calculated move designed to convey to France's European partners a renewed interest in European defense. It was also intended to signal French readiness to pursue that objective through closer coordination with NATO's strategic planning.

Although formally remaining outside the NATO integrated military structure, France was now willing to take part in combined military exercises (e.g., Crested Eagle) in order to improve operational coordination and reciprocal understanding of strategic and tactical priorities, ensure that the movement of French forces dovetailed with NATO plans, and above all communicate both at home and abroad its intention to play an active and integral part in European collective defense.[10] The same policy orientation explains the decision taken in October 1982 to create a new structure of political and military cooperation with the Federal Republic. The same objective also accounts for the muted endorsement of the INF agreement. Describing it as a positive development, Mitterrand saw little cause for "euphoria" and stressed instead the "real danger" of decoupling American and European security. The INF accord provided France with the opportunity to reaffirm the "political" guarantee it had extended to West Germany for the immediate and unconditional support of its security in the event of conflict.[11] The intended message was that France was ready to give European

9. For a detailed, semi-official exposition of France's role in the INF debate, see Bruno Racine, "La France et les FNI," *Politique étrangère*, 53, 1 (Spring 1988), especially 81–84, 86–87.

10. David S. Yost, "La co-opération franco-allemande en matière de défense," *Politique étrangère*, 53, 4 (Winter 1988), 845.

11. See Jacques Chirac's speech to the Institut des hautes études de défense nationale (12 December 1987), "La France et les enjeux de la sécurité européenne," *Défense Nationale* (February 1988), 16.

interests a higher priority in the formulation of French nuclear doctrine.[12]

Despite regular exercises, the creation of a joint defense council, and attempts to forge a common arms procurement policy, there remain serious limitations to the prospects for Franco-German collaboration. To begin with, it is as yet unclear how far France is prepared to go in reactivating its participation in NATO's military planning. Second, it remains to be seen whether the joint initiatives taken so far are primarily political gestures or likely to produce a significant degree of collaboration in conventional defense. Third, it is by no means certain that France is prepared to allow Germany to have its finger in the French nuclear pie. Nor is it clear what processes of consultation and interaction would permit Germany to have a say in an independent European defense system without at the same time provoking the fears and suspicions of other European powers, including the Soviet Union. A privileged arrangement with Germany calls into question France's relations with its other European partners. German reunification will no doubt influence France's long-term strategic assessment and will, at least for the foreseeable future, be the decisive consideration affecting the pace and content of military cooperation between the two countries.

The results of Franco-British discussions have, if anything, been more modest. Agreements have been reached on the use of French ports and highways during maneuvers and use of British ports by French submarines. France has put forward two proposals: joint development of an air-launched nuclear weapon and a program to coordinate targeting of British and French nuclear forces. While accepting the former proposals, Britain has rejected the latter. In responding to French overtures, Britain has kept the door of defense cooperation open, partly as a way of enticing France back into the NATO fold, but has been careful not to open it so widely as to undermine NATO's overriding role in West European security. The underlying British concern appears to be not to do anything that may encourage the United States to scale down its commitments to Europe or reassess the value of the Anglo-American relationship. Britain does not fully share the French and German view, which sees the creation of a second pillar within the Alliance

12. Helmut Sonnenfeldt, "The European Pillar: The American View" in *The Changing Strategic Landscape: Part 1*, Adelphi Papers, 235 (Spring 1989), 99–100.

as an effective contribution to the collective defense burden.[13] There are, however, indications that a united and powerful Germany, and a reduced American military presence in Europe, may prompt a substantial rethinking of British attitudes and policies.

The attempt, then, to construct a European pillar within NATO as the basis of a more independent European security system, is riddled with uncertainty and not a little confusion. In the first place, the leading West European states are far from agreed as to the meaning and content of the European pillar, the importance they should attach to it, or the means by which they might achieve it. The differences become even more striking when account is taken of the preferences of the smaller NATO countries, many of which (e.g., Spain, Greece, Netherlands, Denmark) have become increasingly ambivalent about NATO policies. Several of them have unilaterally abandoned NATO nuclear "tasks" and in varying degrees adopted an anti-nuclear stance, which may have implications as much for a European nuclear deterrent as for NATO's current nuclear doctrines and policies.

To put it more bluntly but no less accurately, the critical but unresolved question is the relationship between a "stronger European pillar" and the United States, particularly at a time when the Soviet threat to Western Europe has lost whatever credibility it may once have had. An alliance based on the twin-pillar concept is by definition one in which the United States can no longer exercise decisive control over Alliance policy. Clearly, the American wish is for the construction of a European pillar that strengthens rather than weakens NATO. Is this, however, a realistic expectation? Has not the idea of a European pillar been conceived specifically as a response to tensions within the Alliance and the perception of America's declining capacity to satisfy European security needs? Is not progress toward the implementation of that idea likely to reinforce and hasten that trend? The relationship between European defense cooperation and American policy is both subtle and complex, and will increasingly be influenced by changing attitudes to the Soviet Union on the one hand and by a reunited Germany on the other.

13. The British security perspective is analyzed at greater length in Stuart Croft, *The Impact of Strategic Defences on European-American Relations in the 1990s*, Adelphi Papers, 239 (Spring 1989), 56.

The Gorbachev Factor

The changing direction of Soviet domestic and external policies during the last few years has had a profound impact on European opinion and cast a long shadow over NATO's strategic thinking. For the "Gorbachev revolution" compounds the already difficult task confronting the Atlantic Alliance: namely, how to redefine NATO's strategic posture and at the same time maintain the widest possible political consensus. That task was immeasurably easier during the Brezhnev years when the Soviet military build-up and the heavy-handed attempt to expand Soviet influence reinforced and legitimated the West's deterrence strategy. Under Gorbachev, NATO faces the prospect of maintaining and modernizing its armed forces at a time when the Soviet leadership has renounced the military ambitions of the past and embarked upon a radical program of economic political change.

How to respond to the Gorbachev challenge has become a difficult and divisive question for NATO. On the one hand, there are substantial elements of West European society that are attracted by Gorbachev's vision of a "common European home" that does away with the enmities of the past, respects the security of all its members, and moves rapidly toward denuclearization. On the other hand, there are those who remain suspicious of Soviet motives or at least argue that the changes introduced by Gorbachev are not assured of success and may simply serve to lull Europeans into a false sense of security. Significantly, official and semi-official responses in Western Europe have now virtually discarded the second interpretation in favor of a more pragmatic approach, which recognizes that the Soviet system is undergoing profound change, that everything possible should be done to encourage it or at least nothing done to frustrate it, and that patient and continuing dialogue with the Soviet Union offers a genuine opportunity for a more stable European and global security system.[14]

What, then, are the practical implications for NATO of Gorbachev's new broom? To explore this question more fully, it is first necessary to review briefly the main elements that constitute the shift in Soviet defense thinking. The long-term vision is of the

14. This is very much the tenor of the recommendations contained in *How Should America Respond to Gorbachev's Challenge?*, A Report of the Task Force on Soviet New Thinking, New York, 1987.

dissolution of the two opposing security systems and their replacement by a new system based on the principle of common security and cooperation between the Soviet Union, Western Europe, Eastern Europe, and the United States. This proposed framework implies the complete elimination of nuclear weapons from European soil, a substantial reduction in conventional forces, and most importantly, the restructuring of armed forces around the principle of non-offensive defense.[15] Leaving aside for the moment the details of the Soviet proposals, the overall thrust of the "new thinking" is to acknowledge that the ever-increasing accumulation of military power is no longer useful, and that the size, structure, and mode of deployment of Soviet conventional forces in Europe are a source of legitimate apprehension on NATO's part. The underlying premise is that in formulating its military doctrines and deploying its forces, each side must first consider its probable impact on the other's perceptions.[16] The attempt to establish a dividing line between an offensive and defensive posture is meant to address this need.

Offensive weapons are said to include tactical strike aircraft, combat helicopters, tactical missiles, search and destroy complements, long-range artillery, and salvo systems. The point about these weapons is that they are particularly well-suited to seizing and holding terrain and inflicting a series of lightning blows on the enemy. The Soviet argument is that priority must be given to reducing this type of armament precisely because it contributes to a climate of suspicion and mistrust and is therefore unusually destabilizing. But over and above the reduction of forces, the "new thinking" envisages changes in military doctrine resulting in the restructuring of forces so as to preclude the possibility of surprise attack by either side.[17] This concept, derived largely from West European research on disarmament and arms control, is premised on the long-term elimination of either side's capacity to mount offensive operations.

As far as nuclear weapons are concerned, the overriding idea is that of nuclear sufficiency, which argues that the build-up of nuclear

15. See Youri Davydov, "L'option double zéro et le sort de l'Europe," *Politique étrangère*, 53, 1 (Spring 1988), 75.

16. The radical implications of this conceptual shift in Soviet defense policy are explored more fully in Seweryn Bialer, "'New Thinking' and Soviet Foreign Policy," *Survival*, 30, 4 (July/August 1988), 291–309.

17. See Edward L. Warner III, "New Thinking and Old Realities in Soviet Defence Policy," *Survival*, 31, 1 (January–February 1989), 22.

forces beyond mutual assured destruction is dangerous and unnecessary and that substantial reductions will ease tensions, lessen the risk of war, and increase mutual security. In line with this general principle, the Soviet Union advocates deep cuts in offensive strategic arms as long as the existing superpower equilibrium is maintained. Although the arsenals of the two sides need not be identical in structure and composition, the capabilities available to each should be roughly equal at each stage of the reduction process. As might be expected, Moscow has tied the twin principles of nuclear sufficiency and nonoffensive defense to the renunciation of space-based weapon systems on the grounds that they undermine strategic stability and are likely to encourage an arms race in both offensive and defensive weapons.[18]

The shift in Soviet defense has until recently suffered from a considerable drawback, namely, the widely shared Western perception that the Soviet Union currently enjoys a sizeable margin of superiority in the conventional balance of forces. To enhance the credibility of the new "defensive" doctrine, Gorbachev therefore opted for unilateral Soviet reductions. In his speech to the United Nations General Assembly on 7 December 1988, he announced plans to reduce Soviet forces stationed in Eastern Europe by withdrawing over the next two years 6 tank divisions, 5,000 tanks, and 50,000 personnel. He also pledged to cut the overall strength of Soviet armed forces by 500,000 and to reduce Soviet forces West of the Urals by 10,000 tanks, 8,500 artillery systems, and 800 combat aircraft.[19] As with previous announcements, Gorbachev's aim was to demonstrate the sincerity of Soviet intentions and maintain the momentum of arms control negotiations. More particularly, he was out to disarm Western critics by depriving them of the argument that the Soviet Union favored denuclearization while jealously guarding its superiority in conventional weapons.

Moscow's psychological advantage was in part offset by the dramatic shift of political fortunes inside Eastern Europe, in particular the loss of the monopoly of political power once enjoyed by communist parties. The radical reorganization of the parties and the purge of hardliners from their ranks, the breaching of the Berlin Wall and the mass exodus of East Germans, the overthrow of the

18. For an official post-INF exposition of the Soviet view, see Dimitri Yazov, "The Soviet Proposal for European Security," *BAS*, 44, 7 (September 1988), 8–11.

19. *New York Times*, 8 December 1988, A16.

Ceaucescu régime, various forms of power sharing, and the associated introduction of multi-party systems in Poland, Hungary, and East Germany, all pointed to the virtual dissolution of the Warsaw Pact. For its part, the Soviet Union responded by acknowledging the new realities and condemning the 1968 invasion of Czechoslovakia as "interference in the internal affairs of a sovereign country," thereby renouncing the Brezhnev doctrine of limited sovereignty.[20]

Domestic ferment had significantly eroded the legitimacy of the Soviet military presence in Eastern Europe. Rapidly democratizing governments in Hungary, Poland, and Czechoslovakia were now pressing the Soviet Union to withdraw its troops from their territory. In varying degrees, all three were calling for an accelerated timetable for withdrawal. The Soviet proposal to recall all its troops from Eastern Europe within five years if the United States and other NATO countries followed suit in Western Europe, was above all an attempt to disguise Soviet military weakness and extract diplomatic advantage from what was rapidly becoming a *fait accompli.*

The United States, which had hitherto been reluctant to match Soviet proposals, now took the initiative. But even before the tumultuous events of late 1989, the perception of Soviet weakness became an influential factor in the Bush Administration's handling of East-West diplomacy. On 29 May 1989, the U.S. president proposed that the timetable for negotiations on conventional force reductions in Europe be reduced from two years (as suggested by Moscow) to six to twelve months, that American and Soviet troops stationed in Europe be cut to 275,000 on each side (this compared with an existing U.S. military force in Europe of about 300,000 troops, compared with some 500,000 troops for the Soviet Union), and the number of combat aircraft and helicopters on both sides be reduced to 15 percent below current NATO levels.[21] By the end of the year, however, President Bush was arguing for much more drastic cuts.

At a meeting of NATO allies in December 1989, he advocated a policy of "deterrence at the lowest possible level of forces."[22] According to unofficial reports, the United States might be willing to reduce its presence by two-thirds, provided that the Soviet Union withdrew the bulk of its forces from Eastern Europe. Further

20. *Washington Post*, 6 December 1989.
21. *Washington Post*, 30 May 1989, 1.
22. *The Age* (Melbourne), 6 December 1989, 6.

evidence of U.S. intentions came with President Bush's State of the Union address in which he proposed that troop levels on each side be reduced to 195,000 and argued for a swift conclusion to arms control negotiations in the conventional, chemical, and strategic fields.[23] These initiatives came on the heels of the Administration's proposed budget, which envisaged the closure of twelve overseas bases (including air bases in Italy, Greece, Turkey, Britain and West Germany) and sixty-six domestic installations.

The drift in U.S. defense priorities may have reflected the perception of declining Soviet diplomatic and military leverage. Perhaps equally important was the economic imperative – the need to reduce America's chronic budget deficit. The substantial cuts in hardware as well as military and civilian personnel contemplated by Defense Secretary Dick Cheney were dependent on a reorganization of the East-West military balance in Europe. One may therefore reasonably assume that the moral and financial support for democracy and self-determination in Eastern Europe was not motivated by purely altruistic considerations. The United States had a considerable stake in Eastern European economic and political reform precisely because such reform offset the effectiveness of Soviet diplomacy in Western Europe and deprived the Soviet Union of the advantage it may otherwise have gained from the economically motivated U.S. military withdrawal from Western Europe. Not to be outdone, Moscow put forward in January 1990 a new proposal calling for an international agreement under which the Soviet Union would withdraw all its troops from Eastern Europe within five years if all U.S. and allied foreign troops were removed from Western Europe during the same period. Through this formula the Soviet leadership sought to combine necessity and opportunity in the hope of containing Eastern European pressure for unilateral troop withdrawals, while at the same time injecting a new variable into the equation of German reunification. The decline in Moscow's bargaining position, however, meant that at least in the short term it had little option but to accept the Bush proposal.

There was in any case an important economic dimension to Soviet defense policy. Gorbachev understood that the transfer of resources from the military to the civilian sector of the economy might in itself be a useful contribution to national security. Yet such transfer was unlikely without the easing of international tensions, hence the

23. *The Age* (Melbourne), 2 February 1990, 8.

importance of arms control negotiations and a more stable political climate. The possibility of expanded economic contacts with the West, particularly in the context of the Soviet Union's stagnating economy, was an additional incentive motivating Gorbachev's reconceptualization of national security. The new flexibility he had introduced in Soviet diplomacy and his readiness to take account of West European interests and anxieties reflected Moscow's desire to treat Western Europe as an independent actor in world politics rather than "a mere satellite of the United States."[24] The wish to exploit differences within the Atlantic Alliance was no doubt a relevant consideration, but so was the recognition of Western Europe's emerging identity and newly found economic muscle.

The net effect, then, of the Gorbachev revolution was to sharpen the dilemmas facing NATO as it tried to redefine its strategic posture. What compounded the problem was that Gorbachev had introduced into Soviet diplomacy a blend of common sense pragmatism and visionary thinking that captured the European imagination. By the same token, he had grounded his proposals and initiatives on a hardheaded assessment of Soviet interests, which probably meant that in its essentials his approach was here to stay. The political disintegration of the Warsaw Pact, coupled with the internal tensions besetting the Soviet Union, may have emboldened the United States to think that it could reap the benefits of the new détente "with little effort and essentially at no cost."[25] There was little reason, however, to believe that Soviet leaders would accept the American interpretation of events, meekly adjust to a diminished status in world politics, or agree to redrawing the European political map in ways deemed prejudicial to Soviet interests. The revolt against Communist rule in Eastern Europe had blunted but not altogether undermined the cutting edge of Soviet diplomacy.

West Germany: The European Melting Pot

Nowhere have the ambiguities of NATO policy and the periodic fluctuations between cold war and détente been more keenly felt than in Germany. The relative decline in America's global ascend-

24. See Jonathan Haslam, "Soviets Take Fresh Look at Western Europe," *BAS*, 44, 4 (May 1988), 38–42.
25. Coit D. Blacker, "The New United States – Soviet Détente," *Current History*, 88, 540 (October 1989), 323.

ancy and the dissolution of the Soviet empire in Eastern Europe, coupled with the rise of anti-nuclear sentiment at home and rapidly changing perceptions of the Soviet threat, have combined to shatter the security consensus that had prevailed in the 1950s and 1960s.[26] A major debate on foreign and defense policy has ensued, particularly in the wake of the INF agreement, with both old and new protagonists in the political arena groping for a new approach, a new *Gesamtkonzept* that might make sense of the radically altered domestic and external environment.[27]

The question that initially gained most prominence was the future of short-range tactical or battlefield nuclear weapons. The NATO summit meeting in March 1987 endeavored to sidestep the issue by omitting in its communiqué any explicit mention of modernization. It merely made reference to "an appropriate mix of adequate and effective nuclear and conventional forces which will continue to be kept up to date where necessary."[28] The vagueness of this language and the confusion as to the proposed timetable for negotiations reflected the unresolved conflict between the exigencies of West German domestic politics and the reluctance of other core NATO states to advance too far down the road of denuclearization. The line of argument used by the proponents of modernization is familiar enough and brings us back directly to the doctrine of flexible response. To offset growing doubts about American strategic assurances it is necessary to deploy theater nuclear weapons in Europe in order "to couple European security with American strategic weapons."[29] According to this view, both longer-range and shorter-range nuclear weapons are needed for this purpose. The need for modernization is all the greater as the most capable longer-range weapons are now banned by the INF treaty.

For all its technical sophistication, the case for modernization soon runs into considerable difficulty. The psychological obstacles were especially difficult to surmount at a time when the Soviet Union appeared ready to negotiate deep cuts in strategic forces, soften its stand on strategic defense, and adopt a nonoffensive

26. The report, *Discriminate Difference*, Washington (January 1988), (commissioned by the Office of the U.S. Secretary of Defense) appears to have had a particularly jarring effect on West German opinion.

27. See Ronald D. Asmus, "West Germany Faces Nuclear Modernization," *Survival*, 30, 6 (November/December 1988), especially 499–505.

28. NATO Press Service, Press Communiqué, M-1 (1988), 13, 2.

29. Hans Binnendij, "NATO's Nuclear Modernization Dilemma," *BAS*, 31, 2 (March–April 1989), 139.

posture in conventional defense. This combination of factors helped to engender "a new German anti-nuclear consensus."[30] Chancellor Kohl made it clear to NATO allies that no West German government could survive a decision to replace the existing Lance missiles with a new system either of greater capability or increased numbers. The compromise to postpone a decision until 1992 gave the different parties breathing space and ensured that the West German federal election would be safely out of the way before a decision was finally made. But it did not solve the fundamental problem underlying the policy of extended deterrence.

Here the evolution in the thinking of the German Right was especially significant. The increasingly prevalent view in the wake of Reykjavik and the INF treaty was that any remaining nuclear weapons on West German soil were likely to make the Federal Republic vulnerable to Soviet superiority in short-range systems, while not sufficiently enhancing the probability of American intervention. As far as the Christian Democratic Union – Christian Social Union (CDU-CSU) coalition was concerned, two strands of thought, which Clemens has labeled "arms-controllers" and "Gaullists," appeared to gain the ascendancy over the "Atlanticists."[31] Although starting from different premises, "arms-controllers" and "Gaullists" both came to the conclusion that over-reliance on the United States was not desirable. For the former, an undue obsession with nuclear weapons would provoke electoral backlash and jeopardize arms control and *Ostpolitik*; for the latter, nuclear modernization promised to make West Germany more, not less, vulnerable. The position of the Atlanticists was further weakened by the unforeseen speed of political change inside the Warsaw Pact countries. Modernization no longer made sense as short-range missiles were targeted against Poland, Hungary, and East Germany, all three at various stages of abandoning communism, introducing a multiparty system, and expanding the role of the market in their respective economies.

The shifting balance of political forces inside East Germany had a quick and profound effect on West Germany. After a brief period of relative indecision, Chancellor Kohl outlined on 28 November 1989 a ten-point plan for German reunification. He envisaged three

30. Thomas Risse-Kappen, "Old German Consensus against New Missiles," *BAS*, 44, 4 (May 1988), 14.

31. Clay Clemens, "Beyond INF: West Germany's Centre-Right Party and Arms Control in the 1990s," *International Affairs*, 65, 1 (Winter 1988/89), 62–64.

broad stages beginning with limited forms of cooperation conditional on constitutional and electoral reform in East Germany, progressing to the establishment of a "confederal structure" and eventually culminating in a fully-fledged federal system.[32] To allay Soviet and European anxieties, Kohl coupled his proposals with support for accelerated agreement on East-West nuclear and conventional disarmament and a reaffirmation of Bonn's commitment to NATO and the European Community.

The East German reaction to the plan was at best ambiguous, which is not surprising given the volatility of the domestic political situation. At first formal reunification was rejected in favor of a looser confederal arrangement. Placing more emphasis on the need to demilitarize central Europe, East Germany proposed that West and East German forces be halved by 1991. Following a visit to Moscow, East German Prime Minister, Hans Modrow, put forward a four-step proposal for a neutral Germany that would eventually enjoy a single constitution and a single government.[33]

The speed with which the reunification concept was unfolding indicated the fluidity of East German politics and also the readiness of both superpowers to entertain the prospect of a united Germany, as long as it was achieved gradually and peacefully. For the United States, the incorporation of a single German state into the Western alliance system was highly welcome, for it promised to entrench American strategic dominance in Europe while at the same time limiting the resurgence of German military power at the expense of other Western allies. To make such an outcome a little more palatable to Soviet leaders, U.S. Secretary of State James Baker raised the prospect of NATO acquiring a more political role by becoming a vehicle for greater economic and diplomatic cooperation with the East and assuming new responsibilities for the verification of disarmament agreements and the resolution of conflicts outside Europe.

For the Soviet Union, a reunified Germany held much less attraction, hence its initial rejection of Kohl's ten-point plan and its insistence that East Germany should remain a distinct and separate state. By the end of January 1990, however, Gorbachev was ready to support the principle of German reunification, while still emphasizing the responsibilities of the four allied powers. Moscow was

32. *The Economist*, 2 December 1989, 60–61.
33. *Los Angeles Times*, 2 February 1990.

now ready to contemplate the process of reunification as long as this did not mean the incorporation of East Germany into NATO. The reformulation of the Soviet position had been carefully crafted to ease domestic pressure on East German leaders, while at the same time playing on British and French apprehension at the prospect of a united Germany holding economic and political sway over much of Europe.[34] Whether German unity could be achieved in a way that reconciled the interests of the two Germanies, the four allied powers, and other European states was open to question. By the same token, though none of the numerous blueprints under consideration was likely to satisfy all relevant parties, the imminent possibility of a German union gave a powerful impetus to the reconceptualization of European security.

Options and Prospects: A Concluding Comment

The foregoing analysis has highlighted several trends, none of which, viewed in isolation, is likely to shift the direction of NATO's strategic outlook. But taken collectively, they may well create the necessary climate for a reassessment of past policies and future options. The first trend, still very much in its infancy, refers to the declining American political and military presence in Europe. Mounting pressure on the U.S. defense budget, growing demands on U.S. military capabilities in the Third World, popular and congressional disenchantment with Europe's apparent refusal to carry a greater share of the defense burden, increasing economic strains with the European commitment, political ferment in Eastern Europe, and a continuing thaw in Soviet-American relations – all these factors are gradually fusing in the minds of America's foreign policy establishment to de-emphasize Europe's role in U.S. military planning and resource allocation.[35]

The second trend relates to the domestic political process in both Western and Eastern Europe, to the changing public mood on military alliances and security issues, the general reluctance to invest

34. European fears arising from the combined effect of a newly powerful Germany and a decaying Soviet empire are graphically encapsulated by R.W. Johnson, "Memories of the Future," *New Statesman & Society*, 5 January 1990, 9–11.

35. These pressures are the subject of careful review in Jeffrey Record and David B. Ravkin Jr., "Defending Post-INF Europe," *Foreign Affairs*, 66, 4 (Spring 1988), 741–43.

greater resources in defense, and more particularly, the desire to reduce current dependence on nuclear weapons. It is clear that budgetary constraints on defense spending will continue to apply in nearly all countries, including France, which has committed extensive resources to the modernization of its nuclear forces. Demographic pressure in most parts of Europe may also severely limit the size of armed forces. The trend is particularly striking in Germany where the *Bundeswehr* is expected to shrink by as much as 10 to 20 percent over the next decade, even without taking into account the restrictions that might flow from an agreement on German reunification.

A third and closely related trend is the appreciable shift in European perceptions of the Soviet threat. Such references as "overwhelming Soviet superiority" and the "gap continues to widen," often used in the past to describe the conventional balance of forces, no longer have much hold over the public imagination. A more critical appraisal of NATO and Warsaw Pact forces has been current for some time in academic and other writings, suggesting that neither side can seriously contemplate attacking the other.[36] This reappraisal of the evidence, coupled with the Gorbachev factor and recent events in Eastern Europe, has put a new complexion on the security dialogue with the Soviet Union.

The three preceding trends have set the stage for a fourth, which may best be described as the reawakening of the previously dormant arms control process. Negotiated reductions in conventional and nuclear arms are now widely perceived to be feasible and desirable in their own right, and also as laying the foundations for a more solid and durable security framework encompassing the whole of Europe.

There remains, however, a fifth somewhat more ambiguous trend, pointing toward the construction of a West European defense community. The ambiguity reflects the ambivalence with which the core European states now view both superpowers and each other. Will a European pillar act as an integral part of NATO and reflect American interests in Europe, or will it serve primarily as an instrument for the assertion of European interests and independence? The same question, cast in slightly different form, can be

36. See, for example, Barry M. Posen, "Measuring the European Conventional Balance: Coping with Complexity in Threat Assessment," *International Security*, 9, 3 (Winter 1985–6), 47–88; John J. Mearsheimer, "Why the Soviets Can't Win Quickly in Western Europe," *International Security*, 9, 1 (Summer 1982), 3–29.

applied to the Soviet Union. Will a West European defense force focus primarily on the Soviet threat, or will it be a vehicle for redefining the East-West security relationship? These remain unanswered questions, as does the extent to which national differences, and the uncertainty surrounding the status of a united Germany, will allow a West European defense identity to emerge in the foreseeable future.

For the next several years, the most promising route would seem to be that of multilateral negotiations. Perhaps one of the most significant, though unexpected, consequences of the Reykjavik summit is the impetus it has given to conventional arms reductions. By raising the prospect of deep cuts in strategic and other nuclear systems, the summit has inevitably turned the spotlight on conventional forces, since these are an integral part of the central balance. The realignment of political forces within the Warsaw Pact countries and the debate about the future of Germany have given added impetus to the prospects for conventional disarmament.

Recent public statements from both sides have stressed the need to establish a secure and stable balance, preferably at the lowest possible level.[37] All of this is not to say that dialogue will be easy or that the numerous technical problems associated with existing asymmetries will not in the end prove insurmountable.[38] Here there may be merit in closely considering one aspect of the Jaruzelski plan first presented in May 1987, which conceives of disarmament and arms control as a complex package rather than a series of discrete negotiating propositions.[39] The plan recognizes that all key elements of the arms control agenda – nuclear, conventional, doctrinal, confidence-building – are equally important and logically connected to one another, but avoids the trap of making progress in one area dependent on progress in another. To do otherwise might well jeopardize progress in all areas.

Two other ideas, to which only passing reference has so far been made, may also facilitate the negotiating process. The first is the notion of "defensive," or "non-offensive" or "non-provocative"

37. See NATO statement, "Conventional Arms Control: The Way Ahead," 2–3 March 1988; "Soviet Offers to Adjust Imbalance of Conventional Forces in Europe," *New York Times*, 24 June 1988, A1–2.

38. For an informed, but moderately pessimistic outlook, see Robert D. Blackwill, "Conventional Stability Talks," *Survival*, 30, 5 (September/October 1988), 429–47.

39. The implications of the plan are examined by Andrzej Karkoszka, "Merits of the Jaruzelski Plan," *BAS*, 44, 7 (September 1988), 32–34.

defense – not a new idea in itself, but one whose application to the European theater has recently aroused a good deal of public and academic interest.[40] Afheldt describes non-offensive defense as "refraining from large-scale offensives and thus from mass transportation of soldiers, weapons and ammunition, and rations over great distances. It means fighting from prepared defensive positions instead of moving to meet the enemy. And it decreases the emphasis on centralized command-and-control capabilities."[41] While different writers give different emphasis to the role of doctrine and recommend different versions of the restructuring of forces, they are all largely in agreement about the value and purpose of a defensive strategy. It would free NATO from the first use strategy for nuclear weapons and enable Europe to adopt a more independent defense policy. It would at the same time delegitimize a strong Soviet military presence in Eastern Europe, thereby strengthening the latter's prospects for greater independence from the Soviet Union.

In the West, the concept has not been formally endorsed by any of the NATO countries, but it has featured prominently in political debate and is strongly supported by the German Social Democrats and the British Labour Party. The established NATO policy of forward defense will clearly have much less relevance for a united Germany. Over the last two years, several Warsaw Pact statements have called for "reductions of the armed forces and conventional armaments in Europe to a level where neither side, maintaining its defensive capacity, would have the means to stage a surprise attack against the other side or offensive operations in general."[42] In a speech to the United Nations General Assembly, Soviet Foreign Minister Edward Schevarnadze urged all sides to adopt the principles of non-offensive defense. The political drama still unfolding in Eastern and Central Europe may steadily narrow the gap between

40. See Jonathan Dean, "Alternative Defence: Answer to NATO's Central Front Problems?," *International Affairs* (Winter 1987–88), 61–82; Andreas von Bullow, "Defensive Entanglement: An Alternative Strategy for NATO," in *The Conventional Defense of Europe, New Technologies and New Strategies*, ed. Andrew J. Pierre (New York, 1986); Andrew Boserup, "Non-Offensive Defence in Europe," in *Defending Europe: Options for Security*, ed. Derek Paul (London, 1986).

41. Horst Afheldt, "New Policies, Old Fears," *BAS*, 44, 7 (September 1988), 26. Horst Afheldt, one of the main writers in this field, heads a working group on non-offensive defense in the Max Planck Society, Starnberg, Germany. His first book on the topic, *Verteidigung und Frieden*, was published in Munich in 1976.

42. "On the Military Doctrine of the State Parties to the Warsaw Treaty," *Pravda*, 31 May 1987.

theory and practice. In any case, the concept is not an all-or-nothing proposition; it is capable of partial or staged implementation. An initial declaratory phase that enunciates a common understanding of defensive military doctrine, operations, and tactics could lead to a second stage involving the elimination of the danger of surprise attack and a large offensive in Central Europe.

The future of European defense has given rise to a wealth of proposals, which now command the attention of governments, experts, and the public at large. But technical fixes, however innovative, must be placed in a political context. To be more specific, denuclearization in Europe, even of a limited kind, cannot occur without addressing the overall character of the East-West divide. Demilitarization and alternative defense policies will make little headway if they are not anchored to political realities and, in particular, to the desire of Europeans on either side of the divide to reassert their identity and freedom of action. This implies a new relationship between Western Europe and the United States on the one hand and between Eastern Europe and the Soviet Union on the other. It also entails a program of cultural, economic, and political bridge-building across the two halves of Europe that not only strengthens existing interdependencies but fosters stable domestic and regional institutions. A European security system must offer a compelling vision of the future if it is to be viable. It must rest on the creation of a new Europe that overcomes the divisions of the past without unleashing new ones. It must widen the security agenda to embrance not only the sense of common vulnerability to conventional and nuclear attack but also the notion of economic and ecological security. The restructuring of the geopolitical equation in Europe is unlikely to succeed unless it firmly enshrines respect for human rights, self-determination, and economic and political democracy.

Bibliography

Adam-Schnaetzer, I. "Transformation of National Sovereignty." *European Affairs* 4 (1989) 47–52.

Allen, D., Rummel, R. and Wessels, W. *European Political Cooperation. Towards a Foreign Policy for Western Europe*. London, 1982.

Agnelli, G. "Europe of 1992." *Foreign Affairs* 68 (Fall 1989): 61–70.

Arbuthnott, H. and Edwards, G. *A Common Man's Guide to the Common Market*. 2d ed. London, 1989.

Armstrong, L. and Dauvergne, A. *L'EUROPE 93 – Tout ce qui va changer pour les consommateurs*. Paris, 1989.

Backer, J.H. *The Decision to Divide Germany*. Durham, N.C., 1978.

Balladur, E. "Investments in Europe." *European Affairs* 2, 4/88 (Winter 1990): 107–11.

Begg, I. "European integration and regional policy," *Oxford Review of Economic Policy* 5 (Summer 1989): 90–104.

Bogdanor, V. "The June 1989 European Elections and the Institutions of the Community." *Government and Opposition* 24 (Spring 1989): 199–214.

Brittain, S. "Britain without currency barriers." *European Journal of International Affairs* 2 (Spring 1989): 17–39.

Budd, S.A. and Jones, A. *The European Community: a guide to the maze*. London, 1989.

Bulmer, S. and Paterson, W. *The Federal Republic of Germany and the European Community*. London, 1987.

Burgess, M. *Federalism and European Union: political ideas, influences and strategies in the European Community 1972–1987*. London, 1989.

Campbell, D. "Multinational labour relations in the European Community." *ILR Report* 27 (Fall 1989): 7–14.

Cecchini, P. *The European Challenge 1992*. Aldershot, 1988.

Cobham, D. "Strategies for Monetary Integration Revisited." *Journal of Common Market Studies* 27, 3 (March 1989): 203–18.

Lord Cockfield. "Beyond 1992 – The Single European Economy." *European Affairs* 2, 4/88 (Winter 1990): 66–74.

Coffey, P., ed. *Main Economic Policy Areas of the EEC, towards 1992: the challenge to the Community's economic policies when the "real" Common*

Market is created by the end of 1992. 2d ed. rev. Dordrecht, The Netherlands, 1988.

Colchester, N. and Buchan, D. *Europe Relaunched. Truths and Illusions on the way to 1992.* London, 1990.

Cooper, M.H. "Europe 1992: danger or opportunity?" *Editorial Research Reports* 13 (Jan. 1989): 18–27.

Corbett, R.G. "The 1985 Intergovernmental Conference." In *The Dynamics of European Union*, edited by R. Pryce. London, 1987.

Corbett, R. "Testing the new procedures: The European Parliament's First Experiences With Its New 'Single Act' Powers." *Journal of Common Market Studies* 27, 4 (June 1989): 359–72.

Cosgrove, K. "1992 and beyond. British literature on the European Community." *British Book News* (Oct. 1989): 694–98.

Curzon Price, V. *1992: Europe's Last Chance? From Common Market to Single Market.* London, 1988.

Dankert, P. and Kooyman, A., eds. *Europe without frontiers. Socialists on the future of the European Economic Community*, New York, 1989.

Dankert, P. "The European Community – Past, Present and Future." *Journal of Common Market Studies* 21 (1982/3): 3–18.

Dean, R. "Nato and Arms Control." *World Today*, 44/12 (Dec. 1988): 201–2.

De Carmoy, G. and Story, J. *Western Europe in World Affairs.* London, 1986.

Devos, T. *Multinational Corporations in democratic host countries. U.S. multinationals and the Vredeling proposal.* New York, 1989.

Dowd, K. "The Case against a European central bank." *World Economy* 12 (Spring 1989): 361–72.

Ehlermann, C.-D. "Le Parlement face à la Commission." In *Le Parlement européen dans l'évolution institutionnelle*, edited by J.V. Louis and D. Walbroeck. Brussels, 1988.

Ehlermann, C.-D. "Europe 1992. Achievement & Perspectives: 1985–89." *Business in the Contemporary World* (Spring 1989).

Etienvre, J.-P. "Europe: 1992 and beyond," *Harvard International Review* 11 (Summer 1989): 6–36.

Featherstone, K. *Socialist Parties and European Integration. A Comparative history.* Manchester, 1988.

Fells, J. and Newman, M. *The European Community and the Superpowers.* London, 1989.

Foschepoth, J., ed. *Kalter Krieg und Deutsche Frage.* Göttingen/Zürich, 1985.

Freedman, L. "Arms control: the Open and Hidden Agenda." *European Affairs* 2, 4/88 (Winter 1990): 36–48.

Gros, D. "Paradigms for the Monetary Union of Europe." *Journal of Common Market Studies* 27, 3 (March 1989): 219–30.

Gros, D. and Thygesen, N. *The EMS - Achievements, Current Issues and Directions for the Future*. Centre for European Policy Studies, Paper No. 35, Brussels, 1988.

Gruner, W.D. *Die Deutsche Frage. Ein Problem der europäischen Geschichte seit 1800*. Munich, 1985.

Gruner, W.D. "Dutscher Nationalstaat und Europäische Integration." In *Deutschland und Europa nach dem 2. Weltkrieg. Entwicklungen, Verflechtungen, Konflikte*, edited by Heiner Timmerman. Saabrücken, 1990: 69–101.

Gwiazla, A. "Some Characteristic Trends in East-West Economic Relations." *Westminster Bank Quarterly Review* (August 1982): 53–61.

Harrop, J. *The Political Economy of Integration in the European Community*. Aldershot, Hants, 1989.

Helm, D. and Smith, S. "The assessment: economic integration and the role of the European Community." *Oxford Review of Economic Policy* 5 (Summer 1989): 1–19.

Heisbourg, F. "Can the Atlantic Alliance last out the Century?" *International Affairs* 63, 3 (Summer 1987).

Hill, B.E. *The CAP. Past, Present and Future*. London, 1984.

Hoffman, S. "The European Community and 1992." *Foreign Affairs* 68, 4 (Fall 1989): 27–47.

Houweling, H.W. and Siccama, J.G. "European Security and the decline of American hegemony: implications for arms acquisition and arms control." *Arms Control* 9 (Dec. 1988): 234–64.

Howard, M. and Beloff, M. "1989: a farewell to arms." *International Affairs* 65 (Summer 1989): 407–17.

Kaiser, K. "A view from Europe: the U.S. role in the next decade." *International Affairs* 65 (Spring 1989): 209–23.

Kettenacker, L. *Krieg zur Friedenssicherung*. Göttingen, 1989.

Knudsen, B.B. *Europe versus America: Foreign Policy in the 1980s*. Paris, 1984.

Kolodziej, E.A. "NATO in a new strategic environment." *Arms Control* 10 (May 1989): 3–20.

Laurent, P.-H. "The European Community: Twelve Becoming One." *Current History* 87 (Winter 1988): 357–60; 394.

Leaman, J. *The Political Economy of West Germany 1945-85. An Introduction*. London, 1988.

Lodge, J. *The European Community and the challenge of the future*. London, 1988.

Lodge, J. "The European Parliament – usurper of national sovereignty or guardian of parliamentary democracy?" *Parliamentarian* 70 (Jan. 1989): 28–31.

Louis, J.-V. and Waelbroeck, D. *Le Parlement européen dans l'évolution institutionnelle*. The European Parliament in Institutional Evolution, Brussels, 1988.

McDonald, F. and Zis, G. "The European Monetary System: Towards 1992 and Beyond." *Journal of Common Market Studies* 27, 3 (March 1989): 183–202.

Malcolm, N. "The Common European Home and Soviet Foreign Policy." *International Affairs* 65, 4 (Autumn 1989).

Marguand, D. "Parliamentary Accountability and the European Community." *Journal of Common Market Studies* 19, 3 (1981): 221–36.

Moreton, E. and Segal, G., eds. *Soviet Policy towards Western Europe: Implications for the Western Alliance*. London, 1984.

Nothumb, C.F. "La Rénovation du Parlement (The Renovation of Parliament)." *Res Publica* 31, 2 (1989): 175–80.

O'Cleireacain, S. "Europe 1992 and gaps in the EC's common commercial policy." *Journal of Common Market Studies* 28 (Mar. 1990): 201–17.

Paleocrassas, J. "Economic and Social Convergence in the Community." *Studia Diplomatica* 42, 2 (1989): 159–70.

Palmer, J. *1992 and Beyond*. Luxembourg, 1989.

Pinder, J. "Economic integration versus national sovereignty: differences between Eastern and Western Europe." *Government and Opposition* 24 (Summer 1989): 309–26.

Poidevin, R., ed. *Origins of the European Integration*. Paris, 1986.

Price, R. *The Dynamics of European Union*. London, 1987.

Rees, W. "The Federal Republic of Germany: a changing security environment." *Political Quarterly* 60 (July/Sept. 1989): 349–56.

Salin, P. "Monetary union or international money order?" *Economic Affairs* 9 (Aug./Sept. 1989): 13–16.

Schackleton, M. *Financing the European Community*. London, 1990.

Scharpf, F.W. "Die Politikverflechtungs – Falle: Europäische Integration und deutscher Föderalismus im Vergleich." *Politische Vierteljahreschrift* 4 (1985): 323–56.

Schwarze, J., ed. *The External Relations of the EC, in particular EC-US relations*. Baden-Baden, 1989.

Sekretariat of the Bundesrat, ed. *Bundesrat und Europäische Gemeinschaften. Dokumente*. Bonn, 1988.

Serra, E., ed. *The Relaunching of Europe and the Treaties of Rome*. Milan, 1990.

Shishkov, Y. "Differences between integration in Eastern and Western Europe: economic and political causes." *Government and Opposition* 24 (Summer 1989): 327–40.

Shub, J.L., ed. *Germany: Keystone to European Security. A Symposium*. Washington/London, 1983.

Smith, S. "Excise Duties and the Internal Market." *Journal of Common Market Studies* 27, 2 (December 1988): 147–60.

Surrey, J. "Beyond 1992: the Single Market and EC energy issues," *Energy Policy* 18 (Jan.–Feb. 1990): 42–54.

Surrey, J. "The Charter as we approach 1992." *Social Europe* 1 (1990): 7–120.

Teague, P. "European Community Labour Market Harmonisation." *Journal of Public Policy* 9, 1 (Jan.–Mar. 1989): 1–34.

Thomaneck, J.K.A. and Mellis, J., eds. *Politics, Society and Government in the German Democratic Republic.* Oxford/New York/Munich, 1989.

Thygesen, N. "The Delors Report and European economic and monetary union." *International Affairs* 64 (Autumn 1989): 637–52.

Thygesen, N. and Gros, D. *Concrete Steps towards Monetary Union.* Brussels, 1990.

Tully, S. "Europe gets ready for 1992." *Fortune* 117 (Fall 1988): 64–68.

Ugeux, G. "Europe sans frontières: the integration of financial markets." *Royal Bank of Scotland Review* (June 1989): 9–24.

Ungerer, H. "The European Monetary System and the International Monetary System." *Journal of Common Market Studies* 27, 3 (March 1989): 231–48.

Walker, W. and Gummett, P. "Britain and the European Armaments Market." *International Affairs* 65, 3 (Summer 1989): 419–42.

Wallenberg, P. "Submit the Single Market to Global Forces." *European Affairs* 2, 4/88 (Winter 1990): 116–19.

Walter, I. "ABB, Airbus, BNN, Bull, Ford, Ikea: trend setters in cross frontier industrial relations?" *Social and Labour Bulletin* (Mar. 1989): 35–38.

Walter, I. "1992: doing business in the European international market." *Northwestern Journal of International Law and Business* 9 (Winter 1989): 463–587.

Walter, I. and Smith, R.C. *Investment Banking in Europe: Restructuring for the 1990s.* Oxford, 1990.

Weatherill, S. "The Free Movement of Goods." *International and Comparative Law Quarterly* 38, 3 (July 1989): 689–93.

Weidenfeld, W. "The Tricky Part of 1992." *European Affairs* 4, 1 (Spring 1990): 59–64.

Weidenfeld, W., et al. *Binnenmarkt '92: Perspektiven aus deutscher Sicht.* Gütersloh, 1988.

Westphalen, J. "1992: doing business in the European internal market." *Northwestern Journal of International Law and Business* 9 (Winter 1989): 463–587.

Wettig, G. "West European integration and pan-Europeanism in Soviet foreign policy." Bundesinstitut für Ostwissenschaftliche und Internationale Studien *Berichte*, 10 (Jan. 1990).

Widmaer, O. "Demographic Change, Labour Force Dynamics and Employment: New Problems and Old Politics?" *European Journal of Political Research* 17, 4 (1989): 501–31.

Wijnand, G. "Try to Put Yourself in His Place." *European Affairs* 2, 4/88 (Winter 1990): 112–15.

Wistrich, E. *After 1992: The United States of Europe*. London/New York, 1989.

Woolacott, M., et al. "Europe tomorrow: the climb to the sunlit uplands." *Guardian* 4 December 1989: 21–24.

Notes on Contributors

Joseph Camilleri is Reader in Politics at La Trobe University, Melbourne. He has published widely on superpower relations, security policy, and international political economy. His publications include *The Nuclear State: Conflict and Control in the Western World (1984)* and *The Australia-New Zealand-U.S. Alliance: Regional Security in the Nuclear Age* (1987). His most recent book is *The End of Sovereignty? The Politics of a Shrinking and Fragmenting World* (1991).

Magnus Clarke is Senior Lecturer in International Relations and Director of Defence Studies at Deakin University, Australia. He has published on a wide variety of topics within these fields, ranging from nuclear warfare in the European context to the diffusion of ballistic missile technology to Third World countries. He is also a prominent media commentator on international affairs.

Jacqueline Dutheil de la Rochère is Professor of Public Law at the University of Paris II and at the Institute of Political Studies in Paris. She teaches EC law and politics. She is currently working on the legal and political implications of a united Europe.

Heather Field is a Director of the Industry Commission in Canberra. She is the author and co-author of numerous publications dealing with EC, U.S. and Japanese agricultural policies and trade, EC enlargement, EC budgetary affairs, and environmental issues.

Wolf D. Gruner is Professor of Modern European History at the University of Hamburg. He has published widely on German and European history since the 16th century, as well as on problems of European integration since World War II. Among his recent books are *The German Question. A Problem of European history since 1800* (1985), *Balance of Power. Past and Present* (1989) and *Federal Forms of German Statehood. From the Hanseatic League to the European Community* (1990).

Christian Hacke is Professor at the University of the Armed Forces in Hamburg. He has published extensively on American and German foreign policy: *Die Ost-und Deutschlandpolitik der CDU/CSU* (1975); *Die Ära Nixon/Kissinger* (1983); *Von Kennedy bis Reagan (1984); Die amerikanische Nahost-Politik* (1985); *Weltmacht wider Willen. Die Außenpolitik der Bundesrepublik Deutschland*(1988).

Martin L. Mruck is Head of the Science Centre in Bonn. He was previously Director of the London Office of the German Academic Exchange Service, specializing in the establishment of international exchange programs within the framework of the scientific community.

Philomena Murray is Lecturer in European Politics at the University of Melbourne and has researched aspects of EC politics in Dublin, Brussels, Bruges, Mannheim, and Florence. Until 1989 she was an Irish diplomat. She has published on the Single European Act and on institutional developments in the EC. She is currently preparing a book on European Union.

Corrado Paracone, who holds degrees in law and political science, is Director of Research Programmes in the fields of technology, industrial organization, new professions and jobs, education and training at the Giovanni Agnelli Foundation in Turin, Italy. He is also Deputy Director at Fiat Automobile Industries in Turin and writes regularly for *Italia Oggi.*

Stuart Rosewarne lectures in Political Economy at The University of Sydney. His research interests include studies in international political economy, labor markets and gendered orders within the political economy, and environmental economics. He is the author of several studies on development within the global political economy. These range from concerns with theorizing capitalist imperialism to studies of the role of the state in international accumulation processes. He is currently conducting research on global restructuring and strategic relations in the post-*pax Americana* era.

Daniel Van Den Bulcke is Professor of International Management and Development at the University of Antwerp, Belgium. He also teaches a postgraduate course at the College of Europe in Bruges and the University of Ghent. He is director of the Centre for International Management and Development, Antwerp (CIMDA). He has published extensively on the activities of multinational enterprises, especially with regard to Belgium and Europe.

Werner Weidenfeld is Professor of Political Science at the University of Mainz, Coordinator of German-American Cooperation at the German Foreign Office, and Vice-President of the German Council of the European Movement. His numerous publications on contemporary Germany and Europe include *Traumland Mitteleuropa* (1988) and *Der deutsche Weg* (1990). He is co-editor of the *Yearbook of European Integration.*

Wolfgang Wessels is Director of the Institut für Europäische Politik in Bonn, Director of the "Dominante administrative" of the College of Europe in Bruges and Professor at the College, and lecturer in European integration at the Universities of Bonn and Cologne. He is co-editor of the *Jahrbuch der Europäischen Integration* and has written books on European institutions, European foreign policymaking, and theories on international and European relations.

Joanne Wright lectures in International Relations and Strategic Studies at the University of Queensland, Australia. She has published several articles on terrorism and a book, *Terrorist Propaganda* (1991). She is currently working on the strategic implications of change in Europe and changing notions of the concept of security.

Index

Index

Human Rights and European Politics
The Legal-Political Status of Workers in the European Community

By Fritz Fabricius

The free movement of labor will be one of the key elements of the Single Market soon to be implemented. One would therefore expect that efforts would have been made to harmonize social policies, especially on the legal status of workers. But the existing EC Treaty contains no provision and the The Community Charter of the Fundamental Social Rights of Workers of 1989 fails to fill the gap. The Charter delegates the socio-political responsibility in almost all points to the Member States. Yet the constitutions of most only refer to general human rights. The author, however, stresses the importance of economic and social human rights which, like human rights in general, have their roots in the Enlightenment, especially in the works of Montesquieu, Adam Smith, and Kant. The author examines how these thinkers' ideas on these topics have been neglected since the 19th century and argues that it is time to revive them. He discusses such hotly debated issues as ownership of the product of work, workers' co-determination, strikes, and lockouts in the light of these ideas. He concludes that it is vital for th Single Market to extend human rights to the social and economic spheres.

Fritz Fabricius is Emeritus Professor of Law, Ruhr-University of Bochum and President of the Committee of Experts for the European Social Charter, Council of Europe, Strasbourg

April 1992
240 pp.
bibliography, index
0 85496 763 X

Europe and German Unification

By Renata Fritsch-Bournazel

The unforeseen end to the postwar period in Europe confronted both the Germans themselves and their neighbors and allies with the need to rethink existing positions and reformulate the relationship between Germany and Europe as a whole. The author of the highly successful *Confronting the German Question* has completely rewritten and updated her material for this new assessment of the situation at the beginning of the 1990s.

It is well documented throughout and uses a broad selection of assessments and statements by both protagonists and commentators to probe this central question of our times.

Renata Fritsch-Bournazel is Senior Fellow of the Centre for International Relations of the Fondation Nationale des Sciences Politiques and Professor of Politics at the Institute d'Etudes Politiques, Paris.

January 1992
272 pp.
bibliography, index
0 85496 979 9
0 85496 684 6 (paperback)

Of Related Interest from Berg

The Idea of Europe

Problems of National and Transnational Identity

Edited by Brian Nelson, David Roberts, and Walter Veit

Europe is both the creator and creation of modernity. Itself successor to a Western Christendom torn apart by religious wars, the Enlightenment vision of a pacified Europe, based on the civil religion of reason and law, foundered in its turn on the forces of national and class conflict released by modernization which plunged Europe into two self-destructive wars. Now, with the dramatic end of the Cold War, Europe no longer stands divided against itself. The prospect of a Europe whole and free is for the first time more than a dream. The essays in this volume examine both the historical dimensions of the European idea and the problems of national and transnational identity confronting European integration in the 1990s.

Brian Nelson is Professor of French and Director of the Centre for European Studies, **David Roberts** is Reader in German Studies, and **Walter Veit** is Associate Professor of German Studies, all at Monash University, Victoria.

April 1992
192 pp.
bibliography, index
0 85496 757 5